THE THEATRE OF
DAVID HENRY HWANG

Esther Kim Lee is associate professor and associate director in the School of Theatre, Dance, and Performance Studies at the University of Maryland, College Park, USA. She is the author of *A History of Asian American Theatre* (2006), which received the Outstanding Book Award given by Association for Theatre in Higher Education, and the editor of *Seven Contemporary Plays from the Korean Diaspora in the Americas* (2012). She was the editor of *Theatre Survey*, the flagship journal of the American Society for Theatre Research, and her articles have been published in *Modern Drama* and *Journal of Asian American Studies*.

Also available in the Critical Companions series from Bloomsbury Methuen Drama:

BRITISH THEATRE AND PERFORMANCE 1900–1950
by Rebecca D'Monté

THE IRISH DRAMATIC REVIVAL 1899–1939
by Anthony Roche

MODERN ASIAN THEATRE AND PERFORMANCE 1900–2000
by Kevin J. Wetmore, Siyuan Liu and Erin B. Mee

THE PLAYS OF SAMUEL BECKETT
by Katherine Weiss

THE THEATRE OF JEZ BUTTERWORTH
by David Ian Rabey

THE THEATRE OF CARYL CHURCHILL
By R. Darren Gobert

THE THEATRE OF MARTIN CRIMP: SECOND EDITION
by Aleks Sierz

THE THEATRE OF BRIAN FRIEL: TRADITION AND MODERNITY
by Christopher Murray

THE THEATRE OF DAVID GREIG
by Clare Wallace

THE THEATRE AND FILMS OF MARTIN MCDONAGH
by Patrick Lonergan

THE THEATRE OF SEAN O'CASEY
by James Moran

THE THEATRE OF HAROLD PINTER
by Mark Taylor-Batty

THE THEATRE OF TIMBERLAKE WERTENBAKER
by Sophie Bush

THE THEATRE OF TENNESSEE WILLIAMS
by Brenda Murphy

THE THEATRE OF
DAVID HENRY HWANG

Esther Kim Lee

Series Editors: Patrick Lonergan and Kevin J. Wetmore, Jr.

Bloomsbury Methuen Drama
An imprint of Bloomsbury Publishing Plc

B L O O M S B U R Y
LONDON · OXFORD · NEW YORK · NEW DELHI · SYDNEY

Bloomsbury Methuen Drama
An imprint of Bloomsbury Publishing Plc
Imprint previously known as Methuen Drama

50 Bedford Square	1385 Broadway
London	New York
WC1B 3DP	NY 10018
UK	USA

www.bloomsbury.com

BLOOMSBURY, METHUEN DRAMA and the Diana logo are trademarks of Bloomsbury Publishing Plc

First published 2015

© Esther Kim Lee, 2015

Esther Kim Lee has asserted her right under the Copyright, Designs and Patents Act, 1988, to be identified as author of this work.

All rights reserved. No part of this publication may be reproduced or transmitted in any form or by any means, electronic or mechanical, including photocopying, recording, or any information storage or retrieval system, without prior permission in writing from the publishers.

No responsibility for loss caused to any individual or organization acting on or refraining from action as a result of the material in this publication can be accepted by Bloomsbury or the author.

British Library Cataloguing-in-Publication Data
A catalogue record for this book is available from the British Library.

ISBN: HB: 978-1-4725-1208-6
PB: 978-1-4081-8585-8
ePDF: 978-1-4081-8557-5
ePub: 978-1-4081-8501-8

Library of Congress Cataloging-in-Publication Data
A catalogue record for this book is available from the Library of Congress.

Typeset by Deanta Global Publishing Services, Chennai, India

CONTENTS

Acknowledgements	ix
Introduction	1

1 The Trilogy of Chinese America: Magic Realism and the Californian Cool — 9
- *FOB* — 12
- *The Dance and the Railroad* — 20
- *Family Devotions* — 26

2 Beyond Chinese America: Love, Death and Resurrection — 35
- *The House of Sleeping Beauties* — 37
- *The Sound of a Voice* — 42
- *As the Crow Flies* — 46
- *Rich Relations* — 49

3 *M. Butterfly* — 57
- The Story and Style of *M. Butterfly* — 58
- The Production of *M. Butterfly* — 63
- Criticisms and Interpretations of *M. Butterfly* — 65
- The Legacy of *M. Butterfly* — 72

4 Identity Politics and Multiculturalism in the 1990s — 75
- *Bondage* — 77
- *Face Value* — 82
- *Trying to Find Chinatown* — 89
- *Golden Child* — 93

5 The Irony and Rhetoric of the Global Millennium — 103
- *Yellow Face* — 107
- *Chinglish* — 115
- *Kung Fu* — 123

Contents

6 Other Critical Perspectives — **129**

'Something Beyond and Above': David Henry Hwang's
Revision of *Flower Drum Song* — 129
Josephine Lee

David Henry Hwang's *Golden* Opportunities — 141
Dan Bacalzo

Butterfly and Locust: *Chinglish* and Asian American
Theatre in the Transnational Context — 152
Daphne Lei

Chronology — 167
Notes — 175
Bibliography — 189
Notes on Contributors — 201
Index — 203

ACKNOWLEDGEMENTS

When I met David Henry Hwang for the first time in March of 2000, I was a graduate student working on a dissertation on the history of Asian American theatre. I met him at a Starbucks near the Lincoln Center in New York City. An inexperienced interviewer with an incomplete knowledge of Hwang's work, I asked him questions that I now see as unprepared and naïve. Hwang, an experienced interviewee, probably saw right through my clumsy errors and obvious nervousness. Hwang, nevertheless, was polite and generous with his time and thoughts. After my book, *A History of Asian American Theatre*, was published, Hwang sent me an email expressing his gratitude for my contribution to Asian American theatre. He truly appreciated the value of theatre scholarship. I met him for the second time in early 2015 as I was nearing completion of this book. This time, I interviewed him at the Signature Theatre in New York City, where we engaged in a lively and casual conversation about his plays. I feel fortunate to have written about a playwright who is accessible and generous both as a person and as a writer, and I give my thanks to Hwang for helping me by granting interviews, sending unpublished scripts, and providing the cover image. Special thanks also go to Tracy Roberts, the studio manager of Eiko Ishioka, who assisted me in obtaining the permission to reprint the cover image.

This book was commissioned by Bloomsbury Methuen Drama, and I would like to thank the series editors Erin Hurley and Patrick Lonergan for giving me the opportunity to be part of the important Critical Companions series on contemporary playwrights. Mark Dudgeon at Bloomsbury Methuen Drama was particularly encouraging and helpful while I prepared the manuscript. The personal attention given by the press made the writing process more meaningful.

In spring 2013, I taught a graduate seminar on Hwang at the University of Maryland, and the students made a tremendous contribution to my interpretation of Hwang's plays. Many of the ideas I include in the book are borrowed directly from our discussions, and much credit goes to them for what may be read as my original thoughts. I wish I could cite them individually, and I hope I have conveyed their ideas accurately. The faculty

Acknowledgements

and staff in the School of Theatre, Dance, and Performance Studies at the University of Maryland were immensely supportive as I made the School my new intellectual home. I enjoyed extemporaneous conversations I had in hallways with colleagues who had deep interest in Hwang's theatre. I give special thanks to Daniel Wagner and Leigh Smiley for showing their leadership by supporting faculty research. With the funding provided by the School, I benefited greatly from working with the graduate assistant Khalid Long and the editor Aaron Tobiason, whose meticulous attention to details improved each draft of this book.

I give my sincere thanks to Josephine Lee, Dan Bacalzo, and Daphne Lei for writing essays that are featured in Chapter 6 of this book. They not only graciously agreed to be part of this important project but actively sought opportunities to meet at conferences as a group to further discuss Hwang's plays. I find my scholarly strength with their support, and I value the collegiality and friendship each has shown me for over a decade.

And finally, my deepest thanks go out to my family, both immediate and extended. My mother-in-law passed away while I was finishing this book, and I was struck by the immediacy and urgency of what Hwang dramatizes of family, ancestry, life and death. To echo what a character says at the end of *Golden Child*, we are part of a larger constellation, and we can be reborn through our family. I dedicate this book to my family, through which I am made anew everyday.

INTRODUCTION

When David Henry Hwang was selected by the Signature Theatre of New York City to be their playwright in residence for the 2013–14 season, many agreed the recognition was fully deserved. Hwang is one of the most important playwrights in contemporary theatre and the best-known Asian American playwright. He has also had a prolific career, writing for film, television, opera and musicals for over thirty years. Alex Witchel of the *New York Times* writes of Hwang: 'Yes, you can win a fellowship from the Guggenheim or Rockefeller Foundations (Hwang has won both) to prove your playwriting prowess, but in the American theatre, nothing tops a Signature season. Among Hwang's predecessors are Arthur Miller, Edward Albee, Sam Shepard and August Wilson.'[1] This was not the first time Hwang was compared to the 'great' American playwrights; as early as 1989, *TIME* magazine compared Hwang to Arthur Miller. In referencing the success of *M. Butterfly*, the magazine states, 'If Hwang can again fuse politics and humanity, he has the potential to become the first important dramatist of American public life since Arthur Miller, and maybe the best of them all.'[2] The Signature Theatre selection reinforced the narrative of success that has shaped Hwang's place in American theatre. According to that narrative, Hwang has become a major American playwright since receiving a Tony Award for *M. Butterfly*, and he is the only Asian American playwright to be produced on Broadway (four times total).

Hwang's success story has, indeed, been seen as the theatre industry's version of the American Dream. Born to Chinese immigrants, Hwang grew up in a Los Angeles suburb with two sisters. His father wanted his children to succeed in America, so he made them speak English at home and prioritized their education above all else. Hwang attended an elite preparatory high school where he was a member of the debating team, and he excelled in playing the violin. Because of his talent with words, his father told him to pursue law. Intending to become a lawyer, Hwang attended Stanford University, but after seeing Thornton Wilder's *The Matchmaker* at the American Conservatory Theatre in his freshman year, he decided to become a playwright instead. He changed his major to English and began to take creative writing classes. Hwang asked John L'Heureux, a novelist and professor of creative writing at Stanford, to read his early plays. L'Heureux told him they were not good and encouraged him to see and read as many plays as possible. He became Hwang's adviser and the two designed a playwriting major within the Creative Writing Department. In 1978, Hwang applied and was accepted to the Padua Hill Playwrights Festival workshop and studied with Sam Shepard and María Irene Fornés. They taught him writing techniques that allowed him to access his subconscious thoughts and to write about what they called 'myths' that had shaped his life. Hwang wrote his first play, *FOB*, as a senior at Stanford, and the play premiered at his dorm. He then submitted *FOB* to the National Playwrights Conference of the Eugene O'Neill Theater Centre in Waterford, Connecticut. Hwang was thrilled to have it accepted to the festival and even more pleased to see *FOB* produced by Joseph Papp, the artistic director of the Public Theater in New York City. Papp would produce two subsequent plays by Hwang and continue to support him. According to Hwang, Papp told him that he would succeed as a playwright in America because he knew how to write comedies, and Hwang knew the statement was especially true for a playwright of colour.[3] After experimenting with different styles and forms of playwriting, he wrote *M. Butterfly* in 1988, a play that prompted critics to associate him with the 'great' American playwrights.

Hwang is not entirely comfortable with this public narrative of success and has at times questioned it. What does it mean to be a 'great' American playwright, and why is there a need to promote one? And why is he the only Asian American playwright to have been produced on Broadway? What is his place in the complex politics of multiculturalism in the American theatre? Does he accurately represent the Asian American community? Hwang, more than others, is aware of these questions and knows what he represents in American theatre. As the only Asian American playwright with a Tony Award, Hwang has been placed in the role of an unofficial spokesperson for Asian American theatre on multiple occasions. He has written plays to interrogate the myths that have influenced him, but he frequently finds himself becoming a myth. Fully aware of his position and influence, Hwang has engaged with the questions that have followed him, but he has also avoided taking overtly political or activist roles. Instead, he has preferred to use his words to articulate the issues he cares about in his plays, interviews, essays and playwright's notes.

In his introduction to the first published collection of his plays, Hwang demonstrates his desire and ability to eloquently express his political and artistic perspectives. In reflecting on his recent success with *M. Butterfly*, Hwang explained that he evolved artistically in what he called 'phases'. Growing up in an affluent Chinese American family, he was first in an 'assimilationist' phase, during which he rejected Chinese and Asian cultures. In college, Hwang explains, he entered an 'isolationist–nationalist' phase, breaking sharply from the past as he became interested in 'working with and writing primarily for other Asian Americans'.[4] His first plays, which he calls the 'Trilogy of Chinese America' and his 'Japanese plays', came out of these first two phases and are detailed in Chapters 1 and 2 of this book. While he does not name the next phase, it can best be described as multiculturalist, as it rejects isolationism and embraces a pluralistic society in which 'different ethnic, political, and social groups co-exist in a state of equality'.[5] Hwang advocated that all writers – regardless of their racial or ethnic background – should develop the ability to write about anything. 'If we are all equally Americans', Hwang declares, 'then we should be equally able to write about many different types of characters.'[6] He wrote *Rich Relations* and *M. Butterfly* influenced by a strong vision of what he perceived as a new horizon in American multiculturalism.

As an experienced debater, Hwang has displayed an exceptional ability to write and speak cogently, and his prose is effective in illuminating the ideas at the core of his plays. His background in debating also explains his ability to see more than one side of an issue and make convincing arguments from all sides. Yet, as a playwright, he relies on his subconscious mind and always leaves his plays open to interpretation by creating ambiguous endings. These two impulses – one highly rational and the other deeply instinctual – coexist in Hwang's mind. He is a dialectical thinker who can hold contradictory thoughts in his mind simultaneously, and he writes plays that require the audience to think in the same way. *M. Butterfly*, for instance, has spawned multiple interpretations, as detailed in Chapter 3 of this book, and the audience must accept the fact that many of these interpretations are equally plausible. The play can be read as an intellectual debate over issues of East versus West and man versus woman, yet at the same time, it is also a tragic love story between two people. In other words, the play forces members of the audience to think critically while also moving them emotionally.

Hwang's dialectical thought process can also be seen in the way he selectively incorporates autobiography in his plays. To him, playwriting allows him full control over his writing, and theatre, unlike film and television, remains the only dramatic medium in which the writer's words are considered sacred. With such a degree of control, Hwang has frequently chosen to reflect his own life in his plays, and playwriting has been his most autobiographical medium. However, his plays do not directly mirror his life, nor do they function as documentaries. Rather, he uses theatre to explore who he is in a variety of contexts, interrogating the factual and fictional in his surroundings. Beginning with his first play, *FOB*, Hwang has incorporated stories from his personal life into fictionalized dramas without making the differences between the two explicit. Hwang has been upfront about using theatre to examine issues closest to his heart, but at the same time, he has distanced himself from his plays by obfuscating the boundaries between fact and fiction. As discussed in Chapter 4, *Golden Child* is about his family's history and is based on the stories he heard from his grandmother; yet he freely changes details of the story in retelling it for contemporary American audiences. In fact, he has revised the play multiple times, trying to strike the right balance between factual history and the emotional impact the play can have on an audience. Dan Bacalzo, in his essay in the last section of this book, discusses the differences between these different versions of *Golden Child* and explores how the play reflects Hwang's view of his family's past.

Yellow Face, as discussed in Chapter 5, is Hwang's most autobiographical play, and the character named DHH learns the hard way what it means to be a well-known Asian American playwright. As he does with other plays, Hwang blends fact and fiction, using the stage to examine how human beings present themselves to others, and how those presentations mutate as their circumstances change. DHH, as a dramatic representation of Hwang, is the most self-conscious and histrionic of his characters and demonstrates that autobiography in Hwang's plays is, like the theatre, both real and illusionary.

The dynamic coexistence of the real and illusion is a recurring theme in Hwang's plays, and he uses theatre as a metaphor to examine the theatricality of life. Hwang is frequently compared to the Italian playwright Luigi Pirandello, whose play *Six Characters in Search of an Author* (1921) is heralded as one of the most important of the twentieth century. In the play, characters break the 'fourth wall' (the invisible 'wall' that separates the stage and the audience) to comment on their fictional existence, and the distinction between the actors and characters is unclear. Hwang prefers playwriting because theatre is the most immediate medium to explore human existence in a live setting. For Hwang, theatre is both a useful metaphor and a controlled laboratory to examine the world he lives in.

In that laboratory, the most meaningful metaphor, for Hwang, is the face. The face is a leitmotif that reoccurs throughout Hwang's oeuvre. The face in his plays functions as a mask – both metaphorical and literal – that characters put on and off: in *Bondage*, the characters' faces are literally covered with masks; and in *M. Butterfly*, Gallimard chooses to put on the Butterfly make-up before killing himself. The face is also a facade intended to hide what is below. It is frequently not to be trusted, and the themes of games and deception are prominent in Hwang's plays. Paradoxically, the face can also reveal who characters really are. Like DHH at the end of *Yellow Face*, Hwang continues his search for his face in order to discover who he really is as a writer, as an Asian American, as a man, and as a human being. The face, like the stage, is a facade that both reveals and conceals the truth.

Hwang says he did not know about the Chinese concept of the face until later in his life, and initially, using the face as a metaphor was not a conscious choice.[7] Although he is aware of his repeated use of the face in his plays, he does not yet know why he has done so. He speculates that the face may be particularly important to Asian Americans, just as the colour of one's skin is critical to the identities of African Americans. Perhaps what distinguish light-skinned East Asians from Caucasians are their faces, which have noticeably different features.[8] Indeed, when Asians were described as 'yellow' in the nineteenth century, the term did not necessarily refer to skin tone, but also to features such as the eyes and the shape of the face. Moreover, Western theatre has a tradition of portraying Asians in yellowface make-up, a theatrical convention involving tapes and headbands to make the actor's eyes slanted. The face, often with elaborate 'Oriental' costumes, is what has marked 'Asianness' onstage for centuries. Hwang is aware of this part of theatre history, as are other Asian American theatre artists who have protested the convention of yellowface make-up in theatre since at least the 1960s.[9]

Asian Americans, like other people of colour, are acutely sensitive to how they look to others and how they are represented onstage and on-screen. Hwang and other Asian Americans grew up looking for Asian faces on television and cringed every time they saw a stereotypical 'Oriental' character played by a white actor speaking broken English, or by an Asian actor playing a demeaning, two-dimensional role. They rarely saw realistic representations of themselves on-screen, and Asian American theatre was founded in part to create accurate portrayals of Asian Americans onstage. To borrow W. E. B. Du Bois's famous phrase, many Asian Americans have a 'double consciousness', a sense of 'always looking at one's self through the eyes of others'.[10] Hwang's characters embody this notion of double consciousness and are self-conscious about how they look to others and how they should act and present themselves. Moreover, Hwang uses the process of self-presentation as a device to create dramatic conflict in his plays. For instance, Song in *M. Butterfly* chooses to act as a woman to deceive Gallimard, and Marcus, a white character in *Yellow Face*, chooses to act as an Asian American in order to feel a sense of community and belonging.

This notion of the presentation of self has been famously explained by Erving Goffman in *The Presentation of Self in Everyday Life* (1959), an important study of how human behaviour changes in different social situations. Scholars of performance studies, such as Richard Schechner, Judith Butler, José Esteban Muñoz and Karen Shimakawa, have expanded on Goffman's notion of self-presentation using theatrical terms such as performance, performed behaviour and ritual. In their studies, identity is in some sense synonymous with performance, and everyday situations are inherently theatrical. Performance studies provides a useful framework to understand Hwang's plays, most of which comment on the theatrical aspects of everyday life and on the mundane truths that can be revealed on a theatrical stage.

In Hwang's plays, both reality and theatre are theatrical and performative. As addressed above, Hwang almost makes the theatre *more theatrical* by using meta-theatrical elements in the style of Pirandello, but he also emphasizes the form of theatre. His style of theatre is formalist, in that the story of each play is intimately linked to its form. In other words, the dramatic structure is not merely a vessel *for* the story but a part *of* it. This attention to form can be seen in his choice to model each of his plays after another playwright's work. *Family Devotions*, for instance, was modelled after Sam Shepard's *Curse of the Starving Class*, while *M. Butterfly* followed the form of Peter Shaffer's *Equus*. Hwang has constantly experimented with different and new forms of playwriting, and he has been drawn to dramatic forms that allow him to showcase characters that are trapped in the structure of the world he creates for them.

For Hwang, the genre that best demonstrates this approach to playwriting is what he calls 'spiritual farce', which he defines as 'God's way of looking at the world'.[11] In a farce, the audience knows what is happening onstage, while the characters' understanding is only partial. The characters' misunderstandings and miscommunications create the comedy that often results in disaster for them but is farcical to the audience. For Hwang, the world is a farce from god's perspective, but a tragedy from humanity's point of view. Applying this idea to theatre, what happens on the stage is ultimately a farce for the all-knowing audience but a tragedy for the characters. Thus, many of Hwang's plays have both farcical and tragic elements, with some, like *Yellow Face*, containing a farcical first act and a darker, more serious, second act.

Hwang's attention to the form of theatre can also be seen in his use of music and movement. He has collaborated with a number of artists – such as the musician Lucia Hwong and the actor John Lone – to experiment with new styles of theatrical expression. To Hwang, music is central to his theatre. With a mother who was a professionally trained pianist, Hwang grew up listening to Western classical music. He can play the jazz violin and was once briefly in a duo band with the Japanese American playwright Philip Kan Gotanda, who played the guitar. Because of his understanding of music, Hwang has been tapped to collaborate on operas and musicals, most notably with Philip Glass (*Voyage*), Elton John (*Aida*) and Phil Collins (*Tarzan*). Hwang has tried a number of times to write his own musicals, and his latest full-length play, *Kung Fu*, began as a musical, as discussed in Chapter 5. He did, however, complete his adaptation of *Flower Drum Song*, a mid-twentieth-century musical by Rodgers and Hammerstein, and Josephine Lee's essay in the last section of this book documents the historical significance of Hwang's work with the musical. The most consistent form of theatre Hwang has developed throughout his career relies on the integration of traditional Chinese opera in his plays. Hwang was first introduced to Chinese opera after writing *FOB*, and he has used movements and sounds from the opera in almost all of his plays. In *Flower Drum Song*, for example, Chinese opera functions as a symbol of the contested sense of cultural authenticity for Chinese Americans. Indeed, Hwang's integration of Chinese opera in otherwise naturalistic plays can be seen as constituting a distinctly Chinese American theatre form. This intercultural form of theatre, which includes non-verbal theatrical elements, has been repeatedly used by Hwang to represent a range of cultural identities.

The following chapters are organized chronologically, following the order of the production dates of Hwang's plays. For plays that are more autobiographical than others, closer attention is given to how they do or do not reflect Hwang's life. Each of the chapters focuses on particular issues and approaches that were important during the time of Hwang's writing, and production histories are provided to further explicate the contemporaneous significance of his dramas. The chapters are followed by three essays by leading scholars of Asian American theatre: Josephine Lee's essay discusses Hwang's adaptation of *Flower Drum Song*; Dan Bacalzo's essay compares different versions of *Golden Child*; and Daphne Lei's essay on *Chinglish* explains Hwang's first bilingual play in the context of Asian American theatre history. Taken as a whole, this book is about David Henry Hwang's plays, and how they have established him as a leading, and even a 'great', playwright in contemporary theatre.

CHAPTER 1
THE TRILOGY OF CHINESE AMERICA: MAGIC REALISM AND THE CALIFORNIAN COOL

When Hwang started his career as a playwright in his early twenties, he was profoundly influenced by the teachings of María Irene Fornés and Sam Shepard, who both emphasize accessing the subconscious. Hwang still writes freehand on a notepad when composing early drafts of his plays. When the draft is finished, he will type the finished version on a computer. By using freehand, Hwang does not edit or censor himself when unexpected or new ideas emerge, allowing his characters to evolve throughout the writing process. His early plays, especially, demonstrate a willingness to allow his subconscious to take over his writing. For instance, in the notes to his first play, *FOB*, he admits that he did not have a structure in mind while writing it: 'With *FOB* I was really influenced by Maxine Hong Kingston's work and my basic notion was, what would happen if these two gods [Fa Mu Lan and Gwan Gung] met in Torrance, California? When I began it, I had no idea what the next word would be. I just went through the woods by myself.'[1] True to the description, the play's plot develops without an obvious agenda.

This sense of being lost in the woods or not knowing where a play is going shaped his early work. While being 'lost', Hwang explored how he could write for the stage. Later in his career, Hwang became more aware of dramatic form and structure. He admits that he does not know how to 'get lost in the woods' anymore, but the early experiments in those metaphoric woods have had a lasting impact on his playwriting style, form and tone.[2] There are two major approaches and styles that Hwang explored as a young writer, and they have had a profound influence on his development as a playwright.

First, realism coexists with non-realism in Hwang's early plays, and the shift between the two is often unexpected. In her book *Performing Asian America: Race and Ethnicity on the Contemporary Stage*, Josephine Lee explains that modern realistic plays have been problematic in their supposedly 'faithful' mirroring of reality. She writes:

> Although realism purports to be a faithful representation of ordinary life, it is in fact a more complex ideological practice, a manufacturing rather than a mirroring of some construct of 'real life'. Less important than how faithful or true to life the play is are the ways in which it constructs relationships between the spectator and the events occurring on stage, relationships that viewing communities must agree on as being 'like life' and therefore meaningful.[3]

Hwang's dramatization of 'real' situations is never stable, and he seems to be sensitive to Lee's criticism of realism. Often in his plays, realism is contested, and Hwang invites the audience to provide multiple interpretations of what is occurring onstage. Moreover, in his early plays, the stage functions as a portal where time and space are fluid. What is seen onstage in terms of setting is naturalistic, but the action can grow surrealistic. He is interested in exploring behind the scenes what the public perceives of realistic settings – whether it is a Chinese restaurant or a mountaintop.

The genre that best describes Hwang's early style of dramatic writing is magical realism. There are many variations of magical realism (also known as magic realism or marvellous realism), and the history of the genre is extensive.[4] In the case of Hwang, the world of his plays includes both fantasy and ordinary life, or to borrow Salman Rushdie's description, Hwang's plays dramatize the 'commingling of the improbable and the mundane'.[5] In *FOB*, the mundane setting of the back room of a Chinese restaurant in Torrance, California, turns into a battle zone for two gods drawn from Chinese American myths. In his plays, there are many indications of the improbable lurking behind the mundane facade. Moreover, the coexistence of realism and non-realism becomes a kind of ritualistic game – a theme he would continue to explore in his later plays as well. And often, Hwang uses Chinese opera to dramatize the non-real and the improbable.

The second characteristic that Hwang explored while developing his dramatic style as a young playwright is what can be described as the 'Californian cool'. Many of his plays are set on the West Coast, and his characters sound like Californians, no matter where the play may be set. For instance, in his second play, *The Dance and the Railroad*, the characters are supposed to be speaking Chinese, but Hwang gives them dialogue that sounds like Southern Californian dialect in both tone and style. They talk informally with quick jabs at each other, and their expressions sound like what one could hear in the 1980s' television shows created in Los Angeles. Hwang deliberately decided to have the Chinese characters speak in the same casual Californian English he grew up speaking and hearing. He did not want to use the pseudo-classical language often used in supposed translations of Chinese language. He did not want his characters to sound like the Chinese characters in the 1970s' television show *Kung Fu*, for instance. He wanted his Chinese male characters to sound cool – Californian cool.

Hwang's exploration of his Californian sensibility was influenced in part by Sam Shepard's plays. In explaining the similarities between the two writers, I borrow a quote from Toby Silverman Zinman, who examines Shepard in relation to what she terms super-realist painters.

> The most obvious and firm link between Shepard and all the major super-realist painters is the California connection. The concern with 'cool' (as in sustained control), with pop culture and its material artifacts – most conspicuously the automobile – and the mythology of the West (true and false) are all present. The pervasive maleness, American-ness, and a certain odd nostalgia for the recent past also link them, as does the powerful exaggeration, the tension inevitably created by 'hype', and a toughness, a hardness, not only in choice of subject matter but in the high-gloss of the surface itself, and in its corollary, an assumption of the importance of surface.[6]

Like Shepard (as described by Zinman), many of Hwang's characters are obsessed with the surface – whether it is the car they drive, the clothes they wear, the house they live in or the face they choose to wear. The glossy surface is often the essence of his characters' identities. Hwang's characters are also haunted by what can be broadly termed the mythology of the recent past, or, as Zinman puts it, the 'certain odd nostalgia for the recent past'. Like Shepard, Hwang has written about the mythology of the West, but he has also written about the mythology he grew up with; most importantly, he was influenced by stories of his family's history, fundamentalist Christianity and the American Dream.

In this chapter, I examine David Henry Hwang's first three plays to gain a better understanding of the styles and approaches that he experimented with as an emerging playwright in his early twenties. In an interview in 1988, he commented that *FOB* was perhaps his favourite play 'simply because it was written so much out of instinct, before I acquired any so-called tools'.[7]

The 'instinct' he showed in *FOB* and other early plays reveals much about Hwang's style of playwriting – both in terms of what he continued to use and what he moved beyond.

FOB

Growing up in a suburb of Los Angeles, David Henry Hwang was taught to assimilate into American culture. He spoke English at home and was exposed more to American popular culture than to what might be described as Chineseness. Assimilation was synonymous with inclusion and belonging in the United States, and it was seen as a way to avoid the stereotype of the perpetual foreigner. To become an American is to lose one's foreignness, and conversely, being a foreigner hinders one's effort to assimilate into American culture. The dilemma of assimilation is a central theme in *FOB*, written during his 'assimilationist phase', which he explains was born of a desire to 'out-white the whites':

> The Asian child sees America defined as predominately of one color. Wanting to be part of this land, he attempts to become the same. The difficulty is, of course, that this is not possible; our inability to become white at will can produce terrible self-loathing. My first play, *FOB*, dealt largely with this dilemma.[8]

In the play, the dilemma of assimilation is embodied by three characters: Steve, Dale and Grace, all of whom are in their early twenties. The FOB (Fresh Off the Boat) represented by the character Steve is contrasted with the ABC (American-Born Chinese) represented by Dale. The third character, Grace, is not labelled as either FOB or ABC and exists somewhere between the two. By triangulating the dilemma of assimilation, Hwang complicates the dramatic conflict and opens the possibility of moving beyond a simple binary (FOB vs. ABC) and towards a more ambiguous articulation of assimilation.

In his 'Playwright's Note', Hwang explains that the play was influenced by the Chinese American writers Maxine Hong Kingston and Frank Chin.

> The roots of *FOB* are thoroughly American. The play began when a sketch I was writing about a limousine trip through Westwood, California, was invaded by two figures from American literature:

Fa Mu Lan, the girl who takes her father's place in battle, from Maxine Hong Kingston's *The Woman Warrior*, and Gwan Gung, the god of fighters and writers, from Frank Chin's *Gee, Pop!*[9]

Maxine Hong Kingston and Frank Chin are two central figures in Chinese American literature, and both have used Chinese mythology to express the Chinese American experience. Maxine Hong Kingston's *The Woman Warrior: Memoirs of a Girlhood Among Ghosts* (1976) received the National Book Award for Nonfiction and was promoted by the publisher as an autobiography, despite the extensive inclusion of the fantastical stories of Fa Mu Lan from Chinese mythology. Many Asian American authors and scholars have questioned the categorization of Kingston's book as an autobiography, and the inclusion of mythology has, in part, led to criticism from one of her most vocal critics, Frank Chin. By 1976, when Kingston's book was published, Chin had written plays about Chinese Americans and was active in collecting and editing works by Asian American writers he endorsed.[10] Kingston, however, was not part of the larger Asian American literary movement Chin was leading at the time. Chin publicly criticized her for misrepresenting Chinese American history and mythology and for writing a 'Christian Chinese-American autobiography' that catered to the 'popular stereotype of the Chinese in white publishing, white religion'.[11]

By the time Hwang wrote *FOB*, he was aware of the public exchange between Kingston and Chin. In 1977, he had watched Chin's play *Gee, Pop! … A Real Cartoon*, which was being produced at the East West Players in Los Angeles.[12] The play featured Gwan Gung as a god who protected Chinese immigrants during different periods of history. Kingston and Chin influenced Hwang equally, and he thought about how he would position himself as a Chinese American working alongside such important voices. Instead of taking sides, he let the mythic characters created by Kingston and Chin clash onstage. The ABC character Dale witnesses the battle between Fa Mu Lan (Grace) and Gwan Gung (Steve). Dale is left alone at the end of the play to make sense of what he experienced. While the ending is ambiguous, what is clear is Hwang's willingness to both draw on and challenge these two preeminent Chinese American writers. By dramatizing the controversy, with the characters literally fighting it out onstage, Hwang explores issues of assimilation and Chinese American history.

FOB is set in 1980 and takes place in the back room of a Chinese restaurant in Torrance, California, a relatively affluent area in southwestern Los Angeles County. In 1980, the Asian immigrant population was steadily growing in

Torrance. The Chinese restaurant functions as a microcosm of Chinese America, as both an imagined and a real place where assimilation is played out in multiple ways. First of all, Chinese restaurants are virtually ubiquitous in the United States. In her book *The Fortune Cookie Chronicle: Adventures in the World of Chinese Food*, journalist Jennifer 8. Lee documents that there are 'some forty thousand Chinese restaurants in the United States – more than the number of McDonald's, Burger Kings, and KFCs combined'.[13] In 1980, as is still the case in the twenty-first century, the Chinese restaurant was the most recognizable place to experience Chineseness in the United States. Such restaurants are also accessible to everyone, allowing patrons from a variety of backgrounds to consume Chinese food and experience a simplified version of the Chinese culture. They are inherently assimilated spaces in which Americanized Chinese food is served for customers who expect predictable dishes such as Almond Chicken and Chop Suey.

Hwang describes the back room of the restaurant as having a 'single table, with tablecloth; various chairs, supplies'.[14] His choice to set the play in the back of the restaurant, rather than its main hall, reveals a theme Hwang would continue to explore throughout his career. He is interested in revealing what takes place behind the scenes – both literally and metaphorically – and in complicating the view the average individual perceives of Chinese America. Most Americans are familiar with the facade and decor of Chinese restaurants, but they do not have access to what happens in the less public reaches of the restaurant. The back room is a private and privileged space for the three characters in *FOB*. It is also a liminal space in which the Chinese American identity can be dynamically defined and contested. For Dale, Steve and Grace, the back room serves as a portal between the familiar facade of the Chinese restaurant and the outside society as they question who they are and where they belong as Chinese Americans. Hwang frequently uses the metaphor of theatre in staging his scenes, and in the case of *FOB*, the back room is analogous to the back stage area, whereas the main hall of the restaurant can be compared to the main stage of a theatre.

FOB begins with a prologue by Dale, who defines and derides the term FOB. Dressed 'preppie', he stands in front of a blackboard and 'lectures like a university professor': 'F-O-B. Fresh Off the Boat. FOB. Clumsy, ugly, greasy FOB. Loud, stupid, four-eyed FOB. Big feet. Horny. Like Lenny in *Of Mice and Men*' (7). Dale declares that boy FOBs are worse than girl FOBs and that they are the 'sworn enemies of all ABC girls': 'Before an ABC girl will be seen on Friday night with a boy FOB in Westwood, she would rather burn off her face' (6). Dale's blatant insulting of the FOB is humorous yet biting, and the scene combines the style of a university lecture with the tone of stand-up comedy, both of which would have been familiar to his college-aged audience members at Stanford University (where the play was first staged). The prologue also demonstrates meta-theatrical techniques that Hwang would use in his later plays. Echoes of Dale's direct address to the audience, with its didactic humour, can be heard in *M. Butterfly* and *Yellow Face*; in each of these cases, the meta-theatrical scene functions as a framing device for the entire play. When the play premiered in New York City at the Public Theater, Hwang found it important to strongly indicate the comedic tone of the prologue. According to Hwang, he had to give the audience 'the permission to laugh' at Dale's lecturing: 'One of the things I found very early on at the [Public Theater] was that with [a] predominantly non-Asian audience, you had to give them the permission to laugh because they weren't sure whether or not they were being offensive by laughing, and so after the *New York Times* came out and said it was funny, then everyone thought it was OK to laugh.'[15] In his review, Frank Rich describes the interaction between Dale and Steve as having 'true comic verve' and finds the climax of act 1 'hilarious'.[16] The comic meta-theatrical framing at the beginning of the play sets the tone for its remainder and influences each interaction between the three characters.

The prologue establishes Dale as a character who thinks he knows more than others: because he is an expert in identifying FOBs, he is certainly not one of them, which, in his eyes, makes him better than the FOB. Like a comedic stock character in the tradition of *Il Dottore* (The Doctor) from *Commedia dell'Arte*, Dale is pompous and claims to have superior knowledge. Predictably, he actually knows less than others and in the course of the play, his ignorance is revealed. Indeed, the play ends by repeating a short passage from the prologue, though everything he says about the FOB the second time around is more questioning than mocking. Dale can be seen as a stand-in for Hwang, who is an ABC himself and resembles Dale in many ways. Hwang's use of humour, then, can be interpreted as self-deprecating with the ultimate goal of self-discovery.

After the audience is introduced to Dale in the Prologue, the first scene begins with a meeting between Grace and Steve in the back room of the restaurant. There is much ambiguity regarding who Grace and Steve actually are and how much they know about each other. On the surface, Grace is Dale's cousin and a student at UCLA, and her family owns the restaurant.

Her main action at the beginning of the play is wrapping a small box, which portends significant meaning throughout what follows. After entering the room unnoticed, Steve introduces himself to Grace as Gwan Gung, the 'God of warriors, writers, and prostitutes' (11). Steve says he is looking for *bing*, a type of Chinese pancake, but it quickly becomes apparent that he wants more than food. Grace may have been expecting Steve but does not show any interest in him and tells him to 'take a menu' (9). Steve has come to the United States with the presumption that everyone would recognize and respect Gwan Gung. To his disbelief, he hears from Grace that no one in the United States even knows who he is and that Gwan Gung 'died way back' (14).

When she is alone, Grace confides to the audience that she is actually Fa Mu Lan, the Woman Warrior. She hides her mythic identity from Dale and Steve while manipulating the situation and arranging for the three of them to meet. While in many ways she acts like a passive character, she is actually the main driver of the play's action. Frank Rich describes Grace as 'not fully written': 'She is supposed to be torn between the poles represented by the men, but more often she just seems vague.'[17] It is certainly true that Grace is a mediator who is neither an FOB nor an ABC, but a little of both. As a character, she may be less developed than the other two, but her vagueness is, in fact, what defines her. As the only female character, she can choose to be neutral and function as a referee between the conflicting forces embodied by the two male characters. She can also be read as the gravitational centre of the play and is most aware of what is happening with the other characters. The main action of the play takes place in a restaurant owned by her family, and Dale and Steve come to her, while she awaits them. When Dale and Steve argue and ultimately disagree over whose car they will use, Grace suggests that they stay and eat at her restaurant. She confines them to her space and continues to observe the men.

The three end up spending the evening together in the back room because Dale refuses to be seen in public with Steve and his limousine. With the beginning of scene 2, the competition between Steve and Dale manifests in several ways, ranging from a spicy food contest to who has a better car. But the main underlying tension between the two men stems from their mutual need for Grace's attention. Both Steve and Dale want to go out with Grace: Steve wants to take her dancing, while Dale argues that they should go see a movie. Steve's desire to go out with Grace can be seen as a typical heterosexual attraction, but Dale's need to be with her is much more complex. Dale initially comes to the restaurant at Grace's invitation, thinking they will be going on a double date. Grace, however, never invited her friend, and when Dale learns that he does not have a date and that he would be the odd man out, he decides to stay, despite his strong distaste for FOBs. Grace seems to have known that Dale would stay and spend the evening with her. Why does he stay when he claims to be a successfully assimilated ABC with a fancy car? Why would he want to spend the evening with his cousin and her FOB date?

Dale has many chances to leave the restaurant, but each time he decides to stay. He may have nowhere else to go, but his main motivation seems to stem from his desire to be with Grace. The relationship between the cousins Dale and Grace is unusually intimate, and there are several moments in the play when Dale touches Grace. Dale competes with Steve for Grace's attention and insists on spending the evening with them. When Steve asks Grace out for a date, Dale makes sure he is not left out. Hwang's triangulation of the assimilation dilemma is represented by the three characters' triangular relationship. Both Steve and Dale desire Grace, who exists between cultures, as well as between the two men. The triangular relationship also represents the gender dynamics prevalent in Chinese American history. During the Chinese Exclusion Era, Chinese women were not allowed to immigrate to the United States, and men vastly outnumbered women in Chinese American communities. Instances of the so-called Bachelor Society, whose members consisted of unmarried Chinese men, formed in Chinatowns across the country. Some Chinese men married non-Chinese women, but the vast majority spent their lives single. Romantic relationships between Chinese men and Chinese women were elusive and uncommon in Chinatowns. When they did date or marry, their relationships carried connotations of incest, given that many Chinese communities were insular and closely knit through kinship and friendship.

The intimate moments between Dale and Grace also mark a subtle shift from realism to magical realism, from the mundane to the improbable. One stage direction reads, 'He strokes her hair. They freeze in place, except for his arm, which continues to stroke her hair' (21). Hwang does not explain why they freeze or how those moments inform the rest of the play. The shift from realism to non-realism can also be seen in the way Hwang uses language. When Grace is left alone onstage for the first time in the play, she speaks about Fa Mu Lan in the heightened tone and style of the narrator in Maxine Hong Kingston's *Woman Warrior*. She then breaks her narration and the magical moment by picking up the phone and calling Dale. She ends the narration with 'No goddess, but woman – warrior woman', and begins her phone conversation with 'Hi, Dale? Hi, this is Grace. ... Pretty good. How 'bout you?' (15). The stark contrast between the two moments and conversational styles exemplifies the coexistence and commingling of the mythic world and the mundane.

At the same time, the moments of the mythic and the mundane are historically specific and patently Californian. Maxine Hong Kingston, who was born in Stockton, California, uses the myth of Fa Mu Lan to tell the story of her growing up as a daughter of Chinese immigrants in California. Kingston identifies herself as a woman warrior in order to reject what her mother and society expected of a Chinese girl and to empower herself as a strong feminist woman. What the woman warrior Kingston has in mind is not the original Chinese mythic goddess; rather, it is Kingston's own story of becoming a Chinese American woman in California. When Grace changes her speech to talk to Dale on the phone, the English dialect she uses is quintessentially Californian – specifically Southern Californian. As noted, this particular dialect is used in most of Hwang's plays, and the dialogue he creates with it is a defining characteristic of his writing style.

The commingling of the improbable and the mundane increasingly intensifies throughout the play, culminating in a climactic battle scene. While Dale watches in utter confusion and awe, Grace and Steve – as Fa Mu Lan and Gwan Gung – engage in a battle onstage. Hwang calls the scene a 'ritual' that 'gradually take[s] on elements of Chinese opera' (43). As I describe elsewhere, the Chinese opera element was added in the 1980 production at the Public Theater.[18] In the original 1979 draft, Grace and Steve play out the battle scene as mythic gods without reference to any Chinese opera movements or sounds. Hwang frames the battle scene as a ritual and a game, implying that the contest is at once predictable and unpredictable, repeated and new. Grace seems to know from the beginning how the ritual is supposed to play out, and she directs Dale and Steve in and out of various moments of history, myth and memory.

Steve begins the battle as Gwan Gung, but when Grace defeats him, he becomes a 'Chinaman' begging for food. The monologue spoken by Steve as a 'Chinaman' echoes the voices of Chinese labourers from the nineteenth century, when laws such as the Chinese Exclusion Act were passed and enforced. Grace gives Steve *chong you bing*, which he eats 'ravenously', and the two reconcile, both as mythic gods and as witnesses of Chinese American history. Steve is an embodiment of the immigration history of Chinese men: he is by turns a nineteenth-century Chinese labourer, the mythic God Gwan Gung and an affluent and westernized immigrant from Hong Kong who, as Josephine Lee describes, is a 'different kind of Asian immigrant' specific to the second half of the twentieth century.[19]

In 'Coda', the play's last scene, Dale begins to repeat the opening monologue, but the language used to describe the FOB (that he is clumsy, ugly, greasy, etc.) loses the meaning and comic effect it conveyed earlier in the play. This ending reveals two important stylistic choices Hwang would frequently make as a playwright. First, the ending is ambiguous. Hwang does not indicate how the actor playing Dale is supposed to deliver these last lines, nor does he specify choices the performer should make when envisioning and creating Dale's state of mind. Obviously, Dale is confused, but is he also angry? How has his attitude towards FOBs changed? What does 'FOB' even signify at the end of the play? By withholding the details of Dale's feelings, Hwang creates ambiguity and openness for those interpreting the play's meaning. He ends the play with a question mark, as if he is asking the actors, directors and audiences to complete the story. The second stylistic choice Hwang uses in *FOB*, as well as in some of his other plays, is the use of a musical structure in organizing the dramatic plot. By calling the ending a coda, Hwang makes it explicit that the play should be examined like a musical score with leitmotifs, repetition and sections. To Hwang, structure and form are central to understanding his plays, and they only become complete – like music – through performance.

After first staging *FOB* in his dorm at Stanford University, Hwang submitted it to the Eugene O'Neill National Playwrights Conference in Waterford, Connecticut. The play was accepted and was produced at the Public Theater in the summer of 1980 with Mako directing and John Lone starring as Steve. Mako was a Japanese American actor and director who spearheaded the growth of the East West Players in Los Angeles for over two decades. He was a leading figure in the Asian American theatre community, and his support of *FOB* was significant to Hwang. Lone's influence on Hwang's playwriting style cannot be overstated: it was Lone who taught Hwang about Chinese opera after being cast in the role of Steve in *FOB*. Lone had been formally trained in Chinese opera in Hong Kong and had worked with Mako at the East West Players in Los Angeles. In fact, it was Mako who cast Lone, and the elements of Chinese opera were added by

Hwang with Lone's help. Hwang, who grew up in an Americanized family more interested in Western classical music than Chinese music, had no prior knowledge of Chinese opera. The production was a success and received a positive review from Frank Rich in the *New York Times*. Rich described the production as an attempt to marry 'the conventional well-made play to Oriental theater and to mix the sensibilities of Maxine Hong Kingston and Norman Lear'.[20] Both Rich and Papp, two immensely influential voices in the American theatre at the time, enthusiastically supported Hwang, support that would provide an essential foundation for Hwang's career in the theatre.

The Dance and the Railroad

Hwang's second play, *The Dance and the Railroad*, received its professional premiere at the Public Theater on 16 July 1981. The play was commissioned by the New Federal Theatre with a grant from the US Department of Education. Focused on education, the play was originally written for young audiences and premiered at the Henry Street Settlement on the Lower East Side in New York City. According to Hwang, the play was performed during the days for 'kids who would get bussed in from schools'.[21] There was a single evening performance, which Rich reviewed positively. Bolstered by Rich's enthusiastic endorsement, the production moved to the Public Theater, where it ran for six months.

The play was the result of a collaboration between Hwang, John Lone and Tzi Ma. Lone directed and choreographed the play, and he also created the production's music. Lone and Tzi Ma co-created and acted the play's two characters, named Lone and Ma. At the time, Tzi Ma was an active member of the Asian American Theatre Company in San Francisco, where Hwang was part of a young group of Asian American theatre artists. While Hwang's early plays were never commissioned by or premiered at Asian American theatre companies, he consistently and deliberately worked with Asian American actors.

While in the battle scene of *FOB*, Hwang had used movements from Chinese opera to dramatize the fantastical and subconscious conflict between two supernatural entities, movements in *The Dance and the Railroad* represent the *reality* of the characters in the play. Whereas Grace and Steve in *FOB* embody the mythic gods for purposes of confrontation and competition, Lone and Ma in *The Dance and the Railroad* perform the movements for aesthetic and philosophical reasons. As the title indicates, dance is the central theme of the play, and the two characters' main actions are conveyed through dance. Hwang had established a creative relationship with Lone when the two worked on *FOB* together, and *The Dance and the Railroad* is a play specifically written for Lone to showcase his virtuosity as a dancer and choreographer. Lone – both as an actor and as his namesake character – embodies Hwang's vision of how Chinese opera could be incorporated within the framework of the more realistic staging familiar to American audiences. Hwang would continue to use Chinese opera both as a theme and a staging technique in his later plays, mostly prominently in *M. Butterfly* (1988) and *Kung Fu* (2014).

In his review in the *New York Times*, Rich describes the play as 'bringing West and East into conflict and unity' and praises the play and the production as 'witty, poetic, and affecting'.[22] Despite his characterization of Hwang as a 'Chinese-American playwright', Rich does not approach *The Dance and the Railroad* as a Chinese American play. Rather, he sees it as an encounter between two Chinese labourers and between two distinct worlds (West and East). While Rich's description is accurate on the surface, it is more revealing to approach the play as a Chinese American work reminiscent of the first wave of Asian American playwriting. During the 1960s and 1970s, the first-wave Asian American playwrights wrote plays that focused on history and autobiography. Frank Chin, for example, wrote about Chinatown in San Francisco, and Wakako Yamuchi wrote about the early Japanese farm workers in Imperial Valley, California, during the Great Depression. Both had experienced the historical basis for their plays first-hand. While I classify Hwang as a second-wave playwright, his early plays echo those of the first. Hwang had read Frank Chin and other first-wave writers and described them as his playwriting role models. It was important for Hwang, especially early in his career, to write plays that followed the path defined by his Asian American predecessors.

Rediscovering history has been an important, shared goal of Asian American writers, artists and scholars, and in the early 1980s, there was still a sense of urgency and a determination to tell Asian American stories. Hwang wanted to dramatize an actual historical incident with *The Dance and the Railroad*:

> The reclaiming of our American past is certainly a priority for Asians. An actual incident, the Chinese railroad workers' strike of 1867, provides the background of this piece. So often 'coolie' laborers have been characterized in America as passive and subservient, two

stereotypes often attached to Asians. The strike is important because it reminds us that in historical fact these were assertive men who stood up for their rights in the face of great adversity.[23]

The key phrase in Hwang's statement is 'our American past'. For Hwang and other Asian American writers, Asian American history had to be reclaimed and integrated into existing narratives of American history. In contrast to Rich's conclusion, it was less important for Hwang to situate Asian American history as a clash between two cultures and more important to emphasize Asian Americans as an indispensable part of the fabric of American history and culture, a goal Hwang pursued in his 'isolationist–nationalist' phase.

In the introduction to *FOB and Other Plays*, Hwang explains that this phase of his development as a playwright followed his 'assimilationist' phase:

> I discovered in college that the assimilationist model was dangerous and self-defeating. ... Living in an Asian American dorm, becoming involved with theater and musical groups of similar focus, I entered what might be considered an 'isolationist–nationalist' phase. I became interested in working with and writing primarily for other Asian Americans.[24]

According to Hwang, he wrote two plays while he was in his 'isolationist–nationalist' phase: *The Dance and the Railroad*, a history play, and *Family Devotions*, an autobiographical play. Despite the separatist connotation of the term 'isolationist–nationalist', his ultimate goal was to establish Asian American history and culture as a distinct yet integral part of American history and culture. *The Dance and the Railroad* is an Asian American history play, and its two characters must be read as surrogates of the Asian Americans who struggled to gain civil rights and enfranchisement as Americans in the second half of the twentieth century.

Hwang's use of Chinese labourer history in the play echoes dramaturgical styles used by other Asian American playwrights of the first wave. While Frank Chin has been a fierce critic of Hwang's popular plays (*M. Butterfly* in particular), Hwang has admitted that his early career was influenced by Chin's plays. There are two major similarities between Hwang's *The Dance and the Railroad* and Chin's plays: both writers masculinize Chinese American history, and both address the survival narrative of Chinese Americans in the United States, which requires the sacrifice of creative forms of expression such as theatre, dance, filmmaking and writing. For both Hwang and

Chin, the Chinese who laboured on the transcontinental railroad are an essential component in Chinese America's origin story and, by extension, Asian America. That story relies on strong male characters who defy the stereotype of Asians being 'passive and subservient', as Hwang puts it in the passage quoted above. The male Chinese American characters created by both playwrights are angry, articulate, cynical and complex. They dream of changing the world, while still recognizing the limits of the reality they live in. They are also artistic types, with piercing observations of the world, and their sensitive minds provide them full awareness of the tragicomic situations surrounding them. In Chin's *Chickencoop Chinaman* (1972) and *Year of the Dragon* (1974), for example, the protagonists of both plays aspire to be strong Chinese American men and try to use their creative talents to change their lives. Ultimately, however, they both fail: Tam Lum in *Chickencoop Chinaman* cannot make his film and Fred Eng in *Year of the Dragon* cannot become a writer.

In *The Dance and the Railroad*, Hwang's characters Lone and Ma play out a similar fate. The play begins with Ma secretly watching Lone practice Chinese opera steps on a mountaintop. Both characters are Chinese 'coolies' conscripted to work on the railroads, though the scenes take place far from the workers' camp. The audience learns that the Chinese workers are on strike to demand better wages and working hours and that Lone has been in the United States for two years, while Ma arrived only four weeks ago. Naive and hopeful, Ma believes that he can earn enough money to return to China and have twenty wives. In this dream, he would practice Chinese opera as a hobby and play the role of Gwan Gung. Lone, in contrast, is disillusioned and cynical, calling other Chinese workers 'bugs'. According to Ma, the workers mock him as the 'Prince of the Mountain' who is 'too good to spend time with them' (58). Ma asks Lone to teach him the dance, not realizing that one must devote a lifetime of study to learn Chinese opera. He wants to merely perform for fun, not become an actor. The uninformed confidence of Ma amuses Lone, who knows that the propaganda about the 'Gold Mountain' in America is false. But he does not tell Ma that there is no 'warm snow' in the winter and that the promise of a year-end bonus is a lie. Instead, he teases Ma sarcastically and tells him to go away. Ignoring Lone's rejection, Ma continues to visit him during the strike. Lone presses Ma to say that the 'other Chinamen' are dead: 'When my body hurts too much to come [to the top of the mountain], I look at other Chinamen and think, "They are dead. Their muscles work only because the white man forces them. I live because I can still force my muscles to work for me". Say it. "They are dead"' (66).

Ma pushes back and insists that the workers are not dead because they are standing up against 'white devils'. After much verbal tussling, Lone agrees to be Ma's teacher, but only until the strike is over.

For the rest of the play, the two characters exercise together, and their interactions are entertaining and humorous. Much of the humour comes from Ma's failure to match Lone both physically and intellectually. When, for instance, Lone imitates a duck convincingly and gracefully, Ma's duck is performed 'mechanically', as described by Hwang in the stage direction. When Ma finally becomes absorbed in his imitation of a duck, Lone sneaks out and returns as a tiger to frighten Ma.

> **Lone**   Grrrr!
> **Ma**   (*As a cry for help*): Quack, quack, quack!
> (*Lone pounces on Ma. They struggle, in character. Ma is quacking madly, eyes tightly closed. Lone stands up straight. Ma continues to quack.*)
> **Lone**   Stand up.
> **Ma**   (*Eyes still closed*): Quack, quack, quack!
> **Lone**   (*Louder*): Stand up!
> **Ma**   (*Opening his eyes*): Oh.
> **Lone**   What are you?
> **Ma**   Huh?
> **Lone**   A Chinaman or a duck?
> **Ma**   Huh? Gimme a second to remember. (72)

This scene is one the funniest in the play, and the physical humour works especially well for younger audiences. But it also dramatizes a central theme Hwang explores in more serious ways elsewhere in the play. Lone, who is painfully and cynically aware of his circumstances, plays with Ma, whose unawareness of his new life in America is both comedic and tragic. While pretending and playing, the two transcend their mundane realities, and what they experience with the audience is hyper-theatrical. In subsequent scenes, the ludic quality of the play increases, culminating in the two characters' complete immersion in the performance of their stories.[25]

The ludic moments allow Lone and Ma to feel alive and temporarily forget where and who they are. These moments are similar to the battle scene in *FOB*, in which the characters enter the mode of magical realism. Similar to Grace in *FOB*, Lone in *The Dance and the Railroad* manipulates the situation to construct the magical moments, intending to teach Ma what is possible outside of their perceived reality. In both plays, Hwang's characters make discoveries about the truth of their lives by physically embodying other entities (such as gods and animals), a technique common to Chinese opera. The stylized and playful movements transport the characters to an imagined world filled with myths, memory and hope for the future. For Lone and Ma, the movements make them feel alive and distinguish them from other 'Chinamen' who cannot escape the control of their white bosses.

When Lone and Ma learn that the strike is over and that they must return to work, they each come to distinctly different conclusions. Lone, after hearing Ma's tale of how he ended up in America, realizes that Ma's history is as important and poignant as the myth of Gwan Gung. The Chinese opera should not restrict itself to myths from China but should also treat the lives of Chinese men everywhere, the same ones Lone had previously disdained as 'dead'. Lone has new respect for the workers because they were able to negotiate better conditions with the strike. 'Maybe I was wrong about them', he admits (87). He asks Ma at the end of the play to take the props down, implying that the dance should not exist separately from the railroad. Lone's arrogance dissipates and is replaced by a new understanding for the workers. For Ma, however, the strike brought only partial success: the workers were able to negotiate shorter hours but only by compromising their compensation. He sees the strike as a failure and realizes that he must continue the fight. In a reversal, *he* calls the workers 'dead men' and says, 'Their greatest accomplishment was to win a strike that's gotten us nothing' (87). In effect, the two characters reverse roles, with Ma refusing to submit to the fate of being a 'coolie' and Lone acknowledging that he is no longer certain about anything. The play ends with Lone dancing by himself, possibly for the last time, on the top of the mountain. Similar to Dale at the end of *FOB*, Lone ambiguously occupies the stage alone at the end of *The Dance and the Railroad*, preventing a satisfying closure to the story and encouraging different interpretations of the ending. Both plays come full circle, and the protagonists end the plays by echoing their beginnings. But the men in each have changed in ways that signal a new beginning.

There are additional thematic and structural similarities between *FOB* and *The Dance and the Railroad*. With the latter play, however, Hwang introduces new styles and approaches to playwriting he would repeatedly use throughout his career. While the play is about actual history, which Hwang is careful to reference, he contemporizes the history with language and humour familiar to his American audiences. Lone and Ma are supposed to be speaking Cantonese in the world of the play, but the actors speak fluent

American English. And while the characters look like Chinese men of the nineteenth century, what comes out of their mouths is colloquial American dialogue, complete with witty sarcasm American audiences can appreciate. In Hwang's *The Dance and the Railroad*, his characters may look like Chinese men, but they speak like young Americans of 1981.

Hwang's characters sound contemporary because of the dialogues he writes, though the delivery of those lines by the actors is just as critical. The style of acting demanded by Hwang's characters is not a naturalistic one, in which the actor convincingly becomes the character. In Hwang's theatre, the actor needs to be visible and present *as* the character. Similar to the Brechtian style of meta-acting, the staging of Hwang's plays requires some distance to exist between actor and character. In such a style, the actor is always conscious of the fact that he is enacting a character, and the audience has to be able see the distance and the self-conscious enactment. This is even truer in *The Dance and the Railroad*, which was written with John Lone and Tzi Ma in mind. The two Asian American actors coexist with the characters onstage, and the play is not only about the story of Lone and Ma, the railroad workers, but also about John Lone and Tzi Ma, the actors.

Family Devotions

When theatre scholar David Savran asked Hwang which playwrights had influenced his work, he identified Sam Shepard as having the greatest impact 'because of the way he juxtaposes reality and myth'.

> [Shepard] is very conscious that there are links to our past and that we, as a country, have a collective history. He attempts to make those connections in his plays. Also, in his preface to *Angel City*, Shepard talks about characters in a different way, in terms of jazz improvisation, rather than developing the character's arc in the traditional fashion. You see almost a collage effect, bits and pieces of the character at different points, butting up against one another.[26]

Shepard's influence on Hwang has been significant. Hwang's use of myth, magical realism, colloquial language, meta-theatrical action, masculinity and the California 'cool' are only a few elements that reveal the similarity between the two playwrights. *Family Devotions*, in particular, follows the single-setting plot structure often seen in Shepard's work. Similar to

Shepard's *Curse of the Starving Class* and other plays, both acts of *Family Devotions* take place in the same setting, and there is no lapse of time between the two acts. Tellingly, Hwang dedicates the play to three people: Ama (his grandmother), Ankong (his grandfather) and Sam Shepard.

Family Devotions dramatizes Hwang's observations of his family in a genre I would describe as tragi-farce. The play is based on an actual event Hwang experienced when an uncle from the People's Republic of China visited his sisters in Bel Air (an affluent suburb in Los Angeles) after being separated for over thirty years. The sisters, Ama and Popo, are zealous Christians, and they remember their brother, Di-gou, as having accepted Christ and spoken in tongues at a young age when they were in China. They want to confirm that he is still a Christian despite years of brainwashing by the Communist Party in China. Each member of the family has his or her unrelenting agenda, and three generations clash onstage with dire consequences.

Set in 1980 in the sunroom of a Bel Air home, the play opens with Di-gou, described as 'an older Chinese man', standing on an outdoor tennis court and peering through a sunroom's glass walls. He exits as Joanne, the daughter of Ama and a resident of the house, enters to attend to a burning barbecue. Joanne's entrance begins a fast-paced scene littered with the overlapping dialogue, miscommunication and meanness that often exists in highly dysfunctional families.

Joanne's husband, Wilbur, is a Japanese American who was voted Mr Congeniality at work. Ama and Popo openly despise him for being Japanese and expect him to 'kill and laugh', just as Japanese soldiers did during the Second World War. Joanne and Wilbur's seventeen-year-old daughter, Jenny, would rather read *Vogue* magazine in her room, but, in order to please her grand-matriarchs, she plays the role of the good Chinese daughter (or the 'Lotus Blossom', as she puts it). Hannah, who is Popo's daughter and Joanne's cousin, is married to Robert, a first-generation Chinese American and a self-made banker. Robert wants to be the centre of attention with his story of success and fame in the United States, but the entire family openly pushes him away. His son, Chester, is in his early twenties and about leave for Boston to play the violin for the Boston Symphony. Chester drifts in and out of the action of the play, never sure whether he wants to stay or leave the family.

In fact, the entire play explores both how a family stays connected and how it comes apart. What has previously held the family together in *Family Devotions* is the mythical story of its ancestors' conversion to Christianity; what pulls the family apart is the revelation that the story was fabricated.

The sisters adamantly believe that the origin of their religious faith began with a certain aunt: back when they were living in Manila, their aunt, See-goh-poh, was the first in the family to become Christian, and she travelled around China to convert local villagers. 'She make this family chosen by God', states Popo.[27] Ama and Popo claim that Di-gou travelled with their aunt and witnessed the miracles she performed. According to Popo, 'Five hundred people accept Christ on these thirty days, and See-goh-poh heal many sick, restore ear to deaf, put tongue in mouth of dumb, all these thing and cast out the demon' (105). Di-gou denies the story they remember and tells them that such miracles and conversions never happened. According to Di-gou, See-goh-poh made up the story of miraculous proselytizing in order to hide her pregnancy and to see her child.

Ama and Popo also believe that Jesus Christ is the main reason for their family's success in the United States, and they are convinced that they are more blessed than others. Christ's blessing, for them, takes the form of materials goods. The play showcases the cutting-edge technology of the early 1980s: a microwave oven, a Beta-max player, a Cuisinart and a tennis ball machine, not all of which the characters in the play know how to operate. Joanne, for instance, says, 'I want to use my new Cuisinart', but admits that she does not know what it does (115). The story of material success functions as another myth that reinforces the family's sense of self-grandeur and exceptionalism. Money is what sets them apart from communists in China and from what Ama and Popo call 'servants'. Being rich, Christian and Chinese proves that they were chosen by God and that they deserve all that they have in the United States. When Jenny discusses potential husbands with Ama and Popo, she receives a long list of criteria that describe a person who would be acceptable to the family: Christian, Chinese, with a good education (Princeton or Harvard) and with a suitable career (such as a doctor, preferably a brain surgeon) (103). Ama and Popo discourage Jenny from pursuing dance and tell her to become a dental technician so she can find a husband they deem worthy.

The character that embodies the worst form of the family's obsession with material success is Robert. If the play is read as autobiographical, Robert represents Hwang's father, who also was a self-made banker who married into a devout Christian family. Robert reminds everyone that he started as a penniless FOB and revels in having achieved his version of the American Dream. In his exchange with Di-gou, Robert declares, 'Us Chinese, we love to eat, right? Well, here in America, we can be pigs!' (120). He then stuffs his mouth with *bao* (steamed meat buns) and stomps on *guo-tieh* (fried meat dumplings) after having intentionally dropped them. Robert wants to show Di-gou that what is precious in China can be casually wasted in America, 'the Land of Plenty' (120). In *FOB*, Grace gives Steve food at the end of the play, and their interaction recalls countless numbers of Chinese labourers who had to beg for food in America. The piece of *bing* eaten by Steve represents hope and opportunity, as well as the survival and perseverance of Chinese immigrants. For Robert, however, food can be stomped on because it symbolizes the excesses of the American Dream. The FOB has achieved his success, and he shows it in the most perverse way. Robert cannot talk about anything other than money and fame, and he does everything in his power to generate publicity. He thinks that any kind of publicity is better than none, and he itches to repeatedly tell the story of how he was kidnapped and became 'famous' because he was featured in newspapers.

The main plot line that drives the play revolves around the 'family devotions' that Ama and Popo want to hold in honour of Di-gou's visit. Everyone in the family is supposed to gather and give testimony about how God has blessed them, but when they take turns speaking, each talks about things unrelated to Christianity. Instead, the entire session of family devotions becomes a chaotic opportunity for each family member to announce what is most important to him or her. It is also a chance to distinguish myth from reality. Popo tells the story of the family leaving China, declaring that it was God's will. Robert insists on relating the story of his kidnapping, a tale the family has already heard too many times. Jenny, who would rather not participate, shares what is essentially the main point of Hwang's play, although the elders misunderstand what she says.

> **Jenny** *(At podium, she begins testimony)*: First, I want to say that I love you all very much. I really do.
> **Popo** *(To Di-gou)*: That meaning is, she loves God.
> **Jenny** And I appreciate what you've done for me.
> **Popo** *(To Di-gou)*: She love us because we show her God.
> **Jenny** But I guess there are certain times when even love isn't enough.
> **Popo** *(To Di-gou)*: She does not have enough love for you. You are not Christian.
> **Jenny** Sometimes, even love has its dark side.
> **Popo** *(To Di-gou)*: That is you.
> **Jenny** And when you find that side, sometimes you have to leave in order to come back in a better way.
> **Popo** *(To Di-gou)*: She cannot stand to be around you. (134)

Jenny's lines are interrupted by Popo, who interprets them as a condemnation of godless Di-gou, and the moment is highly comical. Yet it is also one of the most genuine moments in the play, and it can be read as Hwang's testimony to his own family. Hwang grew up in what he describes as a fundamentalist Christian family, and he denounced the religion while attending Stanford University. If his family is anything like the family in *Family Devotions*, the rejection probably inspired much consternation and heartache. The play can certainly be read as an exaggerated and farcical re-creation of the family's reaction to his denouncement, but at the same time, it is Hwang's explanation of why and how he is leaving his family and its faith. He loves his family, but he must first leave in order to 'come back in a better way', as Jenny states.

Similar to *FOB* and *The Dance and the Railroad*, Hwang frames *Family Devotions* with parallel scenes at its beginning and end. In *FOB*, it is Dale and his lecture about the differences between FOBs and ABCs, and in *The Dance and the Railroad*, Lone's dances bookend the play. In each case, while the scene at the end is similar to the one in the beginning, the ending reveals the stark transformation the play has triggered. The plays' endings leave Dale and Lone alone to question their core beliefs and assumptions. In *Family Devotions*, two characters, Di-gou and Chester, bookend the play. Together they embody Hwang's reasons for leaving the family faith, and they also represent his evolving philosophy and politics as a young American playwright.

Questions of faith and identity are intimately bound up with a common theatrical motif used by Hwang: the face. The opening stage direction reads: 'As the curtain rises, we see a single spotlight on an old Chinese face and hear Chinese music or chanting' (95). The face is that of Di-gou, who watches the family before entering the house later in the act. The last image of the play echoes the beginning, but with Chester rather than Di-gou. The closing stage direction reads: 'Chester stands where Di-gou stood at the beginning of the play. He turns around and looks through the glass door onto the scene. The lights begin to dim until there is one single spotlight on Chester's face. The shape of Chester's face begins to change' (150). The connection between Di-gou and Chester is first established when they are left alone after a frenzied tennis session with a defective ball machine that would not stop. Chester offers to show his violin to Di-gou, saying that, unlike the ball machine, the violin does not have the 'Made in the U.S.' label. In a rare moment of honest communication between characters, Di-gou shares with Chester his stories about his life and why he decided to visit his sisters, and Chester tells him that he is leaving home. While the granduncle is reconnecting with his sisters, his grandnephew is planning to leave the family. Their quiet and tender interaction is at the core of an otherwise outrageously farcical play.

When Chester and Di-gou look at the violin together, the reflective finish on the instrument's backside both reveals and bonds their relationship. Each sees a mirrored image of the other's face, simultaneously similar and different, changing depending on how the violin is held. In one of the most eloquent passages in Hwang's oeuvre, Di-gou tells Chester to study his own face to find the stories of his origins:

> There are faces back further than you can see. Faces long before the white missionaries arrived in China. Here. *(He holds Chester's violin so that its back is facing Chester, and uses it like a mirror)* Look here. At your face. Study your face and you will see – the shape of your face is the shape of faces back many generations – across an ocean, in another soil. You must become one with your family before you can hope to live away from it. (126)

The face is a recurring motif in Hwang's plays, and he uses it to describe and explain his Chinese American identity. In two later plays, *Face Value* and *Yellow Face*, Hwang uses the face motif to further explore identity politics. At the same time, the face functions as one of his primary dramatic devices. The face is like the theatrical mask that shows or hides the truth, and, as Di-gou's speech suggests, the face is essential to Hwang's storytelling. For Hwang, the face is inherently theatrical.

Chester initially dismisses Di-gou's advice, but he realizes later in the play that he already knows the stories written on his own face. During the family devotions, Ama and Popo attempt to convert Di-gou to Christianity and to wash him in the 'blood of the lamb' (141). They knock him down, tie him to the table and begin exorcizing him of demons in front of a neon cross. Joined by Joanne and Hannah, the two elderly sisters whip Di-gou with an electrical cord and demand he acknowledge that See-goh-poh was 'a great evangelist'. When he refuses, Ama chokes him with the electrical cord, almost killing him. Chester, followed by Jenny, rushes inside to release Di-gou, and the ritual takes an unexpected turn. With the barbeque bursting into flames in the background, Di-gou begins to speak in tongues, leading the women to kneel. But Chester begins to interpret Di-gou and tells the real story of See-goh-poh: Di-gou, at the age of eight, witnessed his aunt giving birth. Chester and Di-gou gradually start speaking together, and the latter declares to his sisters, 'Your stories are dead now that you know the truth' (146). Di-gou and Ama then engage in a verbal battle with their conflicting stories as weapons. The battle ends with the death of Ama and Popo, who refuse to believe Di-gou's story.

As with *FOB*, *Family Devotions* culminates in a battle scene between characters embracing two opposing stories of the past. Moreover, both are semi-autobiographical, and both interrogate what it means to be successful in the United States. Read as autobiographies, Dale and Chester represent different aspects of Hwang, who in his early twenties was questioning his assumptions and finding his own voice as a playwright and as an adult independent of his family's influence. The early plays dramatize the internal battles he must have felt while attempting to form his own perspectives on life and theatre. While *FOB* is about his rejection of cultural assimilation, *Family Devotions* is about his search for a new culture, one untainted by dogmatic religion or obsession with material success.

Hwang's characters clash over money, myths and beliefs, but in all cases, the final outcome is ambiguous. In *Family Devotions*, Ama's prayer and exorcism have significant repercussions, and the fact that Hwang dedicates the play to his grandparents complicates any simple interpretation. Chester is trapped in a liminal state: he wants to leave home but has yet to pack; he cannot leave his family yet knows he cannot stay. Di-gou's message to Chester is equally equivocal. Di-gou tells the young man to leave his family in order to come back to it. Ultimately, the play is neither a facile rejection of Hwang's childhood faith nor a mocking condemnation of his father's obsession with fame. Hwang proposes an inclusive understanding of his family by situating his grandparents' and parents' worldviews in the context of a much longer and broader history, explaining their strange behaviour as being guided by perverted and inaccurate family stories. Ama and Popo's deaths should not be taken too literally; rather, they demonstrate that origin stories need to be corrected and demystified. The new story that Hwang tells is one of two men from different generations, Chester and Di-gou, who must leave the past, but will forever be connected because they are part of the same family, and because the shapes of their faces resemble those of their ancestors.

The story Hwang tells in *Family Devotions* is essentially about leaving his own family in search of a new cultural allegiance. For Hwang, that new culture is Californian at its core, and the mode of its expression is theatrical.

When Di-gou announces that he is leaving, he states his desire 'only to drive an American car – very fast – down an American freeway' (149). Di-gou, like Dale, wants the Californian cool, which is symbolized by a fast car and an open freeway. While Di-gou says 'an American freeway', the term 'freeway' is itself Californian, and the fondness of cars is a topic explored by other Californian writers, especially Sam Shepard. The high-gloss of Chester's violin and the fast car in Di-gou's mind epitomize a Californian myth Hwang proposes in his Chinese American trilogy. Together, Dale, Steve, Chester and Di-gou embody aspects of Hwang's vision of the Chinese American man who has the California 'cool' and toughness. He is free to race down that open road, searching for new adventures and creating new myths.

CHAPTER 2
BEYOND CHINESE AMERICA: LOVE, DEATH AND RESURRECTION

The four plays discussed in this chapter are frequently left out of general treatments of Hwang's work. In a popular narrative on Hwang's playwriting career, he is praised for having debuted at a young age with his play *FOB*, and his Chinese Trilogy is recognized as reflecting his strong sense of Chinese American identity. The narrative then focuses on his success with *M. Butterfly* and the Tony Award he received for the play. However, between the trilogy (the last of which was written in 1981) and *M. Butterfly* (which premiered in 1988), Hwang wrote four plays that were significant in helping him develop his craft and style and giving him the experience necessary to write *M. Butterfly*. More importantly, he expanded his subject matter beyond his Chinese American ethnicity and experimented with different styles and forms of theatre.

The fiery ending of *Family Devotions* marked both the conclusion of David Henry Hwang's Chinese Trilogy and the beginning of a new phase in his career. After a farce featuring a burning barbeque and dead grandmothers, Hwang felt free to write about anything that interested him. Having previously dealt with issues of identity, family and history in the trilogy, he was eager to try new forms and styles of playwriting. 'Essentially, I had said everything I wanted to about my immediate background for the time being', Hwang noted.[1] Between 1983 and 1986, he wrote four plays that differ significantly from each other. Hwang continued the practice of modelling his plays on other playwrights' works, finding inspiration in the dramas of Samuel Beckett and Harold Pinter. The questions Hwang asks in the four plays are not variants of 'Who am I?' in the sense of ethnicity, culture or history. Rather, he is interested in exploring existential questions of life and death, as well as the themes of sex and deception. Denouncing the faith of his family led Hwang to also reject the Judeo-Christian theology of life and death and to embrace, instead, decidedly different alternatives. In particular, he was drawn to Japanese stories that blur the distinction between the living and the dead and between the facade and what is concealed beneath.

Characters in *The Sound of a Voice* and *The House of Sleeping Beauties* are mythic and ghostly, and the settings of the plays are otherworldly. At the same time, Hwang wrote them as Asian American plays, intending they be cast with Asian American actors who could speak American English. The dialogue reminds one of Hwang's characters in earlier plays, and the metatheatrical impulse is also present. Ultimately, the plays allowed Hwang to continue exploring his voice as a playwright.

The choice to dramatize Japanese stories is both surprising and intriguing. Japan, as mentioned multiple times in *Family Devotions*, invaded China and other Asian countries during the Second World War, leading Ama and Popo to distrust Wilbur, a Japanese American. Moreover, in the early 1980s, the Japanese mythic stories were not a significant part of Asian American theatre and literature. It was rare in that period for an Asian American playwright to explore the experience of an ethnic group different from his/her own. With his two plays based on Japanese stories, Hwang ventured forth in a new direction in Asian American theatre by writing about Japanese stories as a Chinese American playwright. Hwang includes the two plays in what he calls his 'isolationist–nationalist' phase, which suggests that his vision of Asian American drama was expansive enough to include Asian stories disconnected from the particularities of the Chinese American experience.

Hwang's choice can also be explained by examining the cultural context in which he was working. As Hwang mentions in his interview with David Savran, Japan in the 1980s was seen as being in the 'vanguard' of those 'making some fusion of East and West'.[2] In Europe and the United States, the films and literature of Japan were popular, along with its cars and Sony Walkmans. Hwang was, in many ways, a product of that generation, in that he grew up watching Japanese films and reading Japanese literature. He was also exposed to other creative works informed by Japanese culture, such as the movies of major American filmmakers like George Lucas and Steven Spielberg who were significantly influenced by the Japanese film director Akira Kurosawa. For many artists and writers of the American baby boom generation, Japanese film and literature provided a welcome alternative to European aesthetics and traditions. It should also be noted that the Japanese writer Yasunari Kawabata won the Nobel Prize for Literature in 1968, as did Samuel Beckett in 1969; both writers have significantly influenced Hwang.

In his interview with Savran, Hwang acknowledges that *The Sound of a Voice* and *The House of Sleeping Beauties* were primarily influenced by Japanese literature and film, rather than by Japanese theatre.[3] *The Sound of a Voice* is Hwang's take on Japanese folklore, a genre perhaps best exemplified by Lafcadio Hearn's *Kwaidan: Stories and Studies of Strange Things* (1904), the film version of which (directed by Masaki Kobayashi) was nominated for an Academy Award for Best Foreign Language Film in 1965. Indeed, *The House of Sleeping Beauties* is an adaptation of a novella by the Japanese writer Yasunari Kawabata. Just as *FOB* was inspired by the writings of Maxine Hong Kingston and Frank Chin, what influenced Hwang's two Japanese plays was literature. Also similar to *FOB*, the two Japanese plays were presented in a theatrical form that Hwang would increasingly call 'Asian American' or 'a blend of Asian and Western theatre'.[4] With the help of others, particularly John Lone, Hwang theatricalized literary stories onstage, and he did so by exploring non-verbal elements such as design, movement and silence.

One distinctive feature of contemporary drama is the increased use of silence in plot development, and all of the major playwrights Hwang has emulated – Sam Shepard, Edward Bond, Samuel Beckett and Harold Pinter – use silence extensively in their plays. As Pinter and others have described, there are different kinds of silence. One is literal silence, when nothing is spoken onstage, while another occurs in those moments when what the characters say is less important than what they do not or cannot say. For many contemporary playwrights, spoken language is not to be trusted, often leaving unspoken subtext to advance the plot. Hwang uses silence extensively in *Family Devotions;* for instance, Chester's silence at the play's end reveals his transformation as a character. In fact, the most important moments of the plot are executed in silence throughout the play.

In all four plays discussed in this chapter, Hwang goes even further, using silence as both a central theme and a plot device. He combines Beckett's silence of existential nothingness with Pinter's silence of menace to create distinctive non-verbal moods and atmospheres onstage. In reading and watching the plays, just as much attention must be paid to what characters do not say as to the dialogue itself. Moreover, all four plays feature characters trying to hear echoes of what may exist beyond life. That existence may be embodied by a ghost or a dead mother, but in all cases, characters are haunted by both the sound and the silence of the unknown.

The House of Sleeping Beauties

On 6 November 1983, *The House of Sleeping Beauties* and *The Sound of a Voice* premiered at the Public Theater in New York City under the title *Sound and Beauty*. The two one-act plays were directed by John Lone, who also played Man in *The Sound of a Voice*. *The House of Sleeping Beauties* was the first bill of the double act, and veteran Asian American actors Ching Valdes and Victor Wong played Woman and Kawabata, respectively. Frank Rich, in his *New York Times* review, describes the production as Hwang's 'earnest experiment' with 'an ascetic esthetic mode', but he concludes that the experiment was not entirely successful. He summarizes by suggesting, 'We're keenly conscious of his efforts to duplicate the mood of Japanese literature and theatre. The spare visual and verbal brushstrokes are so artfully applied that effects intended as simple and delicate can come across as synthetic and laborious.'[5] The overall review is mixed, and while Rich predicts that the plays would further Hwang's growth as a playwright, he does not elaborate on how such growth would happen. Of course, Rich had no way of knowing that four years later Hwang would write *M. Butterfly*, a major contemporary play about sex and relationships.

Both of the Japanese plays anticipate *M. Butterfly* in several ways. Most importantly, the relationship between the two main characters in each is defined mainly by traditional gender roles. The Japanese tradition provides the cultural underpinnings for more rigid gender divisions, which Hwang uses to examine how gender is embodied and performed in the game of power and love. In exploring gendered relationships, Hwang's female characters reveal his development as a playwright. In the Chinese Trilogy, female characters such as Grace in *FOB* and Jenny in *Family Devotions* have insightful things to say, but as dramatic characters they are less developed than their male counterparts. And women who are portrayed as strong (such as Ama and Popo) come across as caricatures. The two Japanese plays, by contrast, exhibit more nuanced, complicated female characters. Romantic or sexual relationships are not a major theme of the earlier trilogy, and when relationships are suggested, as in the case of Steve and Grace in *FOB*, the play ends as the relationship begins. Moreover, every time Dale touches Grace's hair, the scene freezes, almost as if Hwang was uncertain what should happen to them. In contrast, Hwang explores what can happen between a man and a woman in the two Japanese plays, and both the male and female characters gain richer personalities as they find themselves in precarious situations.

In *The House of Sleeping Beauties*, Hwang keeps the basic plot of Kawabata's original story by setting the play in 'the house of sleeping beauties', where old men visit to sleep (and only sleep) with beautiful, young, naked virgins who are drugged with a sleeping potion. Kawabata's story is told from the perspective of the protagonist, Eguchi, who initially visits the house mainly out of curiosity, only gradually discovering that sleeping next to the women causes him to recall past memories. He also sleeps better after taking the sleeping pills provided by the house. As an old man close to death, he remembers women from his past – lovers, three daughters, a wife and his mother. His heart is full of regret and sadness, though he also recalls certain moments in his life with fondness. The house is managed by a woman who looks to be in her mid-forties, and her interactions with Eguchi are strictly businesslike. Little is revealed about the woman, who withholds details about the house from the inquiring Eguchi. Her job is to provide beautiful sleeping women to paying men and to facilitate a satisfactory experience for them. Eguchi's narrative focuses on what he feels and remembers as he lies next to the heavily drugged women. Each woman provokes in Eguchi a range of unexpected memories, and he finds himself surprised at what he remembers, leading to a painful self-awareness of how he has lived his life. Moreover, the young women remind him of everything he is not: their lives are only beginning to blossom while his is withering away. At the same time, the mere surface of their limp bodies stands in stark contrast to the depth of Eguchi's lively mind, and he feels, at times, more alive than them. At the end of the story, one of the young women dies, and the woman who runs the house tells Eguchi, 'Go on back to sleep. There is the other girl.'[6] The story ends with Eguchi staring at the remaining girl while imagining what might happen to the dead body.

In Hwang's adaptation of the novella, the author Kawabata is the protagonist who visits the house to conduct research for the story he eventually writes. Eguchi makes an appearance in the form of an acquaintance who tells him about the house and what goes on there. According to Hwang, the play connects the novella, which was published in 1961, with Kawabata's suicide in 1972. Hwang writes in his Playwright's Note that the play is a 'fantasy' and emphasizes that it is not meant to be historical. This blending of actual events with imagined storylines is an approach that Hwang would use repeatedly in his writing career, as can be seen in *M. Butterfly*, *Golden Child* and *Yellow Face*. The play is set in 1972, the year Kawabata surprised the world by taking his own life at the age of seventy-two. In the play, Kawabata is also seventy-two (the same age as Eguchi in the original story), but the Woman (named Michiko) is in her late seventies, much older than in Kawabata's version. The play, then, can be read as Hwang's explanation of the suicide and speculation regarding Kawabata's thoughts during his last days.

In his review of *The House of Sleeping Beauties*, Frank Rich proposes that 'perhaps more important is the play's feminist undertow: Kawabata must move beyond his male ego to partake of the wisdom that Michiko offers him'.[7] While this comment is made almost in passing, it hints at the most prominent aspect of Hwang's growth as a playwright to that point. Hwang takes a story that is told entirely from a man's perspective, in which women are literally silent and immobile, and reconfigures it by drastically altering the older woman's influence on the protagonist. It would be a stretch to label the play as feminist because 'the sleeping beauties' are still subject to the same kind of passive and dehumanizing conditions and because the character of Michiko is not the protagonist. Her role is that of the helper who assists Kawabata in dealing with problems he cannot resolve on his own. Nevertheless, she is portrayed as a complex and savvy woman who knows how to run a successful business by providing what her customers want.

Most men who visit the house suffer from insomnia, so Michiko initially assumes the same is true of Kawabata. However, what ails Kawabata cannot be cured with a potion. He suffers from writer's block and, more importantly, is tortured by a growing conviction that his life must soon end. After several months of visiting the house, Kawabata writes his story with Eguchi in the main role, and in so doing comes to realize that he would like Michiko to help him end his life. Hwang follows the main structure of the original story by having the male protagonist remember moments from the past connected to specific women in his life. His first lover, for instance, broke his heart by marrying another man, shaping his youth in a lasting way. And the memories of his third daughter, the favourite one, trigger feelings of joy and worries over his fitness as a father. In the original version, the narrative ends with the death of one of the sleeping women, an ending that can be interpreted in many ways. Hwang chooses to interpret the ending as a foreshadowing of Kawabata's suicide, a crucial moment in the character's understanding of life and death.

In the third scene of the play, Hwang's Kawabata tells Michiko that he has stopped remembering, explaining, 'When I began coming here, I'd lie awake at nights, too, but I'd love it, because I'd remember … things I'd forgotten for years.'[8] But, increasingly, he can no longer recall the past; instead, he thinks about his friend Mishima, who committed suicide by *hara-kiri* the previous year with the help of his lover. Kawabata asks Michiko if she could do the same for him, requesting a stronger sleeping potion and offering her money. The scene ends with the heavily drugged Kawabata alerting Michiko of the dead 'sleeping beauty' in his room. He wants to leave right away, but he is completely incapacitated and unable to move his body. Drugged and in shock, Kawabata is vulnerable and completely dependent on Michiko. It is at this moment that she helps him see who he really is. 'Look at yourself', she tells him, leading him to the mirror, declaring, 'You can leave now, Mr Kawabata, but as much as you deny it, your face will continue to change, as if your will didn't even exist' (204). She peels away his 'grandstanding', as she puts it, and reminds him he is ultimately a mortal who cannot evade ageing and death. He is like other men, despite what he wants to think of himself. Hwang uses the metaphor of the face once again, but in the case of *The House of Sleeping Beauties*, the face represents life and its ability to reveal various stages, from birth to death. In spite of our efforts, our faces change constantly throughout our lives, and no one is exempt from the inevitability of death.

Scene 4 takes place a week after the end of scene 3, and it departs drastically from the original story. Kawabata has finished writing his story and visits Michiko one last time. He offers her a large sum of money and asks her to 'serve' him. He confides in her, 'As I've slept here, I've grown older. I've seen my sweethearts, my wife, my mistresses, my daughters, until there's only one thing left' (208). His last desire is to die with the help of Michiko. He has decided that she must be the last woman in his life. If the 'sleeping beauties' helped him remember his past, Michiko's purpose is to help him face his own mortality and death. Comforted by her, he falls asleep for the last time, though not before asking her to take care of herself with the money he has given her. The play ends, however, with Michiko drinking the potion-laced tea, implying that she has chosen to die with him.

Hwang rarely provides unambiguous endings to his plays, and *The House of Sleeping Beauties* can certainly generate different meanings. At their core, both the original story and Hwang's play are about life, love, memory and death, but they are also about what exists beneath the surface. Hwang provides texture and depth to the characters of Kawabata and Michiko, who are much more than what they seem at first. The relationship between the two is more complex than a typical friendship or romantic relationship. Before dying, he asks her to put on make-up and a fancy kimono he has bought for her. He wants to make her happy by giving her what she has desired and worked towards all of her life. The make-up symbolizes their futile attempt to change the past, and Michiko knows it is too late for her. The businesslike and callous proprietor in Kawabata's original is replaced with a complex woman who has endured a difficult life. In their last moments together, she finally opens up to Kawabata and tells him the story of her life. Hwang's Kawabata is deeply moved by her life story, and her strength renews him, allowing him to see his own life from a new perspective. Conversely, he helps her remember her past and how she became who she is in her late seventies. At the end, it is her memory that comforts Kawabata. However, exactly why he chooses to die is unclear, as is Michiko's choice at the play's end. Just as the suicide of the real Kawabata remains a mystery (it is rumoured that he was haunted by Mishima's suicide), Hwang's speculative version of what may have happened resists a single, closed interpretation, leaving space for the imagination of the audience and the reader.

The Sound of a Voice

As its title indicates, *The Sound of a Voice* is about sound, and it illustrates Hwang's deep understanding of the musical qualities of live theatre. Hwang's knowledge of music can be traced to his childhood. He grew up playing the violin, and his mother, a trained pianist, was an accompanist with the East West Players. His sister also established a career as a professional cellist. Music was his first introduction to artistic expression, and Hwang's experience playing jazz violin significantly shaped his growth as a playwright. *The Sound of a Voice*, in particular, reveals the influences of jazz in its structure, syncopation and use of improvisation. With the play, Hwang continued his collaboration with Lucia Hwong, who had worked with him on *FOB* as a composer and an onstage musician during performances of the play.

The two characters in *The Sound of a Voice* – Woman (a Japanese woman in her forties or fifties) and Man (a Japanese man in his fifties) – meet as strangers at the beginning of the play. The two develop a relationship filled with unpredictability and danger, but also with beauty and tenderness. The play's nine scenes are set in and near Woman's house 'in a remote corner of a forest', and time is described vaguely as evening, dawn, day, night, etc. The play begins with Woman serving tea to Man, who is travelling through the forest and in need of rest. Man comments on the sound of the tea pouring, which he describes as 'very soothing', to which Woman replies, 'That is the tea's skill, not mine.'[9] Woman's reply can be read multiple ways: she could be modestly understating her skills, or she could be indicating that the tea has the supernatural power to soothe the listener. Either way, Man is affected by the sound. Woman tells Man that she finds the sound of his voice enjoyable for 'the way it moves through the air' (156). This first moment sets the tone for the rest of play, as the two characters' interactions are influenced by sound.

Woman offers Man food and lodging, which Man accepts. She wants him to stay because she dislikes silence and wishes to hear him, both in waking and sleeping. For Woman, silence means loneliness, and she welcomes the opportunity to hear another person, even if that simply means listening to him breathe. For Man, silence causes fear. He tells Woman, 'You see, I can't sleep in too much silence. It scares me. It makes me feel that I have no control over what is about to happen', and she replies, 'I feel the same way' (156). Despite the immediate connection the two characters make, they distrust each other from the beginning, and there is real danger simmering beneath their interactions. Man is at the house because he thinks Woman is a witch who has been killing men after they fall in love with her. Woman is aware of Man's intention to harm her, yet her own intentions are not entirely clear, despite the fact that her actions towards Man seem genuine and even innocent. The paranoia of the two drives the action of the play.

In traditional Japanese ghost stories, time and space are fluid, and ghosts often disguise themselves as beautiful women who never age. They are temptresses, witches and women who haunt men's fantasies. Like an ideal Japanese wife, Woman in *The Sound of a Voice* provides Man with food, lodging, comfort, intimacy and pleasant conversation. Man returns the favour with work that a husband might do. For instance, scene 3 finds him out in the yard chopping wood with his shirt off. In the same scene, he makes her laugh and implies that she is a faithful woman who would never leave him. On the surface, the characters behave like two people about to fall in love. They seem to flirt with each other, and the scene ends with Woman touching Man's body. Perhaps they do fall in love, but it is equally likely that Man is afraid of Woman's seductive and murderous power. When Woman tells Man to accept ageing and learn to like his changing body (i.e. the fattening of the belly), it can be read as a loving and supportive statement. Yet it can mean something entirely different if Woman is indeed a witch who uses the bodies of men to become younger. If Man truly believes that Woman is the witch he is searching for, the scene can be interpreted in yet another way: perhaps he is out in the yard baring his skin in order to seduce Woman and convince her that he is the man she wants.

The play begins as a game of love and deception, where whoever is deceived and falls genuinely in love ends up the loser. In this case, losing means death for the person who succumbs. However, by the end of *The Sound of a Voice*, the rules of the game become ambiguous, and there is no clear winner or loser. The play concludes with Man leaving Woman, who hangs herself after his departure. Yet, Hwang's stage directions do not explain the intentions motivating the characters' actions:

> Man exits. Woman goes out through the door to her room. After a long beat, he reenters. He looks for her in the main room. He goes to the mat, sees her *shakuhatchi* [a Japanese flute]. He puts down his sword, takes off his bundle and coat. He goes inside. He comes out. He goes to the mat, picks up her *shakuhatchi*, clutches it to him. He moves everything else off the mat, sits and puts the *shakuhatchi* to his mouth. He begins to blow into it. He tries to make sounds. He continues trying through the end of the play. The upstage scrim lights up. Upstage, we see the woman. She has hung herself and is hanging from a rope suspended from the roof. Around her swirl thousands of petals from the flowers. They fill the upstage scrim area like a blizzard of color. Man continues to attempt to play. Lights fade to black. (175)

William. C. Boles suggests that Man leaves because he has fallen for her and is unable to kill her: 'He decides to leave her, and she, feeling rejected by his decision, hangs herself. Immediately after leaving, he changes his mind and returns to her, only to discover her dead body.'[10] Hwang certainly allows the play to be interpreted as a tragedy, in which two lovers can never be together. But he also opens the possibility of at least three other interpretations. First, Man could have pretended to care for Woman so as to make her fall in love with him, and when he leaves, she kills herself because of a broken heart. He then returns to confirm the death of the witch or spirit he had set out to kill. With this reading of the ending, all of Man's previous words and actions become suspect, and he emerges victorious, a manipulative and sly man.

Second, Man and Woman can both be seen as manipulatively engaging in a competition in which the one who first opens up and reveals his or her true self loses. In scene 7, for example, Man invites Woman to engage in swordplay with him, daring her to hit him as hard as she can. Initially coy in her customary submissive and modest manner, she quickly demonstrates deftness with the sword. The stage direction reads, 'Woman executes a series of movements with great skill and fierceness. Her whole manner is transformed. Man watches with increasing amazement. Her movements end. She regains her submissive manner' (167). When she sees his shocked reaction, she realizes what she has done and says that she has revealed too much of herself. Man does not tell her that he has also seen her at night looking young and beautiful while walking around with a vase filled with fresh flowers. He tests her, asking whether she has heard stories of 'a face that changes in the night' (169). She dismisses the questions and tells Man that she is the one whose heart has been shattered by travellers who visit her only to abandon her. She tells him to kill her because she cannot bear to have her heart broken again. Man tells her, 'I won't leave you', to which Woman replies, 'I believe you' (170). Using this interpretation, both are being deceptive, and the goal of each is to call the other's bluff. Woman shows Man that she is not an ordinary woman, and Man reveals to her that he knows more about her than she may have realized. Both push and test each other, and with every contest, each reveals a bit more of his or her identity. The game of chicken reaches its climax in scene 8 when Man puts the sword on his throat and Woman threatens to kill him, only to take the sword away. After they play out their brinkmanship, neither emerges victorious.

Finally, the play can also be interpreted as closely following the Japanese ghost folklore that Hwang used as a source. In these ghost stories, female spirits overpower humans, and any man who breaks a ghost's heart cannot escape her vengeance. In *The Sound of a Voice*, the death of Woman can be read as something she had planned all along. If she is indeed a witch or a spirit, the act of hanging herself does not automatically mean death. She could have 'died' every time she had a visitor, and Man's return at the end can signify her victory. She has trapped him as she has trapped other men – perhaps in one of her flowers. His voice is added to the humming sound he heard in the flower petals, and he may experience 'the peacefulness of one who is completely imprisoned' (169). The play ends with Man attempting to play the *shakuhatchi*, trying to make sound to fill the aural void left by Woman's 'death'.

Ultimately, Hwang leaves the ending open, as he does for most of his plays. Any interpretation of *The Sound of a Voice* depends on what a reader or audience member thinks of love, sex, trust and triumph. Similar to a musical performance, the emotional affect of experiencing what occurs onstage creates the meaning of the play. Rather than thinking about what the two characters say or do, the audience is encouraged to listen to the collective sound composed of human voices, breathing, *shakuhatchi*, chopping wood, sword practice, walking and pouring tea. Hwang has often said that plays should be written in such a way that they can only achieve their fullest potential in performance. In other words, plays are not merely about stories and characters; they are also about the form of live theatre.

While *The Sound of a Voice* was inspired by Japanese folklore, literature, and film, the play is also Hwang's interpretation of the story specifically for live theatre. As Boles suggests, the play is about being in limbo, in 'a liminal state where [Woman] exists between time, relationship, and even a consciousness of her current state'.[11] I would extend Boles's observation and explain the play as a study of the liminal space of the theatre itself. On stage, time functions differently, and identities are in constant flux. Even the audience's experience differs from performance to performance. With the play, Hwang exposes the vast possibilities of theatre and invites the audience to interpret events in light of their own experience.

As the Crow Flies

After completing the two Japanese plays in 1983, David Henry Hwang left New York City to travel to Europe, Asia and Canada. He married Ophelia Chong, a Chinese Canadian artist, and the two settled in Los Angeles. His writing expanded to include the mediums of television and film and various genres ranging from sitcoms to epic stories. He did not have another play premiere until 1986, the result of a commission he received from the Los Angeles Theatre Centre to write a companion one-act to *The Sound of a Voice*. The drama he produced, *As the Crow Flies*, opened in a double bill with its predecessor on 16 February 1986, at the Los Angeles Theatre Centre. It was directed by Reza Abdoh, an Iranian American who was known for his work in experimental theatre in the Los Angeles area.

As the Crow Flies dramatizes the lives of an elderly Chinese couple and their interactions with an African American maid who has been cleaning their house for over ten years. According to Hwang, the three characters are based on his grandparents and their housecleaning lady. He describes his grandmother as 'extremely stoic' and 'impenetrable' to the outside world. Hwang wondered about the relationship she had with the cleaning lady and conjectured that the two must have had 'some form of understanding that's developed there'.[12] Moreover, the cleaning lady had two identities: 'She had one name for work, and at home she put on a wig, used another name, and became a different person. This is actually true. I didn't make it up, it was just a matter of accurate reporting.'[13] Similar to *Family Devotions* and *The House of Sleeping Beauties*, Hwang uses factual events and real people as the crux of the plotline, but he freely combines fictional elements and storylines to drastically depart from realism and to enhance the ambiguity of the plays.

In *As the Crow Flies*, the couple, Mrs Chan and P.K., are in their seventies, and the maid, Hannah, is in her sixties. The entire play is set in the living room of 'an upper class home' owned by Mrs Chan and her husband. The play opens with Mrs Chan sitting in a chair and looking out onto a garden while Hannah talks to her. Hannah explains to Mrs Chan that she has two different identities: Hannah Carter, who cleans houses during the day, and Sandra Smith, who is younger and likes to dress up and go out at night. Hannah expects this to confuse Mrs Chan, but Mrs Chan tells her, 'So what? My uncle had six!'[14] Mrs Chan tells Hannah that it is reasonable to think of Sandra Smith as a ghost who takes over Hannah's body. When Hannah says she is scared of Sandra Smith, Mrs Chan demonstrates her knowledge of the 'rules' governing ghosts and explains how they can be prevented from coming inside the house. She describes Chinese traditions that explain how to avoid ghosts, such as having a goldfish in the room or placing a raised step in the doorway. Mrs Chan's confidence is formidable: '[Sandra Smith] comes here, I will fight her. Not like these Americans. So stupid. Never think of these things. Never think of ghost. Never think of death. Never prepare for anything. Always think, life goes on and on, forever. And so, always it ends' (101).

After Hannah exits, her husband, P.K., enters, and it quickly becomes obvious in their comical interchange that he is hopelessly senile and forgetful. He thinks he earlier drove to a golf course for a nice game, though Mrs Chan implies he probably simply wandered around for two hours. Mrs Chan tells him that she saw 'a warning ghost' who cautioned her that another ghost would soon come. The couple believes that the ghost is coming to try to take one or both of them to their death. P.K. tells his wife that there is no way to resist such a ghost when it comes, but Mrs Chan tells him that she will not die, vowing to defy the ghost and resist death. Ironically, it is P.K. who ends up being correct at the play's end, despite his senility.

Mrs Chan's life story is, in fact, a testament to survival and adaptability in a new environment. She left China many years ago to live in the Philippines, which she then left at an old age to join her children in the United States.

'It is all the same to me', she declares, 'Go, one home to the next, one city to another, nation to nation, across ocean big and small' (104). Her statement describes the diasporic condition of immigrants who may live in many places, yet cannot claim one place as their true home. She has a flexible identity that becomes more resilient with the challenges of life, and she continues to fight and run. Sandra, who is played by the same actress who plays Hannah, enters and tells Mrs Chan about a different kind of 'home' the older woman will soon be going to. Sandra first describes Hannah's home, which is 'a dark room' that 'does not move, even as the rest of the world circles "round" and "round, picking up speed"' (106). Mrs Chan initially rejects Sandra's talk of home, but Sandra knows her thoughts – even secret thoughts – too well. She has observed Mrs Chan for years and knows what she sees in the garden day after day.

When Mrs Chan tells her 'I can defeat you. I defeat ghost before', Sandra launches into a monologue that functions as both an allegory of Mrs Chan's life and a death spell (107). Sandra describes a flying crow being chased by two children. The crow tries to prevent their pursuit by throwing disaster and chaos at them, but the children continue on, not knowing why they are doing so. 'Just following a crow, with single dedication, forgetting how they started, or why they're chasing, or even what may happen if they catch it. Running without pause of pleasure, past the point of their beginning' (107). Like the kids, Mrs Chan has been constantly running without any real purpose. In the following exchange, Mrs Chan tells Sandra that she is tired, and she detects 'the scent of home' (107). Just as the children would return home at the end of each day, Mrs Chan ends her life's journey and goes 'home'. Indicating her transition from life to death, Mrs Chan's dress rises into the air, and she is shown wearing a white slip beneath, a convention Hwang would again use to signify death in *Golden Child* (white also represents ghosts in traditional Chinese stories). At the end of the play, Sandra in effect becomes Hannah after removing her wig and dress, and she is also seen wearing a white slip.

The ending, like all of Hwang's endings, is ambiguous. While Mrs Chan moves towards the door to make her final exit from life and the play, Hannah slides slowly into Mrs Chan's chair. The stage direction reads, 'Hannah sits in it, beams' (108). After Mrs Chan leaves, Hannah 'looks around her like a kid with a new toy' (108). The former maid has found a new home in the affluent house she had scrubbed and cleaned for years. When P.K. enters at the very end of the play, he cannot see Hannah, suggesting that she is a ghost. The play can be read as a story about a ghost who helps an old woman leave her life and accept her death, her final home. It can also be read as the tale of a ghost defeating a strong person and claiming her house. Either way, at its core the play is about life, death, home and the adaptability of identity.

Additionally, the play can be interpreted as a story about the experiences of displaced people. Mrs Chan thinks she knows all about ghosts and their rules, but her knowledge is actually relatively limited. In the United States, a new location for her, there are different and unfamiliar rules. She thinks her transnational adaptability is a source of strength, but it also works against her when she realizes that, in secret, she yearns to go home, a destination she can reach only by abandoning her life. The play follows the plot structure of an Aristotelian tragedy, one in which the hubris of the tragic protagonist is the main cause of her demise. Everything that Mrs Chan has done to avoid death by running and fighting ends up meaningless and contributing directly to her tired end.

Despite its short length, *As the Crow Flies* is significant in the trajectory of Hwang's development as a playwright. With the two Japanese plays, he intentionally distanced himself from autobiographical family stories in order to experiment with different forms and storylines. With *As the Crow Flies*, Hwang returns to those stories, specifically those of his grandmother, but he does so in the form and style of the Japanese plays. For instance, there are similarities in the relationships between Mrs Chan and Hannah/Sandra, and between Woman and Man in *The Sound of a Voice*. The characters play a game of trust and power, but the strong bond between them cannot be ignored. Both plays portray characters in a liminal world between life and death, and silence functions to enhance the mood of the setting. The one-act plays he wrote between the years 1983 and 1986 provided the opportunity to experiment with a range of topics in his plays. They also prepared him to write his next full-length play, *Rich Relations*, in which Hwang uses his family story to further explore themes of life, death and love.

Rich Relations

Two months after the opening of *As the Crow Flies* and *The Sound of a Voice* at the Los Angeles Theatre Centre, *Rich Relations* premiered at The Second Stage in New York City. After a two-year hiatus, Hwang returned to the theatre with two plays echoing themes of family, death and resurrection. *Rich Relations* is similar to *Family Devotions* in its exploration of the material and religious influences on his family in Los Angeles. In *Rich Relations*, the play's father character worships both money and Jesus, and the stage is, once again, littered with cutting-edge technologies of the 1980s. While he acknowledged the similarities between the two plays, Hwang intended *Rich Relations* to signal a new direction for him as a playwright. For one, the ethnicity of the characters is not specified in the script, and the production's cast was all white. Frank Rich was the only critic to review the play for the mainstream media, and he underscored the similarities between the two plays. In his review, Rich describes the play as 'tired' and 'stale': 'The problem with this effort is not that Mr Hwang has ventured onto new ground and failed, but the reverse: He has regurgitated his previous work with little fresh inspiration.'[15] To Rich, the play tells basically the same story as *Family Devotions* but without Chinese Americans as the main characters.

While there is some validity to Rich's critique, the significance of *Rich Relations* is not its plot but the fact that it represents a new phase for Hwang, who wanted to move away from the label 'ethnic'. In his introduction to his first collection of plays, Hwang extensively explains the transition, emphasizing the need for new opportunities in the 'multicultural landscape that is the American ideal'.[16] He notes that during his two-year break from playwriting, he came to find the 'isolationist–nationalist' focus of his work limiting and unproductive. It was a phase he had to go through in order to write the Chinese Trilogy and the three one-acts, but its usefulness had run its course. Isolationism, to him, 'runs the risk of reinforcing a dangerous prejudice of the larger society: namely, that minorities are defined first and foremost by race'. He continues, 'America, however, must not restrict its "ethnic" writers to "ethnic" material, while assuming that white males can master any topic they so desire.'[17] The passage reads like a manifesto in which Hwang is granting himself permission to write about characters without regard to ethnic or racial specificity.

Rich Relations was the first play Hwang wrote during the new phase, one that may be called his multicultural or progressive phase. As noted by Rich and others, the play was not a success when it premiered, and Hwang has described it as his first 'flop'. As Hwang has said, the play is not 'great', but he still needed to write it.[18] Moreover, the production process was also troubled. Many unfortunate elements converged to create Hwang's first failure as a playwright, but the experience was momentous for Hwang. In various interviews after the success of *M. Butterfly* in 1988, Hwang was able to look back at *Rich Relations* and explain the importance of the play to his development as a playwright. To him, the experience of failure made his subsequent success possible. He has repeatedly stated that his commitment to playwriting only solidified after the negative feedback, which freed him to write about anything he wanted. Hwang recapitulates this narrative in the introduction to *FOB and Other Plays*, which is the only anthology that includes *Rich Relations*: 'Though not without its detractors, this work remains important to me as the piece which reestablished my commitment to writing. A play about the possibility of resurrection, it did indeed resurrect my own love for work and point the way toward the non-Asian characters that were to follow in such works as *M. Butterfly*.'[19] Indeed, whenever *Rich Relations* is mentioned by Hwang or others, it is identified as the play that solidified his decision to become a playwright and made the success of *M. Butterfly* possible. As recently as 2012, Hwang has stated, 'I didn't know that I was going to be a writer, that that was my life's mission, until I had my first flop.'[20] Paradoxically, the play's failure opened the door to a new, exciting phase in Hwang's career.

While this narrative has been reinforced consistently for almost thirty years, the play itself has received little critical or scholarly attention. It is obviously important to Hwang, which suggests that it is critical to examine the play in its own right, beyond simply discussing the ways it illuminates the rest of his oeuvre. The play reveals Hwang's attempt to expand the scope and depth of his characters and their relationships to each other. In contrast to his previous plays, for example, no character in *Rich Relations* is likeable or redeemable. As Hwang has noted, the play is about resurrection; more specifically, it is about the possibility of redemption for deeply flawed people who find themselves in deeply dysfunctional relationships and awkward circumstances.

Rich Relations is a two-act play set in the 'second living room of a large home in the hills above Los Angeles', and its events occur within twenty-four hours.[21] Similar to *Family Devotions*, the set is a vast house with a view of the outside through floor-to-ceiling windows. There are three ways to exit the stage: a door to the balcony, a door to the rest of the house, and a third door to the driveway. On the stage is a large television that faces upstage, which, along with other electronics in the house, has both symbolic and material significance in the play. Like the tennis ball machine in *Family Devotions*, the machines in *Rich Relations* seem to be autonomous entities. The play opens with Hinson, a man in his early fifties, trying to connect his phone to the television while his son, Keith (late twenties), sits and watches in the living room. In 1986, the technology needed to connect the phone to the television would have been absurdly advanced, so Hinson's attempt to communicate via television can be seen as both curious and comical. His first line – 'Hello? Hello? Can you hear me?' – is a common phrase in the twenty-first century, given the pervasiveness of cell phones. In the context of the 1980s, however, Hinson's actions would have generated laughter.

Hwang wrote the play as a dark comedy, and it is one of his funniest plays. Between 1983 and 1986, Hwang wrote sitcoms for television, experience that is reflected in the humour of *Rich Relations*, which is driven by one-liners and simplistic character types. At the same time, the humour in the play is much darker than that of typical sitcoms, as well as Hwang's previous plays. For instance, Hinson's question 'Can you hear me?' is one of the main questions of the play, and we learn later that Keith has always wanted to hear his dead mother's voice. When he was only five, Keith's mother died after getting hit by a truck. His father's question, faintly heard through the television set, can be funny, but it can also be haunting and tragic. The play begins with the lighter tone of a comedy, yet it increasingly becomes a hyper-real tragicomedy. By the end of the play, even death is absurdly funny.

While Hinson dabbles with his uncooperative television, the audience learns that Keith has returned to his home in Los Angeles after leaving his job as a debate teacher at a boarding school for girls in Connecticut. Keith learns that his aunt, Barbara (Hinson's sister), wants him to marry her daughter, Marilyn. Hinson explains to Keith that the motivation is money: because Hinson is rich, the 'double relations' would allow Barbara a greater claim to his money. Keith balks at the idea of marrying his cousin, but Hinson reminds him that he is a 'real catch' with privileges, manners and a good upbringing. In the next scene, Keith is revealed to be anything but that. He had sneaked into the house of one of his underage students, Jill (who is sixteen). Keith has run away with her after leaving a note at the boarding school confessing to his criminal behaviour. He has returned home not as the successful son Hinson imagines him to be but as a failed teacher who has slept with his underage students.

Jill is described as 'very beautiful', and Hinson likes her immediately. Keith initially thought she was joining him for the weekend, but she left a note for her parents and ran away from home. In their first conversation together, Jill and Hinson share stories of surviving near-death experiences. Hinson had tuberculosis when he was young, but through prayer and the help of his sister, he came back from the dead. And Jill met Keith on a stormy night that almost killed them. Hinson declares to Jill, 'They say I'm supposed to be dead. But I'm not. I had too much personal initiative' (227). The week before, Hinson believes he experienced death itself in a speeding limousine. 'I thought I was going to die', Hinson tells Jill, 'And I did. But I came back' (228). Their conversation is intermittently interrupted by Keith, who wanders in and out of the room as if he does not know what he wants to do. He can be seen as an older version of Chester from *Family Devotions*, and there are many parallels between the two. Both meander around the house, neither completely in nor out of it. While Chester keeps saying he has to pack for his move to Boston, Keith says he has to unpack, which he never does. If Chester is a hopeful and naive young man about to leave home for the first time, Keith represents his older, more experienced self, returning home stripped of his youthful innocence and ideals. Chester searches for his identity (which, thanks to Di-gou's counsel, he begins to find in his own face), while Keith seeks love and redemption.

The fact that Keith is in a relationship with an underage student reveals much about who he is as a human being, and his actions are partly a product of his uncertainty over his own needs and desires. He may be genuinely in love, but the relationship is wrong on many levels. He is torn between a need to clear his conscience and his forbidden desire. After all, he has confessed his deeds in a note to the headmaster before leaving his job, yet he remains with Jill. Adding to his confusion is his aunt Barbara, who pushes relentlessly to marry off her daughter to him. As a character, Keith is the protagonist, but he is passive and unsure of what he needs to do.

Towards the end of act 1, Barbara finally makes her dramatic entrance, and she dominates the action for the remainder of the play. She echoes the grandmothers of *Family Devotions* with her obsessive and warped faith in Jesus and money, and she comes across as a caricatured, extreme version of Chester's aunt. Barbara is one of Hwang's wackiest characters. She enters the house by picking the lock, tells Jill about her husband's live-in mistresses and devours Jill's cheese-puffs. At the end of act 1, she climbs onto the balcony railing and threatens to jump if Keith does not marry Marilyn. Act 2 opens with Marilyn in the living room watching television while listening to Barbara explain that she is about to jump for her. When Jill learns that her parents do not want her to return home, she joins Barbara on the balcony railing so she can have time to think. She enjoys the thrill of daring death, explaining, 'You're in a state of complete excitement. Heart beats faster, senses sharper, your body starts to change. Into a different animal altogether' (249). Barbara eventually climbs off the railing, but her action sets off a series of chaotic events that escalate towards the end of the play.

Barbara engages in a heated argument with Hinson, during which he loudly sings a Christian hymn as she goes on about how he has broken his promise to God to become a pastor. Marilyn, unable to hear the television, turns the volume as high as it will go, and the collective noise created by the three characters seems to make the television to explode. Hwang's stage direction reads: '[Marilyn] throws the remote control to the ground. The TV explodes. Stage blacks out except for erratic flashes of light from the TV screen' (257). After the explosion, Hinson, Barbara and Marilyn immediately notice that Jill has disappeared from the railing and assume that she has fallen to her death. Barbara and Hinson go out to look for her body, while Marilyn stays. Keith enters, unaware of what has happened. For the first time in the play, the cousins open up to each other, confessing their deepest desires and fears. The scene is short, and the relationship between the two is never explored further.

However, the quiet and brief exchange between the two stands out in a play full of noisy busyness. In *FOB* and *Family Devotions*, Hwang dramatizes the relationship between a central male character (Dale and Chester, respectively) and a female cousin (Grace and Jenny, respectively), though he stops short of exploring those relationships in any depth. In *Rich Relations*, the cousins are older and capable of adult conversation. Their parents may see them as pawns for maximizing financial profit and social status, but the cousins know deep in their hearts that they need to find their own ways to navigate the life ahead of them. In *Rich Relations*, the two confess their guilt to each other. Marilyn loved and lost 'someone who played rock "n" roll' and tells Keith that she feels like she has paid her dues. Keith reveals to Marilyn that he did 'something really bad at school' (261). The stage directions indicate he does this while turning on lights and appliances around the house, almost as if he desires to literally shed light onto his sins. He seeks redemption, and Marilyn is his confidant. The word 'rich' in the title of the play can mean both wealth and quality, and it applies most fittingly to the relationship between Keith and Marilyn. They are defined by others in terms of family money, but between themselves, they have a trusting bond as cousins and even friends.

After their talk, Marilyn tells Keith to go outside to look for Jill, and she climbs onto the balcony railing. At this point, the play takes a hyper-real turn. When Keith returns, having apparently seen Jill's dead body, he puts his ear to the ground, while Hinson yells at him to get up. Keith had also put his ear to the ground when his mother died, hoping to hear something. He wanted to raise his mother from the dead, just as his father had been 'resurrected' when he had tuberculosis, and he tries to do the same for Jill. Keith rises, lamenting, 'I can't hear a thing', to which Hinson replies, 'Good, son. No one expects you to perform miracles' (265). Keith proceeds to fully confess what he did to his young female students and screams, 'It's sick! I'm sick!' He then begs his father to bring Jill back, admitting that he loves her. Hinson responds by yelling at his son and kicking him. In their struggle, Keith gets the upper hand and forces Hinson's ears to the ground while shouting, 'C'mon. You always talked about resurrection! OK – do it!' (267). Keith is angry with his father for failing to resurrect his mother, despite the fact that he has become a real estate 'baron' who constantly boasts about his own resurrection. Hinson could not bring his wife back from the dead, and he knows he cannot perform miracles for Jill, either. The father and son continue their fight by smashing all the electronic appliances and machines with golf clubs.

During this rampage, Barbara 'gently' shoves Marilyn from the balcony, but the daughter stops falling and 'miraculously' hangs midair. At the same time, all lights and appliances turn off, making the room dark and silent. While in her midair position, Marilyn delivers a monologue that summarizes the main theme of the play:

> Listen – can you hear it? Behind every noise in the city, every sound we've learned to make, behind the clatter of our streets, the hum of turbines, the roar of electricity – behind all this, there is a constant voice. A voice which carries hope from beyond the grave. It speaks in a fine, clear tone about matters which take our eyes upward – away from things we can touch, away from love made small and powerless. It is a voice which lurks behind every move we make. To listen to it is to rage against the grave, we save our souls, we bring ourselves back from the dead. (270–1)

After the monologue, the lights turn back on, and Jill is found sitting on the balcony in place of Marilyn, who is found safe outside on the driveway. Just as Barbara had performed a miracle to bring Hinson back from the dead, her daughter is now the one to make the resurrection happen. The play ends with the women exiting and the father and son putting their ears to the ground. Keith's last line is 'Ssssh … ', and the last stage direction – 'They remain in this position, listening, as': – literally ends mid-sentence. As previously noted, Hwang always leaves the ending of his plays open; in *Rich Relations*, this denial of closure extends even to his own stage directions.

Keith, at the end, gets what he has wanted. He confesses his sins to his family and witnesses a miraculous resurrection. Most importantly, he tells Jill he loves her when she comes back from the dead. All in all, the play has a happy ending, but many questions remain. Is there true redemption for Keith and the other characters? What does Jill's resurrection signify? Hwang has stated that the play is autobiographical and deals with his family's spirituality. *Family Devotions* is about the inseparable connection between being Chinese, Christian and rich. *Rich Relations*, on the other hand, is about spiritual miracles and material consumption. Hwang wanted to disassociate ethnicity from his family's story, and he was, ultimately, unsuccessful in convincing critics and audiences that the undertaking was worthwhile. Hwang wrote the play as a satire of his family, and he intended the characters to be heightened versions of real people. But it is easy to interpret them not as satirical portraits but as straightforward characters lacking nuance and depth. Without an entryway to empathize with the characters, the play can be seen as much ado about nothing. While Hinson and Keith destroy the expensive electronics and Marilyn pines over the rock band musician, questions remain as to how we are supposed to feel about their actions.

Ultimately, it is difficult to know why the play did not succeed. Did the critics expect Hwang's play to be about Asians (whether Chinese American or Japanese) and were disappointed to see a play about rich, white characters? Was Hwang trying to prove to the audience and the critics that he could write a play with characters who were not defined racially or ethnically, and he could not deliver? Or, did the play flop for reasons that have nothing to do with Hwang's or his characters' racial background? After the play closed, Hwang would quickly redeem himself by writing *M. Butterfly*, the runaway success that has defined him more than any other play he has written. *Rich Relations* and the three one-act plays discussed in this chapter may have been dismissed by many, but they were instrumental in Hwang's development as a playwright. In the four plays, one can see themes of love, deception, death and resurrection that would continue to reverberate in later plays.

CHAPTER 3
M. BUTTERFLY

In May of 1986, David Henry Hwang read a short article in the *New York Times* about a former French diplomat and a Chinese opera singer who were both sentenced to six years in prison on charges of espionage. The two, who were lovers, were accused of spying for China. According to the article, the diplomat, Bernard Boursicot, fell in love with Shi Pei Pu, a famed Chinese opera singer, and the two had a twenty-year relationship that produced a son. Boursicot believed Shi was a woman, despite the fact that Chinese performers are traditionally all men. When the trial judge asked Boursicot how he could have been mistaken for so long, the Frenchman answered, 'I was shattered to learn that he is a man, but my conviction remains unshakeable that for me at that time he was really a woman and was the first love of my life. And then, there was the child that I saw, Shi Dudu. He looked like me'.[1] Boursicot is also quoted in the article as saying that their sexual encounters had been 'hasty affairs that always took place in the dark'. He thought 'it was a Chinese custom'. David Henry Hwang was immediately intrigued by the article and decided to write a play about it.

Hwang intentionally decided against conducting further research on the case because he wanted to imagine how someone could have mistaken a man for a woman for over twenty years. Instead of a documentary drama, the play Hwang had in mind would be a speculative investigation into the mind of the Frenchman. Hwang quickly realized that the story of Boursicot and Shi resembled that of *Madame Butterfly*, the tale of a white man who travels to Japan and has a romantic relationship with a Japanese woman.

While Giacomo Puccini's three-act opera is the most well-known version of *Madame Butterfly,* the story was published and produced in different genres before becoming an opera. The story of *Madame Butterfly* originated with Pierre Loti's autobiographical journal *Madame Chrysantheme*, published in 1887. According to Loti, whose real name was Julien Viaud, the book is based on his actual experience with a Japanese geisha who agreed to a contract marriage with him during his short stay in Japan while a naval officer. Loti's autobiographical account was adapted into an English novella by John Luther Long, an American writer, and it was subsequently adapted into a play by the American playwright David Belasco in 1900.² In Loti's version, the Japanese geisha does not commit suicide but politely says goodbye to her contracted husband when he leaves. It is in John Luther Long's novella that the characters become melodramatic in their attitudes and actions. Loti's character becomes an American named Pinkerton who treats his lover cruelly and breaks her heart. Madame Chrysantheme becomes Madame Butterfly, a tragic heroine. At the end of Long's story, Madame Butterfly commits suicide when she realizes her lover will never return to her. In both Belasco's play and Puccini's opera, the melodramatic plotline and characters created by Long function centrally in enhancing the dramatic effect of the story. In Puccini's opera, the aria sung by Cio-Cio San, 'Un bel dì vedremo', epitomizes her longing and heartache, and it has been recognized as one of the most emotionally intensive arias in opera history.

Hwang wanted to write a play that reverses the roles of Pinkerton and Cio-Cio San; the former would be the victim of the latter in a game of love and power. Earlier plays by Hwang have a similar plot structure, as exemplified by his Japanese plays, in which a power game between a man and a woman drives the main plotline. Hwang has described *M. Butterfly* as a deconstruction of *Madame Butterfly*, which in this case means that his play critiques the opera by using reversal as an important device. At the suggestion of his then-wife, Ophelia Y. M. Chong, he changed the title of his new play from *Monsieur Butterfly* to *M. Butterfly* to make the gender dynamics even more ambiguous.

The Story and Style of *M. Butterfly*

The setting of *M. Butterfly* is described by Hwang as 'a Paris prison in the present', and it includes flashback scenes in Beijing and Paris of the 1960s and 1970s.³ In the opening scene, Rene Gallimard, aged sixty-five, is sitting in his prison cell, while Song Liling appears upstage as a 'beautiful woman in traditional Chinese garb' (1). Song dances in the style of Peking Opera while the music changes from traditional Chinese music to the 'Love Duet' from Puccini's *Madame Butterfly*. While Song dances, Gallimard talks directly to the audience and relates the story of how he ended up in prison. In a self-deprecating and sarcastic tone, he tells the audience that he is a 'celebrity' who has made people laugh around the world. What has made him famous, of course, is his strange relationship with Song, a man whom he long believed was a woman.

Gallimard's actions lead the audience to realize that the story he is narrating is in large part a product of his imagination. It is as if the audience is watching the agonizing fantasy or dream of a man who is unable to overcome the events of his past. He tells the audience that 'In order for you to understand what I did and why, I must introduce you to my favorite opera: *Madame Butterfly*' (5). The scenes move back and forth between the story of the opera and Gallimard's own awkward experiences with women, building to the moment of his first encounter with Song. The initial conversation between Gallimard and Song foreshadows much of what happens to them later in the play. Gallimard praises *Madame Butterfly* as a 'very beautiful story', to which Song replies, 'Well, yes, to a Westerner.' Song continues, 'It's one of your favorite fantasies, isn't it? The submissive Oriental woman to the cruel white man' (17). Song explicitly warns Gallimard how absurd the fantasy is but, at the same time, invites him to the Peking Opera, piquing his curiosity.

Despite Song's warning about his fantasy of the Butterfly, Gallimard succumbs to her eventual seduction and becomes intimate with her.[4] As a young man, Gallimard was unattractive and insecure, and he had to rely on his friend, Mark, to have any luck with women. He married his wife, Helga, to further his career and never felt like a man with white women. Song, on the other hand, makes him feel like he has 'finally gained power over a beautiful woman' (36). Gallimard's self-assurance grows as his desire for Song intensifies, and this new 'aggressive confidence' leads to a major promotion at his job in the French embassy in Beijing (39). Gallimard's new confidence also leads to a brief sexual affair with a young woman, Renee, who has 'a body like those girls in the magazine' (54). While Song does not want to undress in front of Gallimard because of her 'modesty' and refuses to have sex with the lights on, Renee is direct and unafraid of being completely naked with him. But Gallimard finds her too direct and '*too* uninhibited, *too* willing, so as to seem almost too … masculine' (54). Renee can be seen as the embodiment of a particular fantasy of western men and the type of woman Gallimard wished to date as a young man. With the same name as Gallimard, Renee is an echo of internal desires he could never pursue before meeting Song. The older Gallimard has gained the confidence and the status to have sex with a woman like Renee, but he comes to prefer a different fantasy of the perfect woman.

Even as he sits in his prison cell, Gallimard is unable to let go of the fantasy of the perfect 'Oriental' woman. It is evident that despite what happened to him, he enjoys the memories of Song, his Butterfly, and expends significant effort showing the audience how he fell in love with her. The fantasy – and, along with it, his narrative – breaks abruptly when the character of Comrade Chin enters in act 2, scene 3. The stage direction reads, 'Suddenly Comrade Chin enters. Gallimard backs away.' Gallimard asks Song, 'No! Why does she have to come in?' Song replies, 'Rene, be sensible. How can they understand the story without her? Now, don't embarrass yourself' (47). While the entire play is meta-theatrical, which often takes the form of characters breaking the fourth wall to talk directly to the audience, the moment of Chin's entrance stands out as an even more heightened moment of self-consciousness for the characters. Frank Rich, in his review of *M. Butterfly*, compared the play to those of dramatists Jean Genet and Luigi Pirandello, who also wrote plays with characters fully aware of their fictional nature. In such self-conscious and self-referential theatre, the distinction between actor and role is deliberately made ambiguous when characters break out of their expected roles in order to comment on the action of the play.

When Song insists that Comrade Chin must enter the stage to continue with the story, Gallimard turns to the audience and pleads with them to be sympathetic: 'Please – try to understand it from my point of view. We are all prisoners of our time and place' (47). From this moment on, Gallimard loses control over how the story is to be told. Contrary to Gallimard's fantasy, Song is not obedient to the Frenchman and his desires; rather, it is the Communist Chinese government that controls Song and Gallimard. Represented by Comrade Chin, the Communist government forces Song to gather classified intelligence from Gallimard. At the end of the scene, Chin exits, and Gallimard sticks his head out of the stage wings to ask Song, 'Is she gone?' Song tells him, 'Yes, Rene. Please continue in your fashion' (49).

The interruption of Gallimard's narration occurs again when Chin re-enters the stage in act 2, scene 7. Gallimard's fantasy further crumbles, and the play's style moves away from what Song describes as Gallimard's 'fashion' to that of a painfully self-conscious and meta-theatrical documentation of their relationship. Gallimard tells Song, 'I could forget all that betrayal in an instant, you know, if you'd just come back and become Butterfly again', to which Song answers, 'Fat chance. You're here in prison, rotting in a cell. And I'm on a plane, winging my way back to China. Your President pardoned me of our treason, you know'. To add to the injury, Song laughingly reveals to Gallimard, 'I'm an artist, Rene. You were my greatest ... acting challenge' (63).

Because the distinctions between fantasy and reality, and between character and actor, are unclear, the audience is never able to know for sure if the laughing Song represents the real Song Liling, or whether he is still a figment of Gallimard's memory. One can argue that the entire play, including the abrupt breaks in style and tone, is a product of Gallimard's imagination. If that is the case, the cruelty of Song and the two-dimensionality of Chin are attributes conjured up by Gallimard, as well. The nature of Hwang's portrayal of the Chinese characters has led theatre scholar James S. Moy to criticize the play for perpetuating Asian stereotypes. Moy condemns Hwang's depiction of Chin as 'even more stereotypical and cartoonish than the worst of the nineteenth-century stereotypes'.[5] In fact, it is more likely that Hwang intended the characters to act and sound like Gallimard's fantasy. After all, Gallimard has the agenda to make the audience feel sympathetic to his side of the story. If Comrade Chin only exists in Gallimard's memory and imagination, it is hardly surprising to see her represented in the most stereotypical and despicable ways. On the other hand, it is just as likely that the events and characters seen by the audience exist outside of Gallimard's fantasy. Hwang, once again, shows his signature ambiguity in his depiction of the characters in *M. Butterfly*. He steers his audience in and out of many different levels of reality and illusion, opening the play to multiple levels of interpretation. Gallimard's past and present coexist, and it is often unclear what is a product of Gallimard's imagination and what actually happened.

Gallimard continues to narrate his story to the audience during the rest of act 2, which climaxes when Song confronts Gallimard, forcing him to finally see the truth of his fantasy. At the end of the act, Song begins to assume the role of narrator and turns directly to the audience to continue Gallimard's story. When Gallimard interrupts, Song tells him, 'Please, I'm talking' (78). This moment in the play marks a shift in power between the two characters. Gallimard protests, 'You have to do what I say! I'm conjuring you up in *my* mind!' only to hear Song reply, 'I've never done what you've said. Why should it be any different in your mind? Now split – the story moves on, and I must change' (78). What had been Gallimard's story of love and fantasy turns into a nightmare of betrayal and reality. The story must indeed move on, though Gallimard no longer retains control over the story he started. The act ends with Song telling the audience members that he will change onstage and encourages them to take a break, during which Song removes his make-up and changes into a men's suit.

The third act begins with Song, now dressed as a man in an Armani suit, standing in a courthouse being interrogated by a judge about his espionage activities. Now told from Song's perspective, the story of the relationship between him and Gallimard loses the romance and fantasy of the first two acts and turns instead to the technical details of the deception. Song is explicit about how and why he was able to deceive Gallimard into thinking that he was a woman. For example, when the judge asks Song to explain why he was able to fool Gallimard, he answers, 'One, because when he finally met his fantasy woman, he wanted more than anything to believe that she was, in fact, a woman. And second, I am an Oriental. And being an Oriental, I could never be completely a man' (83). In this scene, Song takes an explicitly political stance. When the judge dismisses Song's 'armchair political theory' of the feminine East and masculine West as 'tenuous', Song confidently replies, 'That's why you'll lose in all your dealings with the East' (83). In this interaction, Hwang makes it clear that the play is about the long history of East–West relations, as represented by the story of Song and Gallimard. As a diplomat, Gallimard incorrectly predicted how the Vietnam War would end, and his embarrassing susceptibility to Song's schemes is symbolic of the United States' failure in Vietnam.

By the end of the play, Gallimard and Song have completely switched roles. Gallimard appears in Song's Butterfly wig and costume, while Song controls how the story ends. In the most dramatic and climatic moment of the play, Song disrobes, forcing Gallimard to see the (literally) naked truth. During this scene, Song suggests the possibility that they could have loved as two men without pretence and that perhaps such a relationship is still possible. But Gallimard rejects Song in his true form, declaring, 'I'm a man who loved a woman created by a man. Everything else – simply falls short' (90). With the illusion of his Butterfly gone, Gallimard decides to become the Butterfly himself by taking Song's robes and embodying the role. In the last scene of the play, Gallimard repeats the famous line from Puccini's *Madame Butterfly* – 'Death with honor is better than life … life with dishonor' – and with music from the opera blaring, stabs himself with a knife (just as Cio-Cio San does in Puccini's version).

After Gallimard's suicide, Song appears, the stage direction reading, 'Then a tight special up on Song, who stands as a man, staring at the dead Gallimard. He smokes a cigarette; the smoke filters up through the lights. Two words leave his lips' (93). The two words, the final ones spoken in the play, are 'Butterfly? Butterfly?' Hwang does not specify how they should be delivered, and the question marks further expand the actor's possible interpretations. If Song feels victorious at the end, the words might be laden with cynicism; if he feels sad about Gallimard's death, he could say them with regret. Or, perhaps Song's feelings are more complex, and call for an actor to instil them with all of the pathos expressed in the play. Ultimately, how those two words are delivered can determine the overall interpretation of the entire play. Hwang leaves the ending ambiguous, as he often does, by closing it with a question mark. It is as if he is inviting spectators to provide their own interpretation of what they have just witnessed.

The Production of *M. Butterfly*

In working to get his play produced, Hwang collaborated with Stuart Ostrow, an established theatre producer known for his work on Broadway and musical theatre. Ostrow sent the script to John Dexter, at the time one of the most sought-after directors of theatre and opera. Dexter had directed highly successful productions in London and New York City, of which Peter Shaffer's *Equus* was the most similar in style to *M. Butterfly*. Dexter's experience in directing opera was also advantageous, given the play's relationship to Puccini's *Madame Butterfly* and its extensive use of music and movement. Indeed, according to Hwang, *M. Butterfly* is modelled after Shaffer's *Equus* and *Amadeus*, in that the protagonist narrates his story directly to the audience, alternating between flashbacks and scenes in the present. With Dexter as the director, the production of the play began with Stuart Ostrow and David Geffen as co-producers. John Lithgow was selected to play the role of Rene Gallimard, and B. D. Wong, an unknown actor at the time, was cast as Song Liling after a long audition process. The Japanese designer Eiko Ishioka joined the production team, designing the scenery and costumes.

   The play premiered at the National Theatre in Washington, DC, on 10 February 1988, beginning its pre-Broadway run. Despite high expectations, the review in the *Washington Post* was not positive. David Richards called the play 'curious' and criticized it for being too complicated. In particular, he did not think the play answered certain 'fundamental questions': 'Just what secrets did the diplomat betray? How did he get caught? Was he merely the hapless victim of an astounding scheme or did he, in fact, realize deep down that he was involved in a masquerade and choose to embrace it anyway?'[6] He also disliked how Hwang's dialogue combined casual American English with poetic language, commenting, 'Hwang's slangy dialogue is clearly at war with the dark poetry he perceives in the tale'. In sum, Richards warned his readers that they would not have an 'easy time wending [their] way through *M. Butterfly*'. As reflected in Richard's review, the premiere's Washington reception was, at least in part, met with incredulity, confusion and shock. As Hwang has stated in interviews, the most notable aspect of the premiere was the collective shock the audience expressed when they saw B. D. Wong as Song disrobe and reveal the truth of his sex. The audience 'literally screamed', which Hwang found 'really cool'.[7] Some people in the audience thought they were attending *Madame Butterfly* and complained that there was no singing.[8]

This confused and lukewarm reception did not prevent the production team from moving the play to Broadway. After closing on 6 March 1988, at the National Theatre, *M. Butterfly* opened at the Eugene O'Neill Theatre in New York City on 20 March 1988. According to a blog post written by Hwang, Stuart Ostrow mortgaged his house to finance the production's move to Broadway.[9] Although the production was Hwang's Broadway debut, New York City and its critics were already familiar with him and his earlier plays. Moreover, the theatre audiences of the Big Apple were more accustomed to shocking and confusing plays than those of the nation's capital. The production was hugely successful, running for 777 performances and receiving the Tony Award for Best Play in 1988.

An important factor that contributed to the play's success on Broadway was Frank Rich's review in the *New York Times*. As I mention in previous chapters, Rich had supported Hwang since his playwriting debut at the Public Theatre in 1980 and had identified him as a playwright with much potential. Rich's review of the Broadway production of *M. Butterfly* is mixed, but he once again praised Hwang for his writing talent and describes his imagination a 'one of the most striking to emerge in the American theater in this decade'.[10] Rich dismissed the questions that David Richards asked in his *Washington Post* review by keenly stating that the 'obvious questions such as is she or isn't she, or does he know or doesn't he?' are not pressing concerns for Hwang. Rich explained that the play is as 'intricate as an infinity of Chinese boxes' and described it as 'overt and disguised burlesque deconstructions of *Madama Butterfly*'. Perhaps aware that Washington audience and critics were confused and uncertain what to make of the play, Rich provided, in his review, a detailed interpretation and explanation of Hwang's intentions. Rich summarized what the play is about at its core: 'Instead of reducing the world to an easily digested cluster of sexual or familiar relationships, Mr Hwang cracks open a liaison to reveal a sweeping, universal meditation on two of the most heated conflicts – men versus women, East versus West – of this or any other time.'[11] In contrast to his compliments of the play, Rich was generally critical of the production itself and described John Dexter's directing of actors as 'erratic'. However, he praised B. D. Wong's performance as 'mesmerizing' and compared him to John Lone, who possessed the rare talent of expressing Hwang's theatrical imagination in the most effective ways.

With Rich's endorsement of *M. Butterfly*, the production began to receive wider media exposure, and more people began to take notice. The production was nominated for seven Tony Awards: David Henry Hwang for Best Play; John Dexter for Best Direction of a Play; John Lithgow for Best Performance by a Leading Actor in a Play; B. D. Wong for Best Featured Actor in a Play; Eiko Ishioka for both Best Scenic Design and Best Costume Design; and Andy Phillips for Best Lighting Design. Of the nominations, Dexter and B. D. Wong were awarded in their respective categories, and Hwang received the award for Best Play. The play went on to receive the Drama Desk Award, the John Gassner Award and the Outer Critics Circle Award. It was also nominated for the Pulitzer Prize for Drama in 1989. The play continued to receive a tremendous amount of praise and attention in subsequent years and has been produced around the world. To this day, the play remains Hwang's most successful, and it continues to generate discussions in both the general public and academia.

Criticisms and Interpretations of *M. Butterfly*

M. Butterfly is a quintessentially American play of the 1980s, one that captures the socio–political and cultural climate of its time. The play deals with race, gender, sexuality, Orientalism and the Vietnam War while questioning a range of assumptions made about those topics. As in his earlier plays, the message Hwang proposes in *M. Butterfly* is ambiguous and dialectic. Some critics see it as an angry play that punishes the white man for his orientalist beliefs. It is, after all, Gallimard who dies at the end of the play while Song triumphantly watches his suicide. For others, the character of Song reinforces stereotypes of effeminate Asian men and secretive and exotic Asians. *M. Butterfly* allows both approaches, as well as a long list of alternative readings of the play, which is also notable for generating an impressive number of critical studies in academia. The voluminous and lasting interest in the play after the curtain fell on its final Broadway performance calls for a closer examination of how it reflected the dominant discourses of the late twentieth and early twenty-first centuries.

In the late 1980s, the United States as a country was experiencing the first shots in what would come to be called the 'culture wars'. Politicians, media commentators and scholars have described the country as divided between those who advocated traditional values and those who wanted to see a more progressive and secular country. In his book *Culture Wars: The Struggle to Control The Family, Art, Education, Law, and Politics*, James Davison Hunter describes America of the late 1980s as polarized by 'hot-button' social issues such as women's rights, abortion, homosexuality, gun politics and education. These conflicts continued into the 1990s and were amplified during the presidential contests that led to Bill Clinton's two terms as president. Conservative politicians such as Pat Buchanan and political commentators such as Bill O'Reilly became the spokespersons of the 'traditionalists' who were appalled at what they saw as an assault on American values by the progressives and liberals. They paid particular attention to controversial issues surrounding race, gender and sexuality.

In the late 1980s, homosexuality and the AIDS epidemic emerged as polarizing political issues, with President Ronald Reagan staying silent in the face of increasingly vocal protests by gay rights activists. While there was a general sense of confusion, anger and silence in the public, theatre became one of few public sites to share stories of gay and lesbian people and the health epidemics their community was experiencing. In a few small theatre venues, gay-themed plays began to gain traction, although many of them were limited to alternative performance spaces in New York City and San Francisco. When *M. Butterfly* premiered, it was immediately recognized as one of the very few Broadway plays that explicitly dramatized issues of male-to-male sexuality. While the play was not marketed as being about homosexuality, it was easy for some audience members in the late 1980s to conclude that the ambiguous relationship between Gallimard and Song was actually a homosexual one. In his review of the play, Michael Finegold described it as 'a homosexual love story shot through with social and political ideas', and says of B.D. Wong's performance, 'there is never any doubt onstage that the opera star Song Liling is a man'.[12] Typically, *M. Butterfly* is not categorized as a gay play, though its success on Broadway was quickly followed by what many consider as the renaissance of gay drama in American theatre, best exemplified by Tony Kushner's 1991 play *Angels in America: A Gay Fantasia on National Themes*. By the late 1980s, the American public at large was beginning to engage with questions of sexuality, and the popularity of Hwang's *M. Butterfly* contributed significantly to the growing discourse on the topic.

In academia, *M. Butterfly* appealed to scholars working in various areas of cultural studies, including but not limited to: Orientalism and post-colonial studies, feminism and gender studies, post-structuralism and performance studies. The first scholars to respond critically were specialists of Asian American theatre, and their perspectives were as diverse as the responses outside of academia. Generally, they focused on Hwang's use of racial stereotypes in the play. As mentioned above, James S. Moy criticizes both the play and Hwang for perpetuating the stereotype of the effeminate Asian man. For Moy, the popularity of *M. Butterfly* raises questions about 'whether their acceptance signals, finally, an end to the marginalization of the Chinese or Asians in general'.[13] For Moy, the play presents what he calls a 'system of literary subversions with significant impact for the social'.[14] Moy's criticism stems from the difficult question of how racial stereotypes can and should be challenged onstage. When a stereotype, like the Butterfly, is shown onstage to be deconstructed, it still needs to be shown to the audience, who may misunderstand the playwright's intention. Moreover, the image that replaces one stereotype can become another problematic stereotype. In the words of Moy, Song comes across as 'little more than a disfigured transvestite version of the infamous Chinese "dragon lady" prostitute stereotype'.[15] The play is, for Moy, about the desire of a white man, and his fantasy of the Butterfly continues to live on. After all, the play ends with the death of the Butterfly as embodied by Gallimard, and the stereotype is reinforced, albeit in an inverted way.

In his 'Afterword' in the published version of *M. Butterfly*, Hwang states that using the stereotype of the Butterfly was the key to linking the actual espionage story to the opera *Madame Butterfly*. He notes, 'The idea of doing a deconstructivist *Madame Butterfly* immediately appealed to me. This, despite the fact that I didn't even know the plot of the opera! I knew Butterfly only as a cultural stereotype; speaking of an Asian woman, we would sometimes say, "She's pulling a Butterfly", which meant playing the submissive Oriental number.'[16] But how he went about using the Butterfly stereotype in writing the play and what exactly he means by 'deconstruction' have raised more questions rather than providing satisfactory conclusions. Hwang's approach to stereotypes was to counter them with extreme versions of the same stereotypes. As quoted in Moy's article, Hwang wanted to cut through the stereotype and to provide the 'other extreme and make it so slangy and contemporary that it is jarring'.[17]

One such jarring moment in the play occurs when Song introduces to Gallimard the baby she claims to have given birth to. Song tells Gallimard that the baby would be called 'Peepee', to which Gallimard answers, 'Darling could you repeat that because I'm sure a rickshaw just flew by overhead' (66). When Gallimard suggests naming the baby 'Michael, or Stephan, or Adolph', Song insists that the name will not be changed. Gallimard continues his protest by saying, 'It's worse than naming him Ping Pong or Long Dong or – ', but Song cuts him off (67). This exchange between Song and Gallimard is written as comedic and exemplifies what Hwang means by providing an extreme version of an existing stereotype. One of the oldest stereotypes of the Chinese and Chinese Americans has been how their names sound in English, and Gallimard's comment indirectly references the character of Long Duck Dong, a foreign student from China, in the 1984 film *Sixteen Candles*. The film was immensely popular throughout the rest of the 1980s and the 1990s. The reference to the name in Hwang's play was meant to be a joke for an audience familiar with Long Duck Dong and other popular and contemporary stereotypes of Chinese names.

In 1985, Hwang wrote an article in the *New York Times* with the title 'Are Movies Ready for Real Orientals?' In the article, Hwang provides a brief history of Asian and Asian American characters on television and film and uses that history to advocate for 'real' Asians. Despite the odd and perhaps ironic use of 'Orientals' in the title of the article, he criticizes two-dimensional Asian characters in films such as *Sixteen Candles* and *Rambo*. Hwang poses a challenge to Hollywood by suggesting a test to distinguish between two-dimensional stereotypes and 'truthful' Asian and Asian American characters. Hwang notes,

> Directors attempting to make movies with Asian characters need only ask themselves one question: If this character were white, would he or she seem to be a fully fleshed-out creation? If the answer is no, then minorities are being used as little more than set decorations or special effects, and the film makers are enforcing a double standard that implies that Asians are less than fully human. In the absence of such humanity, all we see on screen is a foreign face.[18]

He ends the article on a hopeful note and states, 'I would like to think that audiences are becoming too sophisticated to buy into the old Oriental stereotypes.'[19] Hwang – like many Asian American writers, artists and intellectuals of his generation – was preoccupied with stereotypes and struggled to subvert them in any way possible. He was fully aware of the legacy and lasting effects of racist stereotypes and was sensitive to the need for more 'real' and 'truthful' images of Asian Americans. Thus, his insertion of ironic jokes about stereotypical Asian names and behaviours in *M. Butterfly* needs to be understood within the full context of Hwang's deep knowledge and sharp critique of the history of 'Oriental' representations in American popular culture.

Moreover, Hwang's use of comedy in dealing with Asian stereotypes in *M. Butterfly* is not significantly different from what other Asian American playwrights – or playwrights of colour in general – have done. Playwrights such as Frank Chin, Philip Kan Gotanda and Diana Son have used extreme versions of stereotypes to parody and satirize popular images of Asians.[20] To Asian Americans, stereotypes of Asians are so far from reality that the only way to present them onstage is to laugh at their absurdities. However, this begs the thorny questions of who is actually laughing with them and who or what is being laughed at. Hwang intended the audience to laugh at the ridiculous stereotype of the baby's name, but an audience may take the stereotype at face value and laugh at what it may perceive as a real name.

Josephine Lee addresses this issue in the chapter titled 'The Seduction of the Stereotype' in her book *Performing Asian America*. Lee writes, 'Although *M. Butterfly* deconstructs stereotypes, it does so by evoking the power that the stereotype still wields.'[21] According to Lee, the play can be read as a parody of stereotypes but also as a play that satisfies the desire to see those stereotypes enacted onstage. In a broader sense, the play explores how 'human desire and the formation of selfhood are rooted in stereotype'.[22] Each character is a stereotype to varying extents, and stereotyping is the only way they can relate to each other. This logic also applies to the audience members, who cannot enter the world of the play without bringing their preconceptions of people and culture. When watching the play, audience members may laugh at Gallimard, but they may also sympathize with him, as he asks them to, while finding pleasure in watching him become the Butterfly stereotype. Like the characters in the play, the audience is seduced by the stereotypes and implicated in their creation onstage.

This implication of the audience raises further questions about how effective Hwang is in deconstructing stereotypes and narratives of Asians and East–West relations. What is being deconstructed, and do audiences recognize the process of deconstruction? Hwang does not provide a definitive answer but, instead, allows each audience member to incorporate his or her presumptions in interpreting the play. One of the most frequently asked questions about the play is whether Song truly loved Gallimard. This question was asked once again when Hwang was the keynote speaker at the Comparative Drama Conference in April 2014 in Baltimore, Maryland. Hwang's answer to the question reveals much about what the play should do to an audience member. In his reply, he explained that the answer depends on what each audience member thinks of Pinkerton's true feelings towards Cio-Cio San in *Madame Butterfly*. If the audience member believes that Pinkerton, deep in his heart, loved Cio-Cio San despite his cruel actions, the reverse is true in *M. Butterfly*. In other words, the interpretation of the play would be contingent upon the interpretation of the power dynamic between the two characters in the opera.

For many scholars, the indefinite and contingent construction of relationships and identities in *M. Butterfly* illustrates the theories of post-structuralism in cultural studies. Dorinne Kondo, in her article '*M. Butterfly*: Orientalism, Gender, and a Critique of Essentialist Identity', writes that the play 'subverts notions of unitary, fixed identities'. She writes, 'Far from bounded, coherent, and easily apprehended entities, identities are multiple, ambiguous, shifting locations in matrices of power.'[23] The study of identity formation was a central topic in the 1990s, and many scholars from different academic disciplines questioned what they called 'essentialism', the idea that a person is defined as a single, unchanging identity, as Cio-Cio San is described solely as a Japanese woman. Scholars increasingly emphasized intersections of different facets of identities, including gender, race, ethnicity, sexuality and class, to name only a few. Moreover, different intersections are located in the intricate power structure (or matrices) of society. To phrase Kondo's statement in another way, *M. Butterfly* is about shifting identities and power relations and shifts that are possible because the characters' identities are not fixed or unitary. A white man can become a Japanese woman, and a Chinese man can become a fantasy. Identities are no longer about 'being' but about 'becoming', and that 'becoming' is constantly changing.

Kondo's essay uses *M. Butterfly* to explain emerging ideas of identity in the 1990s, and what she writes about has more to do with the actual, lived experiences of identity and less to do with dramatic characters in a fictional play. Song and Gallimard are, after all, not real people, and in theatre, the onstage transformation of a character is not uncommon.

Kondo's purpose is to project theories of post-structuralism on the play and to investigate how identities might intersect in real life. Similarly, other scholars have used Hwang's *M. Butterfly* to expound on and to illustrate various theories of postmodernism, gender studies and other fields of study that were dominating academic discourse in the 1990s. Karen Shimakawa, for instances, uses the concept of postmodernism, as described by Jean Baudrillard, to analyse the use of space and role-playing in the play. Her article also applies Judith Butler's well-known theory of 'performative acts' to explain the efficacy of *M. Butterfly* in enabling 'the progressive politics of the performative acts of gender/ethnic identities'.[24] By performative acts, Judith Butler means that gender is performed and constructed, rather than being innate or natural. Using metaphors of theatrical role-playing, Butler and others have described gender as rehearsed, repeated and enacted. In this sense, *M. Butterfly* provides a heightened and hyper-theatricalized illustration of Butler's theory, and many scholars have expounded on the concurrent themes that run in both the play and Butler's writings.

While many in academia have celebrated the play as an intelligent exploration of socio–political issues, others criticized what they saw as Hwang's reactionary and misogynistic politics. Gabrielle Cody was one of the first to explicitly describe the play as misogynistic and to question the ending. Cody takes particular issue with B. D. Wong's interpretation of Song Liling, in that he is not convincing in his enactment of a female, but her chief criticism of the play has to do with how the female gender is represented in the power game between Gallimard and Song. To become a 'woman', in other words, is to be inferior and the loser, and she finds Hwang's portrayal of becoming a 'man' equally simplistic and problematic. Cody argues, 'Gallimard becomes a "woman" out of failure and shame. Butterfly remains a "man" out of anger and revenge. Hwang's rejection of human complexity in his characters leads one to wonder why he chose this story'.[25] As Cody sees it, in the world Hwang creates, it is impossible for a man and a woman to coexist or reconcile without 'one having power over the other'. In the play, the last image presented to the audience is that of a dying woman, the very fantasy of beauty and sacrifice that the play supposedly attempts to deconstruct. When Gallimard dons the Butterfly costume and declares his 'vision' of the 'Orient', he becomes the Butterfly. His last lines in the play are: 'I have a vision. Of the Orient. That deep within its almond eyes, there are still women. Women willing to sacrifice themselves for the love of a man. Even a man whose love is completely without worth' (92). Cody reads Gallimard's last lines and self-punishment as reactionary and asks whether that is the only ending the character could have arrived at.

Scholars such as Cody interpret *M. Butterfly* as a largely realist play that should be seen as representing the world outside of the theatre. Such an interpretation requires Song to look like a real woman, and the relationship between the two main characters has to make sense with a reasonable suspension of disbelief. Others, such as Kondo and Shimakawa, interpret the play as a theatrical illustration of the fast-changing notions of gender and other identities and not necessarily as reflective of reality. Depending on how the play is interpreted, it can be criticized for misrepresenting women or praised for accurately showcasing how womanhood and sexuality are changing. Hwang's nuanced play readily opens itself to both sets of interpretations, and the play remains a fertile ground for discussions between scholars and critics.

The Legacy of *M. Butterfly*

M. Butterfly is the most anthologized Asian American play to date, and it has been produced around the world. The Broadway production directed by John Dexter was exported to London in March of 1989, with the British actor Anthony Hopkins as Rene Gallimard and the Singaporean actor G. G. Goei as Song Liling. Hopkins had performed in *Equus*, directed by John Dexter in 1974 on Broadway; Hopkins's appearance in *M. Butterfly* further suggests Peter Shaffer's influence on the play and the production. The set design by Eiko Ishioka, portrayed on the cover of this book, was replicated in the London production.[26] In 1990, the production toured North America and opened at the Roman Viktyuk Theatre in Russia in May. The play has since been revived in multiple cities and venues, including the Singapore Repertory Theatre in 1999 and the Sejong Centre in Korea in 2012. The film version of the play, written by Hwang and directed by David Cronenberg, stars Jeremy Irons as Gallimard and John Lone as Song. It was produced by David Geffen, who owned the production rights. Geffen's vision of the film was different from Hwang's, and Cronenberg emphasized the erotic relationship between Gallimard and Song, virtually ignoring the political and meta-theatrical perspective that is at the heart of Hwang's play.[27] As a screenwriting novice, Hwang had little control over the film's direction, which ended up telling a much more serious and tragic story than the play. In an interview, Hwang described the film as 'the director's movie' and added, 'It wasn't well received, and now I keep thinking that we should have done it my way.'[28]

More than any other play, *M. Butterfly* has shaped the legacy and reputation of David Henry Hwang as a playwright. The title 'Tony-Award-Winning Playwright' is mentioned every time he is introduced, as if the honour permanently changed him as a playwright. He also became an inadvertent spokesperson and representative of Asian American theatre. In various interviews, he articulated the importance of including Asian Americans in American theatre while being – ironically – the sole Asian American playwright most could name. The success of *M. Butterfly* would have a lasting effect on the subsequent plays Hwang would go on to write in the 1990s and beyond.

CHAPTER 4
IDENTITY POLITICS AND MULTICULTURALISM IN THE 1990s

In 1990, while *M. Butterfly* was still running on Broadway, David Henry Hwang received a phone call from the actor B. D. Wong. The call was about a new musical that was being imported from London, set to open on Broadway with a white actor in yellowface make-up in the starring role. The musical, *Miss Saigon*, would feature Jonathan Pryce playing a Eurasian character with his eyes taped up and skin bronzed. The convention of yellowface make-up in European and American theatre and film has a long history and has for centuries involved white actors pulling their hair or taping their eyes to make them look slanted or 'oriental'. The choice to cast Pryce in the role and to use yellowface make-up was seen as an accepted theatrical convention in London, but in the United States, both the casting and the make-up caused a controversy. Asian American theatre was founded partly in reaction to the practice of yellowface in the 1960s and the 1970s.[1] Asian Americans had protested yellowface on-screen and onstage for decades, and by the early 1990s, many thought the practice was all but eradicated in the United States. Because of his visibility and name recognition, Hwang became a major spokesperson in the controversy surrounding *Miss Saigon*. He spoke against the casting of Pryce and aligned himself with others who wanted to rid American theatre of what they saw as a racist casting convention.

Hwang quickly found himself in the middle of a whirlwind, involved in one of the most publicized controversies in contemporary American theatre. Hwang would later write about this experience in *Yellow Face*, which I discuss in Chapter 5. As signalled in this semi-autobiographical play, his involvement in the *Miss Saigon* controversy had a significant impact on his writing throughout the 1990s. After the *Miss Saigon* controversy died down, Hwang looked back to his activist experience with mixed feelings. He did not feel comfortable having sided with only one side of the controversy and found validity in the views of some he had fought against. He told Kevin Kelly of the *Boston Globe* that he sympathized with both sides of the issue:

'It's real hard for me to pick between artistic freedom on one hand and discrimination on the other.'[2] As foreshadowed by this statement, Hwang would spend the 1990s discovering deeper complexities in political issues, personal choices and playwriting styles.

All of the plays he wrote during the decade question assumptions he held during the 1980s, and he experimented with different dramatic structures and styles. None of the plays from this period could match the success of *M. Butterfly*; indeed, the next play he wrote, *Face Value* (1993), ended up being the biggest flop in his playwriting career. After the failure of *Face Value*, Hwang met with more bad news when the 1993 film version of *M. Butterfly* was not well received. He also wrote a series of original screenplays, many of which were never made into films. Of these, *Golden Gate*, released in 1994 and starring Matt Dillon and Joan Chen, received mostly negative reviews. Despite the setbacks, Hwang was optimistic for the future, and he began to think differently about race, multiculturalism and identity.

In 1993, Hwang married Kathryn Layng, whom he began to date after divorcing his first wife. When they met, Layng was a young actress who had graduated with a BFA in theatre from the University of Illinois at Urbana-Champaign. A beautiful blonde, she was an understudy for the role of Renee in the Broadway production *M. Butterfly*. His interracial marriage would have a significant impact on Hwang's changing perspectives of the world, and he continually incorporated these experiences into his work. Layng pursued a career in television acting early in their marriage, and she was cast in the role of Nurse Mary Margaret 'Curly' Spaulding in the popular television series 'Doogie Howser, M.D.' For a while, the couple maintained a bicoastal lifestyle, with a beachfront house in Los Angeles and a duplex on the Upper West Side of New York City. When their family grew with the birth of a son, they settled down in an apartment in New York City.[3]

The success of *M. Butterfly* had given Hwang celebrity status in the theatre community, and he enjoyed many opportunities to write for a variety of genres. He received prestigious commissions for new plays and was courted to write for television. Hwang continued his collaboration with the composer Philip Glass with *The Voyage* (1992) and worked as the librettist for *The Silver River* (1997), a chamber opera composed by Bright Sheng. In 1998, he was commissioned by Trinity Repertory Company in Providence, Rhode Island, to write an adaptation of Henrik Ibsen's play *Peer Gynt*. The production was directed by Stephan Muller and opened on 3 February 1998. Overall, the decade of the 1990s was significant in the development of

Hwang's career as a playwright, and his vision for the new millennium can be found in all of the plays from that period. This chapter focuses on the four original plays he wrote during the 1990s and traces the major themes and issues Hwang wrestled with during this important decade.

Bondage

Bondage premiered on 1 March 1992, as part of the 16th Annual Humana Festival of New American Plays at the Actors Theatre of Louisville. The play is Hwang's most optimistic and least ambiguous play. Its structure is similar to that of his Japanese plays and *M. Butterfly*, and the main theme in *Bondage* echoes those of his earlier plays, as well. Like Man and Woman in the Japanese plays or Song and Gallimard in *M. Butterfly*, the two characters in *Bondage* engage in a high-stakes relationship of power and love. In earlier plays, such relationships end tragically and ambiguously, and Hwang uses them to dramatize the futility of love in relationships built on power and secrets. In *Bondage*, Hwang dramatizes a couple that accomplishes what his previous characters could not by shedding all pretence and honestly falling in love. If earlier plays are about Hwang's doubts regarding love and honesty between a man and a woman, *Bondage* is about a willingness to believe that all things – including love – are possible in the new decade and the new millennium.

The play is set in an S&M parlour in the San Fernando Valley, a California region known as the capital of the pornography industry. Hwang returns to California for the play's setting, though the choice is unusual in other ways. His earlier plays set in California are about his family or Asian American history, and the settings have a particular purpose in foregrounding his Chinese American identity and heritage. The spatial setting of *FOB*, for example, is inspired by his cousin's Chinese restaurant, while *Family Devotions* and *Rich Relations* are set in fancy houses that can be read as symbols of the financial success of Hwang's family in America. *Bondage*, in contrast, is set in a location far from his family's dwellings. The S&M parlour is, nevertheless, still a theatrical space where one must perform multiple roles. Similar to the backroom of a Chinese restaurant in *FOB* or the balcony in *Rich Relations*, the parlour functions as a portal and a theatricalized place where characters must engage with questions of who they are, who they pretend to be and who they would like to become.

Bondage addresses these questions directly by having its two characters, Mark and Terri, play out different racial roles in an S&M setting. The play begins with Terri, a dominatrix with a whip, and Mark, chained to a wall, talking about what they are about to start. Both wear face masks and hoods, concealing their racial identities from each other and from the audience. Terri works at the parlour, and Mark is her regular customer. They have known each other for about a year. Mark begins the play with the question, 'What am I today?'[4] Terri tells him that he is a Chinese man named Mark Wong, and that she is a blonde woman named Tiffany Walker. She teases him by saying, 'I've seen you looking at me. From behind the windows of your – engineering laboratory. Behind your horn-rimmed glasses. Why don't you come right out and try to pick me up? Whisper something offensive into my ear. Or aren't you man enough?' (253). Thus begins the day's session for Mark and Terri, and it quickly becomes obvious that they have played this game a number of times. The two are familiar with each other's tactics, needs, desires and weaknesses.

Mark's weakness is love, and his professions of love for Terri – regardless of the racial role she plays – are his admission of defeat in their game of power. Mark calls the three words, 'I love you' the 'ultimate humiliation', and tells Terri, 'A woman like you looks on a declaration of love as an invitation to loot and pillage' (260). He does everything he can to avoid such humiliation, while Terri's job is to 'pry those words' from his lips in order to humiliate him (260). In their first phase of role-playing, Mark asks Terri whether it is okay for him to love her. Terri replies, 'C'mon, this is the 1990s! I'm no figment of the past. For a Chinese man to love a white woman – what could be wrong about that?' (254). Mark begins to say he loves her when she cuts him off and says, 'It's not real likely I'm gonna love you' (254). Terri tells Mark that she could never love an 'Oriental man' because she is not attracted to them. While a hardworking 'Oriental' man might fulfil her mother's fantasies, she could never get excited by him. Terri seems to think that Mark has already said he loves her, in which case her rejection of him would cause humiliation, the effect she wants. But Mark tells her that he never got to finish his sentence and actually say 'I love you'. As a blonde, white woman, Terri was supposed to have an easy time dominating and humiliating Mark, and she implies that she always gets the upper hand in their games. The incomplete sentence, however, puts Mark on top, and Terri admits that she 'turned total victory into personal embarrassment' (255). If this exchange is the first round in their competitive match, Mark comes out the winner.

Terri's failure is caused not by her mistake of cutting Mark off before he could finish saying 'I love you', but because she breaks the fantasy to self-consciously acknowledge her failure to dominate. When Mark tells her, 'Try not to break down again in the middle of the fantasy', Terri replies, 'I had a very bad morning. I've been working long hours' (257). Although Mark and Terri are in an S&M parlour, where continuity of role-playing and fantasy is key, the two break character to talk to each other not as fantasy lovers but as a dominatrix and her customer. Within the setting, the characters are meta-theatrical and self-aware. Hwang, once again, uses meta-theatrical techniques reminiscent of Pirandello to make transparent how characters and dramatic narratives are created and constructed onstage. However, unlike *M. Butterfly*, in which Gallimard is painfully aware of how his story is supposed to end, *Bondage* follows two characters that are making up the script as the play progresses. They are both the characters and the authors of the play.

In her next iteration of role-playing, Terri continues to have trouble staying in character. It is Mark who prods her to continue, declaring, 'This is a fantasy palace, so goddamn it, start fantasizing!' (257). Terri pushes herself to role-play in order to please her customer, though she does so by spewing out stereotypes of Asian men. When Mark explains that Asian men can be exciting and even dangerous, Terri immediately thinks of the Chinese Mafia and a Vietcong soldier and asks him whether he is one of them. If Mark is not a Chinese gangster or a Vietcong, Terri tells him, he would have to be a nerd. Mark wants 'something in between': 'Just delinquent enough to be sexy without also being responsible for the deaths of few hundred thousand US servicemen' (259). Terri flatly tells Mark that the parlour deals only with 'basic, mainstream images', implying that such an 'in between' image of an Asian man is not possible in their game. Mark submits to Terri, admitting that no woman could love an Asian man. He is humiliated and gets down on all fours, ready to be whipped.

Mark wants to be humiliated and whipped by Terri, and she thinks he is satisfied. But unlike the other days, this one is different for Mark. He reminds Terri that he has not yet said 'I love you' and tells her he will not say it. Terri thinks he will, as he has on other days, eventually say the three words and experience the 'ultimate humiliation' (260). She teases him by saying how easy it is to make him say the words. Despite their efforts, the two have difficulty staying in their S&M roles consistently and instead bicker about what is at stake. Does Mark, deep in his heart, really love Terri, the dominatrix, and do his declarations of love in their role-playing actually express his true feelings? Is Terri getting tired of Mark's desire to explore social issues through S&M activities? Does she find pleasure in the game they play, or does she see it as just a job that pays the bills?

To do her job well and consistently dominate Mark, she tells him that she is a black woman and that he is a white man. After Mark admits defeat, Terri moves onto another racial combination and tells Mark that he is an Asian man while she is an Asian woman. Each time Terri changes the racial identity of their characters, Terri gets the upper hand, and Mark finally says, 'All right! You win! I love you!' (269). Whatever his race, Mark expects to be defeated by Terri because she understands how the power structures of race and gender can be manipulated to her advantage. Mark is ready to be punished, but Terri surprises him by not giving him what he wants. She tells him, 'Punishment is, by definition, something the victim does not appreciate. The fact that you express such a strong preference for the whip practically compels me not to use it. *(Pause)* I think I'd prefer ... to kill you with kindness' (272). Terri understands that Mark's biggest fear is being exposed as himself and being made vulnerable by a woman, but she also knows that his fear might also be a secret desire.

Terri begins to kiss Mark's body, taking his 'no' as a 'yes', in keeping with the sadistic game. She continues to touch him erotically and slowly removes her costume, except for her hood. When she is stripped to her bra and panties, she commands Mark to remove her hood, which would give him the ultimate victory according to their 'rules of engagement' (278). At that moment, Terri is also quitting her job at the parlour. Mark disobeys her final command and takes his hood off instead. He is an Asian man, and the first thing he tells her is, 'I love you'. Terri then takes off her hood, revealing herself to be a Caucasian woman. Instead of rejecting him, as she has done numerous times before, she tells him that he is beautiful. As Mark removes the rest of his costume, Terri asks him, 'Was it all so terribly necessary? Did we have to wander so far afield to reach a point which comes, when it does at last, so naturally?' (278). In their last moment, Mark touches Terri's hair, and each character gazes at the other's face as the lights fade.

Mark's touching of Terri's hair mirrors a similar moment in *FOB*, when Dale touches Grace's hair and the scene freezes. In *FOB*, Hwang does not explore the moment further and leaves its interpretation to the audience. Do Dale and Grace, who are cousins, share an intimate moment, and if so, is Hwang signalling that their relationship is incestuous and forbidden? Or does the frozen moment signify Hwang's uneasiness in tackling issues of love and sex in his early twenties? Either way, the touching of hair causes the scene to freeze in *FOB*, but in *Bondage*, Hwang has the two characters gaze at each other's faces. As mentioned in previous chapters, Hwang repeatedly uses the face as a metaphor of identity and all of the historical and existential meanings that come with it. In *Family Devotions*, Di-gou tells Chester to study his face because 'the shape of your face is the shape of faces back many generations' (126). Mark, as an Asian man, also has a face with a specific history and ancestry, while Terri brings her own lineage and experiences. Hwang has them look at each other's faces to symbolize the honest encounter between two human beings who love each other. Their hoods and masks are literally off, allowing them to shed all of the pretences that prevented them from truly seeing one another.

The tender moment at the end of the play can be read in a number of ways. First, it can be seen as an endorsement of the same type of interracial love that Hwang himself was experiencing while writing the play, a coping mechanism for handling the anxieties of dating a white woman. Plays written by Hwang before *Bondage* are about the failure of love and relationships, and interracial love in *M. Butterfly* stands out as the most disastrous of all of the relationships Hwang has dramatized. In *Bondage*, Hwang finally allows his characters to fall in love without a tragic ending. However, it is also possible to read the play and the ending critically, as Jon Rossini convincingly does in his article, 'From *M. Butterfly* to *Bondage*: David Henry Hwang's Fantasies of Sexuality, Ethnicity, and Gender'. Rossini notes that the Asian men in both *M. Butterfly* and *Bondage* are portrayed as the 'crisis' in interracial relationships marked by 'the power of whiteness and heteronormativity'.[5] In other words, the play assumes that Mark, as an Asian man and a minority, is 'already in the masochistic position', always at the mercy of those in power.[6] In this reading of the play, Mark embodies the stereotype of the passive Asian man, and the space of the S&M parlour can be seen as one that reinforces the power structures that privilege whiteness. In short, the play can be interpreted either as a light-hearted rumination on interracial love in the 1990s or as a psychological study of fetish, desire and subconscious assumptions of race and gender.

On another level, however, the play is about Hwang's anticipation and anxiety surrounding the 1990s and the new millennium. As the mouthpiece of Hwang, Mark tells Terri that he worries about the coming millennium: 'Because it feels like all labels have to be rewritten, all assumptions reexamined, all associations redefined. The rules that governed behavior in the last era are crumbling, but those of the time to come have yet to be written' (227). At the very end of the play, Mark asks Terri whether she would have dated him if they had first met outside of the S&M parlour. Terri answers, 'Who knows? Anything is possible. This is the 1990s' (279). In the play, the 1990s are portrayed as the decade leading up to the new millennium, a time during which many things – including race, gender and relationships – will change. In reviewing the play at the Humana Festival, Michael Grossberg of the *Columbus Dispatch* declared that *Bondage* was the most successful play of the festival and described it as 'risky'. He praised it for being 'politically incorrect' while celebrating multiculturalism: '[Hwang's] sly sendups of racial and ethnic stereotypes affirm our common humanity and individuality rather than our separateness.'[7] In this sense, the play celebrates the 1990s and all of the new possibilities that the new decade might bring. Whether it is interracial love (as suggested by Mark's reference to the film *Jungle Fever*) or a redefinition of racial roles, the themes in the play are centred around the current topics of the 1990s.[8]

Face Value

After the lasting success of *M. Butterfly*, Hwang and Stuart Ostrow wanted to sustain the momentum with a new play that would be produced in a large Broadway venue. The production, *Face Value*, was budgeted at $2 million, and it had a pre-Broadway tryout in Boston in February 1993. Expectations were high for Hwang and Ostrow. Could they reproduce the sensation created by *M. Butterfly*? Would Hwang continue to shape the history of contemporary American drama? In the early 1990s, the US economy was in recession, and 1992–3 was a slow season on Broadway. In an article about *Face Value* in the *New York Times*, Hwang's new play was described as a hopeful sign that things would pick up on Broadway. In quoting Rocco Landesman, the president of Jujamcyn Theaters, the article notes, 'The occasion for [Landesman's] optimism was the announcement that David Henry Hwang's new play, "Face Value," would begin previews on 9 March at, as expected, a Jujamcyn house.'[9] Jujamcyn Theater was (and remains) one of top three producing companies of theatre in New York City. It was expected that *Face Value* would be produced at one of the Broadway theatres it owned, most likely the Eugene O'Neill Theatre, where *M. Butterfly* was performed

777 times. With the investment of Jujamcyn, Hwang and Ostrow had every reason to believe that *Face Value* would be another Broadway hit. Moreover, the production was directed by Jerry Zaks, a well-known director who had directed the Broadway production of John Guare's *Six Degrees of Separation*, a comedy about racial politics.

Much to their disappointment, the run in Boston at the Colonial Theater did not go well, and the reviews were overwhelmingly negative. William Boles summarizes them in *Understanding David Henry Hwang*:

> The *Christian Science Monitor*'s April Austin had little positive to say, noting that the plot was so convoluted that she 'got lost trying to explain it to a colleague'. It featured 'pointless wackiness', suggesting that 'farce isn't his forte'. More important, his desire to theatricalize the racial issues created a play that 'fails to register as either comedy or protest' because 'it skims across important issues without once dipping below the surface'. Iris Fanger of the *Boston Herald* was equally dismissive, describing the experience of watching the play as 'squirmy viewing'. Hwang's writing was problematic, with its 'zingy one-liners that Hwang throws off as if he's the next Neil Simon' and 'preachy lessons'. Most troublesome was the play's structure. As Fanger noted, 'The climax comes at the first act curtain, leaving the second act to meander in search of a reason to keep the audience in its seats.'[10]

Hwang and Zaks tried to rescue the play with a new version, and B. D. Wong replaced Dennis Dun in one of the lead roles. Broadway previews of the new version began on 9 March 1993, at the Cort Theatre, but it closed after eight performances. The official reason given by the producers to explain its closing was 'lack of box-office interest'.[11] The production's financial losses were significant, and Hwang found himself facing the largest flop of his career.

In an interview with Kevin Kelly of the *Boston Globe*, Hwang stated that he had wanted to write 'a farce about mistaken racial identity as early as 1989'.[12] After his experience with the protests surrounding casting in *Miss Saigon*, Hwang realized that he could use the scenario of a Caucasian actor performing in yellowface as the main plotline for a play. In the same interview with Kelly, Hwang explains that the *Miss Saigon* controversy 'was an example of someone masked who was actually in the face of another race.

There was a protest among Asian actors, a disruption of the actual show, and I started to think, "Hmmm, if I put Asians in whiteface ...". Then and there the plot device started to make itself known to me'.[13] Hwang decided to use this device to write his first farce. According to Boles, the literary inspirations for the play were two Joe Orton farces – *Loot* and *What the Butler Saw* – which, as Boles puts it, 'not only featured slamming doors, mistaken identities, and hanky-panky but also provided biting criticism of English society and government institutions in the 1960s'.[14]

Each time he writes a new play, Hwang seeks to model it after a form he has not previously used, and *Face Value* was his first attempt at writing a farce. There are certainly elements of farce in plays he wrote in the 1980s: parts of *Family Devotions* and *Rich Relations*, for instance, have scenes that use farcical situations for comic effect. All of Hwang's plays have comedy, and from the beginning of his career he has been compared to playwrights who specialize in comedy. However, farce, as a genre, is difficult to master, even more so when the main topic of a play is as serious as racial politics in the 1990s and the expectations are so high. Kelly articulates the complexity of this difficult task when he observes that *Face Value* is 'bugged as much by the expectations that have trailed *M. Butterfly* as it is by Hwang's inexperience in a new dramatic form'.[15] Farce is arguably the most difficult form of comedy, and if it is not first and foremost funny, it is a failure, regardless of how true or convincing the main message might be.

In *Face Value*, Hwang makes all characters ridiculous and all races equally silly. The play begins in the apartment of Linda Anne Wing. Linda and Randall Lee are both Asian American actors in their late twenties or early thirties. The two seem to be friends, and Randall may be in love with Linda, although she tells him flatly that she does not date Asian men. In the first scene, the two transform themselves into white people. With thick make-up and 'sandy blonde wigs', they scheme to pass as whites in order to execute a surprise protest on the opening night of *The Real Manchu*, a Broadway musical. Randall is convinced that the main, white actor of the musical, Bernard Sugarman, stole his job by playing an Asian role in yellowface make-up. In the first of his many rants, Randall declares that he could have brought 'some truth to that role' while acknowledging that the musical is 'racist, sexist, imperialist, misogynist'.[16] Both Linda and Randall denounce the musical as a 'disgusting piece of crap', though their protest is intended to focus solely on casting choices and 'that offensive yellowface' (1).

From the start, the absurd irony of racial politics is presented in the play. Randall and Linda are upset because they did not get an audition for the musical, yet they protest yellowface by putting on whiteface. Despite their complaints about the content of the musical, it is very likely that the two would have accepted roles, were they offered to them. Randall and Linda think that looking white will make it easier for them to gain admittance to the theatre. Once they are in, they will charge the stage and say to Bernard: 'You are the only gook here, we are human beings', after which they would reveal themselves as Asians – 'yellow and proud' (2). The second scene introduces Bernard Sugarman, a white actor who is clearly bothered by the protests against him yet convinced that he could really become Fu Manchu. He is consoled by Andrew, the producer of the musical, and Marci, the stage manager. Andrew is white, and Marci is African American. Bernard is portrayed as a less-than-intelligent actor who often confuses his real identity with the characters he plays. Andrew enables Bernard by telling him: 'After playing this part, you sympathize with Orientals! The very fact that you're wondering if our show might be bad for Asians proves how good it is for them!' (5). Bernard replies, 'I do think I understand now how it feels to hate all white men' (5). To Bernard and Andrew, they are practising their artistic freedom while the protesters outside are the intolerant extremists. Both Andrew and Marci call Bernard the 'emperor' to help him get into his character. Marci talks to Bernard in Chinese, which she has been studying, in order to convince him that he actually *is* Chinese. Bernard thinks the key to his full transformation is the face make-up, and both Andrew and Marci promote this self-delusion. Bernard describes putting on the make-up as 'a ritual', and explains that the new face gives him a new identity.

Bernard's self-delusion is aided by Jessica Ryan, a blonde, white actress who is described as wearing 'a sci-fi Vegas rendition of an Oriental harem outfit' (8). She is the embodiment of the ditzy blonde stereotype who wants to sleep with the lead actor and is naive enough to believe that Bernard, as Emperor Fu, has real sex secrets from the Orient. Jessica tells Bernard, 'Don't even speak English. I expect you to astound me with your Oriental love technique' (12).

The actress who played Jessica in the Boston previews was Jane Krakowski, who has played similar ditzy blonde characters both onstage and on-screen throughout her career. The character of Jessica is uncannily similar to another of Krakowski's roles, that of Jenna Maroney in the television sitcom '30 Rock'. Jessica, like Jenna, does not give a second thought to having casual sex, even with married men, for the sake of narcissism and self-promotion. Most importantly, the way Krakowski plays Jenna Maroney on television is very much in the vein of Hwang's meta-theatrical comedy. In other words, Jane Krakowski – as a beautiful, blonde actress – knows all about the stereotype of the ditzy blonde and embodies her character perfectly, all the while making it obvious that she is only pretending. Such a meta-theatrical style of acting would have worked well in *Face Value*.

All the characters in *Face Value* have varying degrees of self-awareness, a quality many critics have described as inspired by Pirandello, and the characters often talk directly to the audience in asides. Female characters are generally more aware of the fact that they are in the world of a farce, while most of the male characters – like Bernard – cannot tell the difference between what is real and what is pretend. The confusion is even more complicated when the audience is introduced to Glenn Ebens and Pastor, two white supremacists who sneak into the dressing room through a bathroom air-conditioning grate to sabotage the performance. The fictional name Glenn Ebens recalls the real name of Ronald Ebens, who, with his stepson Michael Nitz, fatally beat Vincent Chin in 1982 in Detroit, Michigan.[17] In *Face Value*, Hwang combines multiple layers of reality (ranging from pure fiction to real history) and complicates the combination with characters who may or may not know in which reality they are living.

Glenn and Pastor believe that Emperor Fu is a real threat, and they intend to assassinate him to protest multiculturalism and other liberal politics that they believe diminish white men's influence in the world. Glenn thinks that the musical glorifies 'the very symbol of the yellow peril – Fu Manchu', and it is his job to fight it: 'Well, we've killed 'm in 'Nam. But they're still around – bugging us! The next Asian war will be fought here at home!' (13). His sidekick, Pastor, is anxious and prone to crying, although he is supposed to be 'a guardian of the Christian faith' (13). Hwang portrays the two men as crazy white supremacists wielding real guns and claiming Christianity to promote their racists views. The confusion between reality and fiction is symbolized by Glenn's real gun, which looks exactly like the theatrical prop used by Bernard. Then again, Glenn's 'real' gun is a prop in Hwang's play, and it looks just like the other 'fake' guns that are supposed to be fictional props in the musical within the play. This is supposed to be confusing, both to the characters and to the audience.

Face Value, in essence, is about theatre itself. All of Hwang's plays have meta-theatrical elements, and many of his settings resemble a stage within a stage. The restaurant backroom in *FOB* and the prison in *M. Butterfly* function as hyper-theatrical settings within the worlds of the plays. In *Face Value*, a fictional stage is literally presented on the actual stage of the theatre venue. The device of a play-within-a-play has been used extensively by other playwrights throughout theatre history, and Hwang is certainly not the first to write a play about theatre and characters who do not know what is real and what is not. However, *Face Value* is literal in relating performances of fictional characters onstage to performances of race in real life. With the play, Hwang wanted to dramatize how race is performed by everyone, rather than being an essential part of who we are. By making the performance hyper-theatrical and meta-theatrical, Hwang asks the audience to see the absurdities in identifying ourselves exclusively in terms of narrow definitions of race.

All characters are parodied as hypocritical and self-righteous with narrow worldviews of racial politics. In defining themselves as Asian American activists, Randall and Linda are parodies of those who take a few classes in Asian American studies and then blame white racism for everything that is wrong in their lives. At the same time, Randall and Linda perpetuate the very stereotypes they protest: Linda does not want to date Asian men and Randall wants to play the role of Fu Manchu. Bernard and Jessica are parodies of unintelligent and narcissistic actors whose only interests are fame and recognition. They are white, but if they could become famous, they would play any role – including the most racist and sexist types. Moreover, as white actors, they are in a position of power to choose what roles they can play. Glenn and Pastor, mouthpieces of conservative extremists, do not realize how theatre works. Ironically, however, they become theatrical characters themselves when Bernard starts to believe that they are eunuchs in his imaginary world. Andrew and Marci only want the opening of the musical to go smoothly, and they are willing to play all sides in the game of racial politics to achieve that goal.

Much of the comedy in the play derives from mistaken racial identities as the eight characters interact with each other: Jessica thinks Randall is white and falls in love with him; Bernard mistakenly pities Glenn and Pastor for being 'Eurasian' eunuchs; and Glenn thinks Linda is white and calls her 'sister'. In their interactions, the characters discover that they have many things in common. Both Glenn and Linda hate the musical and want to disrupt the show, and Randall and Jessica find each other attractive in the oddest way. As the play progresses, these multiple iterations of mistaken racial identities spiral out of control, and Jessica seems to express Hwang's feelings when she declares to the audience, 'I feel like we're trapped on an endless loop that could play itself into infinity without a drastic measure!' (37). Hwang does not have a neat solution to the confusion he has created. Jessica seems to speak for Hwang once again when she says to Linda, 'I don't blame you for getting confused. Who can keep track of the subtle distinctions people make nowadays? I mean, even up close, how many of us can tell a Swede from a Finn' (41). The statement is obviously a joke, but it is, in essence, the main point of the play: when seen from a broad perspective, the racial distinctions characters insist on preserving are absurd and even farcical.

The musical manages, somehow, to start, and Linda is finally able to disrupt it by going onstage to say the line she has practised. However, she delivers it incorrectly and, frozen with stage fright, blurts out 'We are not the gook here, you are human beings' (47). Glenn then goes onstage and succeeds in stopping the show with violence. Andrew, in his desperate attempt to manage the chaos, takes the stage to tell the audience that it is time for intermission – for both the fictional musical and *Face Value*. At the beginning of the second act, Glenn and Pastor hold Bernard and Linda hostage and demand to be put on television. It is at this point in the play that the characters become fully aware of the fact that they are mere characters. Linda, after playing the role of a hostage, suddenly rises to tell the audience, 'Ladies and gentlemen I just can't go on with this play. I've been feeling for some time now ... this is such a negative portrayal of an Asian woman' (50). And Pastor comments, 'Wow, This is totally ... Pirandellian. I mean, the audience, they probably can't even tell right now whether we're really ad-libbing, or reciting actual lines' (51). The characters then bicker about racism, sexism, biases against actors and what is and is not considered politically correct. This scene can be seen as an intelligent and perhaps inevitable intervention in what was becoming an impossibly complicated play. But it can also be seen as an acknowledgement of failure on the part of Hwang as the playwright, who allows his characters to protest against their creator and express frustrations over the stereotypes they have had to play.

After they vent their anger, the characters decide that they will return to the world of the play. They continue to mistake each other's racial identities as they had done before Linda's Pirandellian interruption. However, the second time around, the jokes of mistaken racial identities grow tiresome, and the play becomes more serious. Shots are fired from both the 'real' and fake guns, and Glenn threatens to kill all the Chinese people in the group. To confuse him, the rest of the cast all become 'Chinese' by putting on Oriental costumes and yellowface from the musical. They succeed in confusing and apprehending Glenn with the help of Pastor, who confesses that he does not believe that race exists. Pastor tells Glenn that race is 'all some crazy fantasy – and a pretty funny one, too!' (97). The play ends with the revelation and resolution of all racial misunderstandings, and the characters wash the make-up from their faces. Despite getting shot during the frenzy caused by Glenn, Randall seems to be fine. Like a true comedy, the play ends with the formation of three couples, all of them interracial: Randall and Jessica, Linda and Bernard, and Andrew and Marci. Pastor blesses the couples and bids the audience goodnight. The last moment shows the couples sharing 'wedding kisses', with Pastor spreading his hands over them, the sound of falling water heard in the background.

Kevin Kelly of the *Boston Globe* compares the ending of the play to Shakespeare's *A Midsummer Night's Dream* but also calls it 'cheesy' and impossible to salvage. He is pointed in his criticism of the play: 'The problem here, in comedic terms, is that Hwang isn't very funny. The ironic sensibility may be humorous but his delivery is neither sharp nor droll.'[18] Perhaps it was impossible to create an effective farce about mistaken racial identities in the meta-theatrical style of Pirandello's plays. As Kelly predicted, the play could not be salvaged, despite Hwang's attempts to rewrite it. Hwang reacted to the lasting impact of the play's failure by later writing *Yellow Face* in order to understand what went wrong with the production of *Face Value*. As I will discuss in the next chapter, Hwang does so by inserting a version of himself into his play to investigate how race can be made funny and farcical without losing its seriousness.

Trying to Find Chinatown

With both *Bondage* and *Face Value*, Hwang wanted to dramatize how race is an artificial construction made by society and how interracial marriage challenges and unsettles racial categories. He continued this line of thought with *Trying to Find Chinatown*, a short, one-act play that premiered at the Actors Theatre of Louisville as part of the 20th Annual Humana Festival on 29 March 1996. The play is set on a street corner on the Lower East Side of New York City in the 'present', and features two male characters. Benjamin Wong, in his early twenties, is biologically Caucasian and is blonde and blue-eyed, yet he was adopted by a Chinese American couple and raised in the Midwest and identifies himself as Asian American. Ronnie Chang, in his mid-twenties, is biologically Chinese, but he finds his cultural roots in blues music and calls himself 'The Bow Man'. The play opens with Ronnie, dressed in 'retro-1960s clothing' with 'a few requisite 1990s body mutilations', playing an electric violin on a sidewalk for money. He plays what Hwang describes as 'Hendrix-like virtuoso rock "n" roll riffs'.[19] Benjamin enters and listens to the music, applauding when Ronnie is finished.

The first conversation between the two characters reveals much about their personalities: Benjamin is a naive and polite midwesterner, while Ronnie is a foulmouthed and rude New Yorker. Benjamin asks Ronnie for directions to an address, and the latter tries to help until he realizes that the address is in Chinatown. Ronnie immediately gets angry and bursts out to Benjamin, 'So why is it that you picked me, of all the street musicians in the city – to point you in the direction of Chinatown? Lemme guess – is it the earring? No, I don't think so. The Hendrix riffs? Guess again, you fucking moron' (287). Ronnie assumes that Benjamin singled him out because of his race and rejects the stereotyping he perceives. Benjamin, surprisingly, understands Ronnie immediately and says, 'Brother, I can absolutely relate to your anger' (287). Benjamin then gives a long speech about the plight of Asian Americans in the United States and how stereotypes of Asian Americans hurt the community in real ways. Shocked, Ronnie asks Benjamin where he learned 'all that'. Benjamin answers that he took Asian American studies at the University of Wisconsin, Madison, and that he wanted to 'explore [his] roots': 'After a lifetime of assimilation, I wanted to find out who I really am' (289). Benjamin talks and sounds like an Asian American who has experienced racism throughout his life. He also says he hungers to know more about his ancestors who 'built the railroads' (289).

Ronnie reminds Benjamin that he is white and that what he just heard sounds like 'some kind of redneck joke' (289). Benjamin then tells Ronnie that race is not just about skin colour and explains that he was adopted by Chinese American parents at birth. In his hometown of Tribune, Kansas, he is known as Benjamin Wong and a Chinese American. Ronnie is not convinced that race is something one can choose: 'You can't just wake up and say, "Gee, I feel black today"' (290). Benjamin says he is looking for a home and a community, which he assumes Ronnie already has because he is Chinese American. Ronnie rejects the assumption and counters the argument by describing his home and community in terms of musical influences. While playing the violin, Ronnie explains in a monologue that the lineage he identifies with most is found in the history of jazz and the blues. He knows his history well, and that history is unrelated to his race or the colour of his skin. For Ronnie, the history of the music he plays is 'crowded with mythology and heroes' that inspire pride, and he asks rhetorically, 'Does it have to sound like Chinese opera before people like you decide I know who I am?' (291).

After Ronnie's monologue, the two characters stop talking to each other. Ronnie plays 'a jazz composition of his own invention' while Benjamin listens for a while. The play ends with Benjamin's monologue about finding the street and the building he was looking for. The old tenement was where his father was born, and the audience learns that Benjamin's father had died six months earlier. His father never wanted to return to the Chinatown 'ghetto' where he grew up, but Benjamin brings the memory of his father back to his old home. In the last lines of the play, Benjamin tells the audience: 'To this place where his ghost, and the dutiful hearts of all his descendants, would always call home. (*He listens for a long moment*) And I felt an ache in my heart for all those lost souls, denied this most important of revelations: to know who they truly are' (293). By returning to his father's birthplace, Benjamin can honour the memories of his father and grandfather and feel one step closer to knowing who he truly is.

In the final stage direction, Hwang indicates that Ronnie and Benjamin 'remain oblivious to one another' (294). The two do not directly interact, though Benjamin's last monologue is delivered with Ronnie's music in the background. In effect, the words of Benjamin's monologue become the lyrics to Ronnie's violin melody. As is the case in Hwang's earlier plays – such as *The Dance and the Railroad*, the Japanese plays, and *Bondage* – Hwang often dramatizes two characters that come from opposing sides of a debate, whether personal or political. In all of the aforementioned cases, the characters have a profound influence on each other, and they often switch places or points of view. Such a reversal does not happen in *Trying to Find Chinatown*, however. One reason may be that, unlike in the earlier plays, *Trying to Find Chinatown* is only ten minutes long, which does not allow time for extensive character development. Another reason may be that Hwang uses the play to pose a question, rather than to explore a debate to its logical end. While Benjamin delivers his last monologue, Hwang describes Ronnie's style of music in the form of a question: 'As [Benjamin] speaks, Ronnie continues playing his tune, which becomes underscoring for Benjamin's monologue. As the music continues, does it slowly begin to reflect the influence of Chinese music?' (293). Hwang opens the possibility for Ronnie to start using Chinese music in his jazz violin performance, but the fact that the stage direction is posed as a question does not reveal the playwright's commitment to one particular position.

Ronnie may be starting to reconsider his position on culture and race based on his conversation with Benjamin, and his music may, in turn, inspire Benjamin to rethink how he defines his own identity. This is, of course, speculative and only one possible interpretation of the play's ending. However, Hwang clearly seems to be asking if race can be chosen. What makes one Asian or Caucasian? What is more important in racialized identities: biological traits or cultural influences? Who is more Asian American: Ronnie or Benjamin? What defines identity: being or doing? These questions drive the action in *Trying to Find Chinatown*, and Hwang is suggesting that cultural identity is increasingly becoming a matter of personal choice. With Ronnie and Benjamin, Hwang envisions what some would call a post-racial society, one in which racial identities are incidental, not essential.

The play works well as an intellectual exercise, and it is based on the changing realities of American politics in the 1990s. There have been cases of white children adopted and raised by Asian American parents, and Asian Americans who think and talk like Ronnie are abundant in New York City. Hwang also juxtaposes what he calls his 'isolationist–nationalist' phase, embodied by Benjamin, with the multicultural or 'pluralistic' phase that was celebrated in the 1990s and fuelled by hope at the prospect of the coming millennium. At the same time, Ronnie can be seen as representing Hwang's 'assimilationist' phase. Like Dale in *FOB*, Ronnie does not want to be identified as foreign or different, preferring to be a cool and hip American. Echoing Steve in *FOB*, Benjamin mentions Gwan Gung as the deity he recognizes as the god of warriors; Ronnie, like Dale, does not know who he is talking about. Ronnie is similar to Hwang in that both grew up as musicians trained in western styles and lacked direct knowledge of Chinese culture or history. Like Ronnie, Hwang played the jazz violin in his twenties and identified more with the blues than with Chinese music. Hwang learned Chinese theatre as a young playwright, and he began to incorporate Chinese music as his artistry grew. Perhaps Hwang sees his younger self in Ronnie and recognizes the potential for both of them to change as artists, an optimism captured in the stage direction posed as a question.

However, *Trying to Find Chinatown* is different from *FOB* in one critical way. Ronnie, as dramatized by Hwang in 1996, is different from Dale of 1979. In 1996, a Chinese American jazz violinist with body piercings and a foul mouth was hardly a strange sight in New York. While he would have stood out as an anomaly in 1979, in 1996 Ronnie represents the growth and diversification of the Asian American population. In fact, when the play was performed in Singapore in April of 1996, it was seen as a play that evoked the diverse population and culture of Singapore and other cosmopolitan and multicultural locales around the world. In interviews with Singaporean news outlets, Hwang articulated the 'mutability' of identity and described his characters as living in 'the grey areas between those presumably fixed categories'. He also noted in the same interview that 'rigid definitions, whether they apply to issues of culture or gender or some other category, also seem … somewhat malleable'.[20] *Trying to Find Chinatown* asks where 'home' is for each of the audience members, without reifying 'fixed categories' of culture and race. In doing so, Hwang celebrates the possibilities of a post-racial society, but he also implies that Asian American identity is conditional and might perhaps be unnecessary in the future.

Golden Child

Golden Child was Hwang's first full-length play to be produced after *Face Value*, and is a return to themes of autobiography and family. For one, the birth of his first child, Noah, had a significant impact on Hwang's perspectives on family, history and culture. According to Hwang, *Golden Child* was inspired by his great-grandfather, who was the first in his family to convert to Christianity around the turn of the twentieth century. While it is loosely based on his family story, the main plot points of the play are factual. In his notes to the published version of the play, Hwang describes *Golden Child* as a reimagination of 'the wrenching changes [the great-grandfather] set into motion, which forever changed the world of his three wives (Chinese society of that era was polygamous) and one of his daughters'.[21] With *Golden Child*, Hwang echoes the ending of *Trying to Find Chinatown*, in which Benjamin, with Ronnie's music in the background, remembers his father and grandfather, seeking to know who he is and to connect with the ghosts of his ancestors.

Golden Child is about Hwang's personal journey to find who he is and who his ancestors are, and he chose to tell that story in the style of Russian playwright Anton Chekhov. Initially, he had wanted to model the play after Brian Friel's *Dancing at Lughnasa* (1990), a memory play set in Ireland's countryside. Like Friel's play, the early version of *Golden Child* featured poetic monologues throughout the play. As Hwang developed the script, however, the monologues were replaced with action, and the play began to depart from Fiel's example. He found a better model in Chekhov's plays, specifically in the way the Russian playwright dramatizes minute details of his characters' lives, revealing in them both comedy and tragedy. As early as 1993, while working on *Face Value*, Hwang had wanted to write a play in the style of 'a very small, Chekhovian piece'.[22] With *M. Butterfly* and his other two-character plays, Hwang had demonstrated his ability to write Brechtian style drama that engaged with dialectical and political ideas. With his new play, he wanted to pay attention to 'small details that make up an individual life' and deal with 'small things that break your heart'.[23] He repeated this comment when *Golden Child* was produced at the Public Theater in New York City: 'I wanted to write something detailed and less directly political.'[24]

At first, he did not know he was going to write about his family, but his search for self-knowledge and ancestral history took him to a project he had worked on when he was ten years old. He has told the story of that project in numerous interviews, and it has become the indispensable background for the play. The story goes like this: when he was ten years old, his maternal grandmother, who was living in the Philippines at the time, fell gravely ill. He wanted to capture her memories of his family's past before she passed away, so he took an audio-recording device and visited her. 'As an American boy, growing up in Southern California', Hwang explains, 'these stories somehow seemed very important to me.'[25] After returning to Los Angles, he wrote her story into a ninety-page 'novel' he titled *Only Three Generations*, which he copied and distributed to his relatives. His grandmother, instead of passing away, recovered and lived a long life with Hwang's family in California. In fact, at the age of ninety-one, she attended a performance of *Golden Child* when it was presented at the South Coast Repertory.

In 1995, as a thirty-nine-year-old man, Hwang returned to the story and began to collaborate with his ten-year-old self to write a new play.[26] The story Hwang has consistently told of his visit to the Philippines functions as a framing device for the play. Indeed, the play cannot be separated from Hwang's autobiographical story of how he came to write it. In contrast to the consistency of Hwang's personal backstory, the script of the play has gone through numerous revisions. Hwang was given the opportunity to develop it at multiple venues, and each time, he made significant changes to the script. In particular, Hwang has changed how the story of the past is framed within the story of the present. Dan Bacalzo's essay in the last section of this book details the different versions of the play and examines how the changes reflect Hwang's nostalgic view of his family's past. Given Bacalzo's thorough study, it is unnecessary to go into the specifics of how Hwang has continued to revise the play. However, a general assessment of the changes Hwang made is necessary to understand the play's significance. For the most part, the description and analysis of the play I provide below refer to the version presented on Broadway and published by Theatre Communications Group in 1998.

The play was commissioned by the South Coast Repertory theatre company in Costa Mesa, California, and premiered on 17 November 1996, at the Joseph Papp Public Theater. The production was created by 'the original *Sunday in the Park with George* team', as Laurie Winer of the *Los Angeles Times* puts it.[27] The team included James Lapine as the director, Tony Straiges as the set designer and Richard Nelson as the lighting designer. The play was then further developed in production at South Coast Repertory and the John F. Kennedy Centre for the Performing Arts in Washington, DC. Reviews of the Public Theater production were generally positive. Ben Brantley of the *New York Times* described the play as 'likable, educational and, at times, very poignant', but he found it lacking in emotional connection between the present and the past.[28] The same production opened at South Coast Repertory in January of 1997. Hwang continued to develop the play, trying out different narrative frames and tones. For the Kennedy Centre production, Hwang insisted on emphasizing the comedy of the play, which ended up being, in his words, 'glib and shallow'.[29] Most reviewers of these earlier productions identified the play's lack of emotional affect as a weakness, despite Hwang's attempts to model it after Chekhov's plays. Hwang continued to seek a balance between Chekhovian laughter and pathos as he further developed the play at the Singapore Repertory Theatre and the American Conservatory Theatre. Finally, on 2 April 1998, the play opened on Broadway at the Longacre Theatre. It was Hwang's first return to Broadway, ten years after the opening of *M. Butterfly*. The long development process Hwang enjoyed with *Golden Child* is rarely granted to a playwright; it seems Hwang wanted to avoid the mistakes he made with *Face Value*, and he was cautious in taking the play to Broadway. During that long process, Hwang was able to fine-tune the 'small moments' in the play to maximize the emotional impact he wanted to have on the audience.

In the version presented at the Public Theater, the play begins with Andrew Kwong, the main character, in a taxi ride in Manhattan on his way to the JFK airport to attend his grandmother's funeral. Andrew is worried about becoming a father for the first time. While in the taxi, he hears the voice of his grandmother, who tells him, 'Time to cast out demons of your anger.'[30] The set then becomes a grand Chinese house in 1918, and the actor who plays Andrew becomes the character's great-grandfather, Tieng-Bin. The actress who plays Andrew's grandmother becomes her younger version (she is Tieng-Bin's daughter). The story of Tieng-Bin is based on Hwang's great-grandfather and the different personalities of his three wives. Tieng-Bin's desire to convert to Christianity is the central story of the play, which ends in the same taxi as it began. As Bacalzo explains in his essay, the Broadway version cast the veteran actor Randall Duk Kim, who is older than Stan Egi, the actor who played Andrew in the Public Theater version. With Kim in the lead role, the older Andrew is visited by his mother, rather than his grandmother. In the 2012 version at the Signature Theatre, Hwang once again changed the framing narrative of the play to reflect his new perspective on his family.

Given the fact that *Golden Child* is an autobiographical play close to his heart, it is not surprising that Hwang has continued to revise the framing narrative. As his life has changed, Hwang has looked back on his family's past with changing expectations, which have led to a deeper understanding of his past. At its core, however, the play has stayed constant. While the specifics of the story may have changed, the play has always been about the theme of fundamentalism. In his interview with Steven Drukman of the *New York Times*, Hwang states, 'As a playwright … what I object to right now is any form of fundamentalism, whether it's nationalistic, religious or ethnic.'[31] When he was twenty-four, Hwang rejected his family's fundamental Christianity, which he wrote about in *Family Devotions*. In the play (discussed in detail in Chapter 1), Ama (the grandmother) is portrayed as a ridiculously fundamentalist Christian, and she serves as the target of Hwang's criticism of his family's religion. Chester (who represents Hwang) identifies with Di-gou, the uncle from China who is not a Christian. Di-gou tells Chester to study his face in order to see the many generations that came before him. *Family Devotions* ends before Chester can complete the journey, before the study of his face can reveal his family's past encoded in it. In a sense, *Golden Child* begins where *Family Devotions* ends. Andrew in *Golden Child* is like Chester's older self, in search of his family's past and worried about the new family he is about to start.

Just as Hwang rejected Christianity because of its fundamentalism, his great-grandfather, Tiong-Yee, rejected Chinese ancestor worship and other traditional practices for the same reason. Christianity, for Tiong-Yee, was modern, radical and liberating. As he approached middle age, Hwang realized that rejecting fundamentalism was much more complex than he had thought. With *Golden Child*, he wanted to show that his family's conversion to Christianity was 'neither completely "good" nor "bad"'.[32]

In the play, Eng Tieng-Bin, who represents Hwang's great-grandfather, returns from a three-year trip to Manila where he ran a business and encountered westerners and their way of life. At his home in a village near Amoy in Southeast China, his three wives are busy preparing for his return. The first wife, Siu-Yong, is traditional and proud; the second wife, Luan, is calculating and willing to do anything to capture Tieng-Bin's attention; and the third wife, Eling, is beautiful and the love of Tieng-Bin's life. The three wives bicker about everything, ranging from their house duties to how servants should be disciplined. Much of the comedy in the first act derives from their interactions, as each competes to be seen as the ideal wife who is humble and dutiful, as demanded by tradition. As Luan declares, 'humility is power' in their household, and they must manipulate the situation to be perceived as the most humble wife.[33] Being seen as most humble would make a wife the most honourable, as well, and honour would give her the upper hand in their power struggle. In the dinner banquet scene, the wives take turns praising each other and downplaying their own accomplishments. The more they are successful at praising others, the more honourable they seem, yet when they are praised by others, they must do all they can to humbly deny the compliments at all costs.

The Chinese characters' language in the play is mostly casual American English, though the audience understands that they are actually conversing in Chinese. The characters speak with appropriate formality, but slangy English phrases are often inserted for effects that are both comical and familiar for American audiences. For instance, when Luan praises Siu-Yong excessively, she is scolded, 'What are you – retarded?' (15). The style of language and the interactions between the characters recall Hwang's approach in *The Dance and the Railroad*. In both plays, the characters are Chinese, but the ways in which they talk and behave are American. The only non-Chinese character, Reverend Baines, speaks in broken English to accentuate his lack of language skills in the world of the play.

In *Golden Child*, the character written to be most sympathetic to an American audience is Ahn, who is the first wife's ten-year-old daughter and Tieng-Bin's favourite child. She calls herself the Golden Child because she has been told that she brings good luck. The play is essentially about how she was affected when her father decided to adopt Western ways. The changes she experiences symbolize the entire family's transformation. When Tieng-Bin announces that he will be modernizing the family, his first act is the unbinding of Ahn's feet. The first wife, Siu-Yong, reacts in horror, but Tieng-Bin calls the Chinese custom of binding girls' feet 'outdated' and 'barbaric' (28). Siu-Yong warns that without bound feet, Ahn will not be able to marry and will suffer 'a lifetime of loneliness' (29). She adds to this warning a condemnation, one as assertive as a wife can be in her culture: 'Men. You dream of changing the world when you cannot even change yourselves' (29). To her surprise, it is Ahn who decides she does not want to wear the foot binds. After Tieng-Bin commands Siu-Yong to remove the binding, he hears 'the spirits of his ancestors' warn him: 'To betray your ancestors is to cut your own heart from your body' (29). The first act ends with the agonizing screams of Ahn as strips of cloth are removed from her feet, while Tieng-Bin prays at his parents' altar, asking for forgiveness.

Throughout the play, the spirits of the ancestors wield real power in the Eng household. Each character has to pray to his or her parents' altar, make offerings to appease them and ask for their protection. Tieng-Bin's prayer of forgiveness at the end of the first act demonstrates his dilemma in converting to Christianity. He sincerely believes that his ancestors' spirits are watching over him and that he is committing a great offence by wishing to pray to a foreign god. At the same time, he has many reasons to reject the old ways and to embrace the modern changes he witnessed while staying in Manila. For one, modernization would be good for his business, and he would be in a better position to support his family and the village. He also wants to educate his daughters and to give his children the opportunity to learn about the world outside of China. Most importantly, Tieng-Bin dreams of being married only to Eling, and he wishes to live privately, outside of the traditional, polygamous household. His love for Eling is the main motivation that drives his desire to convert. In total, these multiple reasons are impossible to separate, and together, they are compelling enough for Tieng-Bin to reject his ancestral obligations.

The second act begins with the visit of Reverend Anthony Baines, a British missionary whom Tieng-Bin invited to educate his family about Christianity and Western ways of life. Luan, the second wife, eagerly attends the lessons with the full understanding that Tieng-Bin's conversion to Christianity would require him to have only one wife. Siu-Yong and Eling avoid the reverend in fear that he is a 'white devil' who will bring a curse to the family.

Identity Politics and Multiculturalism in the 1990s

Siu-Yong staunchly opposes her husband's demands to modernize the family and increasingly isolates herself in her room with an opium pipe, which she uses to escape a reality she cannot control. Luan, on the other hand, eagerly embraces Western culture and Christian beliefs and shows up to a Bible studies session in a Western outfit she ordered from a catalogue. She laments the fact that her bound feet will not fit into the matching high-heeled shoes. Eling is intrigued, but she is afraid to reject her ancestors and does not know whether to side with Siu-Yong or Tieng-Bin, both of whom have power over her. Earlier in the play, she had surprised Tieng-Bin by wearing a Western nightgown when they were alone. She is willing to change her clothes and music preferences, but when it comes to changing whom or what she should worship spiritually, she is torn.

When the second act begins, Eling is eight months pregnant, and Reverend Baines has been visiting as long. With Siu-Yong in hiding in her room with her opium pipe and Eling unwilling to show up to the Bible studies sessions, Luan has full control of the situation and the future of the Eng household. Her wish is to become the only wife when Tieng-Bin converts to Christianity. She succeeds in soliciting Reverend Baines' support for her cause in exchange for convincing Tieng-Bin to be baptized in front of the entire village. She also makes Tieng-Bin turn against Siu-Yong. Ahn had been attending Bible studies at the request of Siu-Yong, who wanted her to spy on her father and the reverend. Luan leaks this information to Eling, who inadvertently tells Tieng-Bin. In a rage, Tieng-Bing destroys Siu-Yong's opium pipe and ancestral altar, which Ahn witnesses. As he stands next to the heap of destruction he has created in her room, he makes a pronouncement: 'I have made my decision. Or you've made it for me. I *will* be baptized. And all the family altars will come down at once' (49). As Siu-Yong keenly observes, Tieng-Bin is, deep inside, a traditional man. The way he enforces his will over his family represents the exercise of a fundamentally traditional sort of prerogative.

Siu-Yong chooses the most humble way out of her unhappy life by committing suicide. With the help of Ahn, who does not fully understand her mother's actions, Siu-Yong ingests a lethal amount of opium. Her suicide scene is staged concurrently with the baptism scene of Tieng-Bin, Luan and Eling; while the husband rejects his traditions and worships a foreign god, his first wife becomes a ghost that will haunt his house. Siu-Yong returns to punish Eling for telling their husband about Ahn's spying duties. Eling dies in childbirth, and Tieng-Bin is left with Luan, the wife he can neither respect nor love. He thinks that he is being punished for rejecting his ancestors and becoming an 'individual' in the Western sense of the word. He tells Ahn, 'I should've listened to your mother', in expressing regret over forcing his family to change. However, it is Ahn who comforts her father and says that she has decided to believe and follow 'this new God, the one you brought into our home' (60).

Ahn tells Tieng-Bin, 'Papa, we must all be born again', which the older Ahn repeats to Andrew, her son (60). The notion of being 'born again' is a central theme in the play, and its meaning applies not only to religion but also to all belief systems that can be both fundamentalist and liberating. Hwang recognizes that belief systems – whether Christianity or Confucianism – have the power to limit people's actions, but they can also free them to explore new ways of thinking and living. *Golden Child* is about coexistence, the cyclical nature of the zeitgeist and how specific choices made by one generation have lasting effects.

Hwang gives validity to both traditional Chinese ancestor worship and Christianity by allowing the possibility of both belief systems exerting real power in people's spiritual lives. In fact, his family has found a way to integrate both belief systems for their benefit. In the opening scene of the play, Andrew tells the ghost of his mother: 'You're a Christian, Ma. Christians don't come back from the dead.' Ahn replies, 'You forget – I am *Chinese* Christian. Best of East, best of West' (6). In the play, Ahn's choice to believe in the Christian god is a form of ancestor worship. She wanted to follow her father's path, and her prayers to Jesus were an acknowledgement of her gratitude for being liberated from foot binding. Andrew realizes this at the end of the play: 'So – whenever you opened a Bible, or said a prayer to Jesus, you were actually making an offering ... to your father. In spite of everything, you love him so much' (61). Andrew makes peace with his family's history and with the baby who will become his Golden Child. The play, in turn, is Hwang's ancestor worship and his way of using the ritual of theatre to honour his family's past. In his notes to the published version of the play, Hwang states, 'Looking back upon the twists and turns of this journey, I sometimes see it as an American playwright's act of ancestor worship. ... Undoubtedly, returning to this material allowed me to invent many sides of numerous conversations, and to remember my forebears the way I know best: upon the stage' (ix).

The play ends with Andrew's monologue addressed to his unborn child. The motif of the face, which Hwang has repeatedly used in his plays, prominently appears again at the end of *Golden Child*. As Andrew's wife (who is played by the same actress who plays Eling) sleeps next to him, he says: 'I watch your mother sleeping, knowing you are growing inside her. And suddenly the room is filled with spirits – so many faces, looking down on me. And on each face, a story, some I have been told, some I can only imagine, and some I will never know at all' (62). As the monologue continues, Siu-Yong and Luan appear onstage, and the last image of the play is that of his wife holding him with Siu-Yong, Luan, and Ahn sitting on their bed. The ending echoes the final scene of *Family Devotions* and reinforces the similarities between the two plays. In *Family Devotions*, Hwang has only Chester's face remain onstage as the last image of the play and indicates in a stage direction that 'the shape of Chester's face begins to change' (150). What began in *Family Devotions* manifests fully in *Golden Child*, and Andrew realizes that his face will, one day, 'join this constellation' of faces (62). Moreover, Andrew, who represents Hwang, is surrounded by women whose stories have become part of who he is.

The Broadway production of *Golden Child* featured an impressive cast of veteran Asian American actors. Randall Duk Kim, the noted Shakespearean actor, played the role of Tieng-Bin, and Tsai Chin, best known for her performance as Auntie Lindo in the film *Joy Luck Club*, played Siu-Yong. The actress Ming-Na Wen, who was also in *Joy Luck Club*, played Eling, and Kim Miyori played Luan. The actor who received the most praise from critics was Julyana Soelistyo, who originated the role of Ahn from the beginning of the development process. She was nominated for a Tony Award for Best Featured Actress in a Play, and her onstage transformation from an eighty-year-old woman to a ten-year-old child was recognized as a highlight of the production. For the 2012 revival of *Golden Child* at the Signature Theatre in New York City, Soelistyo played the role of the first wife. Overall, critics found the cast and the design elements of the 1998 Broadway production stellar but gave mixed reviews to the play and James Lapine's directing. Nevertheless, the play was nominated for a Tony Award for Best Play in 1998 and went on to be produced at other major venues, including the Seattle Repertory Theatre (1999) and the East West Players in Los Angeles (2000). When Signature Theatre selected Hwang to be their playwright in residence for the 2012 season, he had the opportunity to revive two of his earlier plays; he chose *Golden Child* and *The Dance and the Railroad*. The former was produced on the larger stage and was directed by Leigh Silverman, whom Hwang has collaborated with a number of times. Hwang states in a video interview that he thought the Broadway production may have gotten 'short-shrift' and thought the 'bookend' story of the present time was always 'really problematic'.³⁴ He wanted to continue to rewrite the play and to discover its potential in ways he could not do during its Broadway run. In the new version, the actor who plays Tieng-Bin also plays Hwang's younger self, the ten-year-old who visited his ill grandmother in the Philippines to record her story. Hwang is more direct in framing the play as an autobiographical one and inserts himself as the person who wrote, and continues to write, the story of his family. In the new millennium, Hwang would become more comfortable in being a character in his plays, most poignantly in *Yellow Face*, which I discuss in the next chapter.

CHAPTER 5
THE IRONY AND RHETORIC OF THE GLOBAL MILLENNIUM

With his background in music, David Henry Hwang sought opportunities to work in opera and musical theatre throughout the 1990s. He had worked with Philip Glass on a few occasions, but he also had his eye on large-scale Broadway musicals. The new millennium opened with several such opportunities for Hwang. He was invited to co-author the book for *Aida* (2000), with music by Elton John and lyrics by Tim Rice, and was the writer of the book for *Tarzan* (2006), with music and lyrics by Phil Collins. In 2000, his adaptation of Richard Rodgers and Oscar Hammerstein II's *Flower Drum Song* opened at the Mark Taper Forum in Los Angeles, with the Broadway star Lea Salonga as the lead actress. The production was received well by Los Angeles critics and audiences. With an updated cast, the musical moved to the Virginia Theatre on Broadway and opened on 17 October 2002. Unlike the West Coast critics, New York City critics did not like the updated version of *Flower Drum Song*, and it closed early on 16 March 2003. Many factors contributed to the musical's lack of success on Broadway: the musician's strike in early March had shut down Broadway musicals; New York City critics nostalgically preferred the original 1958 version; and the size of the production was a constant problem. The musical was originally scaled for Broadway, but because of investment issues, it was downsized for a smaller space at the Mark Taper Forum. When it was then moved to a larger space on Broadway, the intimacy of the musical – which many in Los Angeles liked – was lost. It nevertheless received Tony Award nominations for Best Book of a Musical, Best Costume Design and Best Choreography.

Josephine Lee's essay in the last section of this book compares Hwang's *Flower Drum Song* to the original version, and it details how Hwang changed the storyline while retaining the original songs. She convincingly argues that Hwang's version celebrates Asian American performers and their legacy in American history. William C. Boles, in his book *Understanding David Henry Hwang*, thoroughly contextualizes *Flower Drum Song*'s creation and reception, and he situates it convincingly in the broader context of Hwang's oeuvre. The musical is clearly one of Hwang's most important theatrical works, and it deserves the close studies provided by Lee and Boles.

In 1999, around the time Hwang was working on *Flower Drum Song*, he was invited by the Disney Theatrical Group to work on the musical *Aida* as a 'creative consultant'.[1] The musical had an unsuccessful pre-Broadway run in Atlanta, and the creative team was eager to revise it. When Robert Falls became the musical's new director, Hwang was asked to join him as a co-author of the book. Hwang, with Falls and Linda Woolverton, worked to revise the script. To Hwang, this invitation was initially surprising. In an interview, he stated, 'It's a little surprising, in a sense. To this day, I never imagined working on a big musical. I subsequently became interested in them, but I'm not your standard go-to guy when it comes to big musicals.'[2] Hwang also appreciated the willingness of the creative team to see him as more than an Asian American writer: 'It was something sort of impressive (that) they were not pigeonholing me by race, by going to an Asian-American writer for something that isn't Asian.'[3] When Hwang was asked to rewrite the script, he welcomed the opportunity to work on a large-scale Broadway musical. In the revised script, he focused on the triangular relationship between the three main characters and on the tension between love and politics.

According to critics, the new version, which premiered in Chicago, was more serious and lacked what some described as the 'cartoonish' elements that were in the Atlanta version. In reviewing the Chicago premiere, Chris Jones of *Variety* pointed out the most significant contribution the writers made in the revision process: 'With the cartoonish approach from the show's premiere Atlanta stand banished along with the original title, the Chicago production is far more dignified. Along with David Henry Hwang, Falls had the inspired idea of adding an outer frame set in the Egyptian room of the Metropolitan Museum of Art. (Since people do actually talk in museums, the currently mute frame would work far better with a few judiciously chosen lines.)'[4] The revised version of *Aida* included a narrative framework in the same meta-theatrical style as some of his earlier works, including *M. Butterfly* and *Golden Child*. In many of his plays, the main story is told as a recollection within the framework of the present time and space, and the same device is used to tell the story of *Aida*. In *M. Butterfly*, the framework is the prison cell, while in the Broadway version of *Golden Child*, it is Andrew's bedroom. In *Aida*, the present-day museum functions as a narrative framework to provide a context to the main story set in ancient Egypt.

Hwang's work with *Aida* signified a broad acknowledgement of his ability as a writer and unequivocally demonstrated his skills in writing in a new genre. The success of Hwang's version also affirmed that his playwriting style could effectively enhance dramatic effects. With a reputation as a "book-doctor," as Chris Jones describes him, Hwang found more opportunities to work on musicals. In 2005, he signed a contract allowing him to retain the copyright to the book he would write for the theatrical version of Disney's animated film *Tarzan*. The copyright not only gave Hwang the artistic freedom to write his own version of the story, but it also gave him an important share of the musical's profits. Although it received mixed reviews during its Broadway run and closed early, it did well in other countries, especially in Germany where it ran for five years.

The musical was noted for its elaborate design and aerial choreography, and Ben Brantley of the *New York Times* declared it 'insistently kinetic'.[5] The production was marketed as family-friendly, and Hwang's book was described by David Rooney of *Daily Variety* as having 'the clean, uncomplicated lines necessary to communicate across the footlights and play to the broadest possible age range'.[6] Although their reviews varied, critics agreed that the musical is about universal themes of family, loss, love and identity. It is easy to see why Hwang was drawn to the story of Tarzan, who is, after all, an outsider with an identity crisis, a theme Hwang has written about since his first play. Like a number of Hwang's characters, Tarzan does not feel he belongs anywhere, and he must adapt in order to survive. Moreover, Hwang's script had many of his signature styles, such as slangy American language and a sitcom-like sense of humour. In his review, Brantley, who did not like the production, criticized Hwang's script as having an 'abrasively wiseguy tone'.[7] It is notable that Brantley's negative review of the musical implicitly acknowledges Hwang's unique style of musical writing, a style that is consistent across his non-musical plays, as well. Although the stories of *Aida* and *Tarzan* are not originally Hwang's, his scripts must be considered as an important part of his oeuvre and interpreted in the context of his straight plays.

In this chapter, I focus on plays written by Hwang between the years 2000 and 2014. In 2001, he wrote *Jade Flowerpots and Bound Feet*, a short, one-act play, which was part of *The Square*, a theatrical project conceived and curated by Lisa Peterson and Chay Yew.[8] Hwang's *Jade Flowerpots and Bound Feet* is about a writer who looks white but claims to be an Asian woman. She wears a black wig and a *cheongsam* (a traditional Chinese dress) and calls herself Kwok Mei-li. She writes pseudo-memoirs about the old world of China in the style of Maxine Hong Kingston's *The Woman Warrior* and Amy Tan's *The Joy Luck Club*. As hinted by the title, Mei-li's books discuss how Chinese women suffered at the hands of traditional Chinese men and Japanese soldiers, and she claims her memoirs are 'the absolute truth'.[9] She is challenged in the play by Beth, a representative from 'Amazon Dot Com Publishing'. Beth wants to meet Mei-li to verify her ethnicity in order to follow her company's 'policy of meeting all multicultural authors face-to-face' (577). When Mei-li insists that she is part Asian and that her stories are authentic, Beth makes her take a blood test for 'scientific verification' (578). The play ends with the medical technicians watching her blood fill the vial.

Jade Flowerpots and Bound Feet reiterates themes explored in *Bondage* and *Trying to Find Chinatown*, particularly the socially constructed nature of race and cultural authenticity, and whether, in the new millennium, individuals can choose their own identities. Like Benjamin in *Trying to Find Chinatown*, Mei-li (whose real name is Ashley Winterstone) can claim to be Asian and invoke the authority of her heritage. However, Hwang does something new in *Jade Flowerpots and Bound Feet* and introduces ideas he would explore in his next full-length play, *Yellow Face*. The one-act play parodies authors who claim authority and authenticity of any sort, as well as a publishing industry that profits from selling books about 'authentic' history. The play is also, in part, a commentary on Hwang himself. Hwang, as an Asian American playwright, has written about the Chinese American experience and about his ancestors in China. *Golden Child*, after all, is about the first woman in his family to have her feet unbound. Hwang makes his presence known in *Jade Flowerpots and Bound Feet* when Mei-li asks, 'What does "authentic" mean anyway? For instance, let's just say – what if we weren't real people, what if we were fictional characters, would we be authentic?' (578). Beth, after a pause, says, 'Not if we were written by a man' (578). The man Beth references is, of course, Hwang himself. He is asking whether the two female characters can be authentic if he, as a man, is authoring them. In *Yellow Face*, Hwang amplifies this kind of self-conscious intervention by the playwright.

In the new millennium, Hwang has shown a deeply satiric attitude towards race and identity politics. The satire in his recent plays is much more nuanced and complex than the farce he attempted in *Face Value*. He continually revisits issues of identity and culture, and each iteration adds additional layers of meaning. And he has expanded the notion of culture beyond Asian America; with his travels to China and other parts of the world, Hwang has become interested in transnational and intercultural topics. He has continued to use playwriting to explore autobiographical subjects, but the plays he has written in the new millennium demonstrate his desire to branch out and engage with more global and cosmopolitan themes.

Yellow Face

As an individual, David Henry Hwang has broken the race barrier in mainstream American theatre by becoming the first and only Asian American playwright to be produced on Broadway. He has also been an articulate spokesperson for Asian American theatre. But his career trajectory raises a number of questions that deserve further exploration. Is he a 'token' Asian American in mainstream theatre? How else do we explain the fact that he continues to be the only Asian American playwright to be produced on Broadway? Moreover, Hwang's career did not necessarily begin in the Asian American theatre community. Rather, he made his theatrical debut at the Public Theater with the help with Joseph Papp, and *M. Butterfly*, his most famous play, does not have any Asian American characters, nor does it dramatize what can be called the Asian American experience. Yet, Hwang has been tapped to speak on behalf of Asian American theatre, and during the height of the *Miss Saigon* controversy, he was the individual newspaper articles identified as a representative of Asian American theatre. Hwang found his unofficial role as an Asian American spokesperson uncomfortable. He also recognized the irony of being pigeonholed and labelled as 'an Asian American playwright' while having written plays (such as *Bondage* and *Face Value*) questioning that very label.

Hwang engages with this irony in his semi-autobiographical play *Yellow Face*. The play was originally developed at the Lark Play Development Centre in New York City and was supported by the Stanford Institute for Creativity in the Arts at Stanford University. The production, directed by Leigh Silverman, premiered in May 2007 at Los Angeles's Centre Theatre Group/Mark Taper Forum, in association with the East West Players in Los Angeles and the Public Theater in New York City. The play received an Obie Award in Playwriting and was a finalist for the Pulitzer Prize for Drama. The play has since been revived at a number of venues, including Silk Road Rising in Chicago, the Guthrie Theater in Minneapolis, Theater J in Washington, DC and the National Theatre in London. In 2013, Jeff Liu adapted and directed a YouTube version of the play produced by the YOMYOMF Network.[10]

The play, as Hwang describes it, is a 'mock stage documentary' that chronicles the major events in his life since he received a Tony Award for *M. Butterfly*. Linda Winer of *Newsday* calls it a 'quasi-mock-autobiographical docudrama'.[11] At first, Hwang wanted to 'fix' *Face Value*, a play that failed as a farce about mistaken racial identities. He wanted to find a way to allow the audience to laugh at racial politics and multiculturalism while not dismissing the importance of race in the everyday lives of Asian Americans. In his interview with Jack Viertel, Hwang explains how the play came to be written:

> I'd been wanting to fix my play *Face Value* for the past 17 years, but I couldn't figure out how to do it. Then I started thinking about the stage documentary form – making it a mock stage documentary that would poke fun at some of the absurdities of the multicultural movement. It seemed easiest to poke fun at myself, since that way I would be offending only me. Then I figured the play would begin and end with two fairly public events – the *Miss Saigon* thing … and the charges leveled against my father in the late '90s.[12]

As he developed the play, it increasingly became about his father, who was ill with colon cancer and passed away in 2005 before the play premiered. *Yellow Face* has become Hwang's tribute to his father. The play deals with the casting controversy that surrounded the musical *Miss Saigon* in the early 1990s, as well as his father's involvement in a campaign finance scandal during the re-election of former President Bill Clinton. Hwang also writes about his relationship with his father who came to the United States to pursue his American Dream.

Reflecting the development of the play, the first act is about Hwang's involvement with the *Miss Saigon* controversy and the writing of *Face Value*. In contrast to the light-hearted and comical first act, the second act dramatizes the 1990s version of the 'yellow peril' that seriously affected Hwang's father.[13] The two acts together present different aspects of racial politics in the United States: one is absurd, artificial and farcical, while the other entails dire consequences, including charges of treason. In *Face Value*, Hwang also explores the farcical side of racial politics, though he does so without giving its darker side a full consideration. In contrast, *Yellow Face* provides a more nuanced and complex portrayal of how race and politics are intertwined. The play is also about the intermingling of fact and fiction, and of reality and fantasy. Hwang combines factual events and people with fictional ones, integrating them to deliberately confuse who or what is 'real'.

All of the background stories and subplots are based on Hwang's experience, but the main storyline is fictional.

At the centre of the play is a character named DHH, the dramatic alter ego of Hwang, and he dominates the play's main action. DHH is identified as an Asian American playwright who received a Tony Award for Best Play for *M. Butterfly*. With the exception of DHH, all the other characters are played by actors who portray multiple roles. Most of the characters are based on actual people in Hwang's life and career, and Hwang uses real names for some and invented ones for others.[14] At the beginning of the play, DHH is portrayed as a successful young playwright who confidently condemns racist practices in the theatre. In an early scene that shows the Tony Award ceremony, DHH predicts in his acceptance speech that the 1990s would bring radical changes and that the era of racist casting of Asians in theatre and film was over: 'Asians have consistently been caricatured, denied the right even to play ourselves. Well, it's a new day in America. We're entering the 1990s, and all that stops now!'[15] As a celebrity, he then gets pulled into protesting the casting of Jonathan Pryce in *Miss Saigon*. In private, he feels conflicted about condemning an artistic choice made by the musical's producing team, but he also decides to write a play that mocks yellowface casting. In a moment of hubris, however, DHH mistakenly casts a white actor in the role of an Asian American character in his play *Face Value* and finds that while he can hire an actor for his ethnicity, he cannot fire him for the same reason (because of Actors' Equity Association rules).

In order to hide the embarrassing mistake he has committed, DHH convinces the white actor, Marcus G. Dalhman, to change his name to Marcus Gee and to pass as a Eurasian. In one scene, Marcus and DHH attend an event at the 'Asian American Resource Centre' on a college campus and are questioned by a group of Asian American students who demand to know Marcus' ethnicity. DHH explains to the students that Marcus is Eurasian from Siberia with 'Russian Siberian Asian Jews' as ancestors. Encouraged by Hwang, Marcus tells the students about the difficulties he encountered as an actor, and he begins to feel a sense of community with Asian American students.

> **Student #3** Marcus, as an actor of Jewish Siberian heritage – have you faced a lot of barriers?
> **DHH (*To Marcus*)** Sure you have. You can tell them.
> **Marcus** Well, uh, before this, my career was sort of going nowhere. I mean, directors just didn't seem to know what to do with me.

>   **Student #1** Bastards!
>   **Marcus** Last November, I went in on this commercial call. They had me back five times. Five times! And in the end, you know what they told me? They said I didn't 'look right'. (*Gasps all around.*)
>   **Student #2** That is so racist! (31)

With the students' support, Marcus begins to identify with them as an Asian American. Much to DHH's disgust, Marcus thanks him for giving him a 'community' he could belong to. This scene can be read as a parody of angry student activists, but the real butt of the joke is DHH, who must perpetuate the lie of Marcus's 'Asianness' in order to save face. In doing so, it is DHH who ends up practising the very racist casting practices he had criticized during the *Miss Saigon* controversy. In *Yellow Face*, DHH not only casts a white actor in an Asian role but also inadvertently helps him find his 'community'.

As the play progresses, Marcus increasingly sees himself as Asian American and becomes a celebrated figure in the Asian American community. DHH publicly defends Marcus to avoid embarrassing himself and says, 'Nowadays, it's so hard to tell' (9). But in private, Hwang is mortified. With the fiasco he has created with Marcus, Hwang finds himself the worst kind of hypocrite and deceiver. And the more he tries to clean up the mess he has made, the worse the situation becomes, as he spirals downward into the seemingly bottomless complexities of racial politics. While he questions identity politics, DHH understands why they are sometimes needed. He envisions a world in which everyone can choose to be anyone, but at the same time, he knows such agency tends to favour more powerful groups. A white person can pass as an 'Asian', but someone who looks like DHH can never be accepted as white. While Marcus feels a genuine sense of belonging in the Asian American community, DHH increasingly grows confused about what community he belongs to. While he is excellent in the job and desires to be an 'Asian American role model', he is increasingly uncomfortable as a spokesperson for Asian American theatre. The play shows DHH set adrift, uncertain where he belongs, yet surrounded by people who expect him to represent his 'community'.

DHH succeeds in firing Marcus from the cast of *Face Value*, but he is appalled to learn that a new production of the musical *The King and I* will star Marcus Gee, who is heralded as ethnically 'authentic'. The first act of *Yellow Face* ends with the spectacle of Marcus as The King in the musical's 'Shall We Dance' number. DHH is even more disturbed to discover that

Marcus is dating his ex-girlfriend (who is Asian American) and suspects that the actor is not only claiming to be Asian American but in fact wants to emulate him, the Asian American role model. DHH's dream of being an Asian American role model has turned into a nightmare about a white person who wants to become his replica. Frustrated, DHH calls Marcus' mother to ask for her help in revealing the truth: 'In interviews, he's telling people he actually has Asian blood. As his mother, doesn't that bother you?' (48). The mother's reply echoes the post-racial themes Hwang writes about in earlier plays such as *Bondage* and *Trying to Find Chinatown*: 'David, this is America – where race shouldn't matter. I didn't even know about the racism Asians still face today. But Marcus raised my consciousness. He told me it doesn't matter what someone looks like on the outside' (42). In his earlier plays, Hwang imagines a utopic future in which race would be a choice, and everyone could become whatever he or she wished; in *Yellow Face*, however, his alter ego finds it impossible to accept a world where a white person could become Asian American.

DHH's nightmare turns ironic as the second act begins, and the play's style shifts from a 'mockumentary' to a more serious documentary. In the second act, the main story of the play shifts to a character named HYH (DHH's father, who shares the initials of Hwang's actual father, Henry Yuan Hwang). HYH, like Hwang's father, was the founder and CEO of Far East National Bank, and he comes under investigation for allegedly violating campaign finance laws. During the re-election of President Bill Clinton, a number of Chinese Americans were targeted for giving money to the Democratic Party. Conservative congressmen accused them of working with the Chinese government and held hearings to uncover what they believed was a national threat. In *Yellow Face*, Hwang uses actual quotes from such politicians to show how the scandal was a 1990s version of the 'yellow peril', one that characterized China as the biggest threat to the United States. For instance, Representative Tom DeLay is quoted as saying, 'There's a high probability this is money from foreign[ers] … if you're friends with a guy named Johnny Huang [or Marcus Gee] … and you have friend[s] by the name of Arief and Soraya, and I cannot even pronounce [these] name[s] … Cheong Am, Yogesh Gandhi, Lap Seng Ng – (*Tries different pronunciations*) Ng? … Ng?' (50). In the politician's logic, Chinese Americans are, in secret, loyal to the Chinese government, and their support of the Democratic Party is motivated by their desire to gain political influence and benefit China. The investigation targeted donors who had Asian-sounding names, regardless of their actual ethnic backgrounds.

In the play, both HYH and Marcus Gee had given money to the Democratic Party, and both had become targets of investigation. As a banker, HYH comes under intense scrutiny, though he initially savours the media attention he receives. Quickly, however, he realizes the gravity of the scandal. Hwang writes HYH as a self-made man whose life mission was to pursue the American Dream. HYH believed in American ideals and celebrated his success in his adopted country. When HYH is accused of aiding the Chinese government and deceiving the United States, however, his dreams and idealism shatter. He never recovers from the shock of being betrayed by the country he had loved all of his life. When his cancer worsens, HYH rejects experimental treatments in one of the most revealing and moving moments in the play:

> I used to believe in America, but now, I don't anymore. I don't even put my money into minority banks anymore, because the system doesn't play fair. I put my money into mainstream banks, where at least it will be safe. (*Pause*) When I was a kid in Shanghai, my favorite star of all was Jimmy Stewart. He was so kind, always doing things for other people. And when the chips were down, he would give it to the bad guys, tell them off, and everyone would listen to him. When I started the bank, I thought, Now, I can be Jimmy Stewart, too. But when I try to stop those guys who are after me, I can't beat them this time. I'm not Jimmy Stewart after all. (64)

HYH thought he could be Jimmy Stewart, but he realizes, on his deathbed, that his beloved country sees him only as a threatening foreigner.

HYH's disillusionment is accentuated by the unfair reporting of the *New York Times* (which in real life also targeted David Henry Hwang for having served on the board of his father's bank). In fact, the newspaper almost functions as a character in the play. Hwang quotes extensively from it, and it influences how the narrative of the 1990s unfolds in the play. In a poignant scene, DHH has a hostile exchange with one of the paper's reporters (the character's name is NWOAOC, 'Name Withheld on Advice of Counsel'). NWOAOC asks DHH about HYH, with the assumption that the 'Chinese banker' has committed a crime. DHH corrects him by stating that his father is a 'Chinese American banker' and that there is a difference between the two titles. DHH tries to educate the reporter about his father's loyalty to America, but NWOAOC implies that there is an inherent conflict in being 'Chinese' and 'American', while 'there's no conflict between being white and being American' (61). DHH tells him, 'You know, you're going to make a fascinating character' (61). DHH's anger and frustration, which had been building up to that moment, finds an outlet, and he vows to write about the exchange in a play. In this sense, *Yellow Face* can be read as Hwang's act of intellectual and artistic vengeance against the racism he saw in the newspaper's coverage of his father.[16]

Yellow Face dramatizes another instance of questionable journalism by the *New York Times*, which in 1999 actively perpetuated false accusations against Wen Ho Lee, a Taiwanese American nuclear scientist at Los Alamos National Laboratory. As explained in *Yellow Face*, Lee was accused of espionage and served nine months in solitary confinement without ever being convicted. When he was finally released, the presiding judge apologized for the unfair treatment he received. Hwang ties his father's experience to that of Wen Ho Lee, suggesting they are both part of a broader, national trend, what Frank Rich calls 'the Washington witchhunt'.[17] The two men were both stereotyped and victimized as perpetual foreigners, and their suffering stemmed from being Asian Americans in the 1990s. Hwang had thought stereotypes of Asians were vanishing from American society, as he confidently declared when receiving the Tony Award, but he had to face the painful fact that the ordeal of his father's illness was probably worsened by such prejudice.

Unlike HYH, Marcus Gee is able to escape the accusations of having made illegal donations by revealing his true identity as a white American. In fact, DHH tells him to 'take off [his] mask' and expose their lies in order to debunk the accusation: 'Can you imagine? How idiotic all their investigations will look? Once the American public learns that in their determination to find evil Chinese spies, this government spent millions of taxpayer dollars – just to end up going after … a regular American?' (65). In taking off Marcus' mask, DHH also removes his own: DHH is willing to 'lose face' and be revealed as a liar in order to clear his father's name. At the end of the play, HYH's death is announced, and the congressional investigation ends. DHH is left alone onstage with Marcus, who tells him that he, like HYH, willed himself to become a new person. In a meta-theatrical moment, Marcus asks why DHH created him. DHH first resists the questions and states that he wanted to keep the 'ambiguity about reality versus fiction – through the end of the play', but he ultimately admits to the audience that Marcus is a fictional character created by him.

In answering Marcus' question, DHH uses the metaphor of masks to articulate the anxiety he has felt as someone who has been expected to represent his community.

> Years ago, I discovered a face – one I could live better and more fully than anything I'd ever tried. But as the years went by, my face became my mask. And I became just another actor – running around in yellow face. (*Pause*) That's where you came in. To take words like 'Asian' and 'American', like 'race' and 'nation', mess them up so bad no one has any idea what they even mean anymore. (68)

DHH writes a happy ending for Marcus, but his own fate is uncertain. The play ends with the lines: 'For Marcus, the play ends. And I go back to work, searching for my own face' (69). With this ambiguous ending, Hwang again declines to provide any closure. DHH tells Marcus that when one's father dies, 'You start making his dream your own' (69). HYH dreamed of living in a world in which he could be Jimmy Stewart, and in that world, Marcus could become Asian American.

In *Yellow Face*, as he does in *M. Butterfly* and *Face Value*, Hwang uses the theatrical stage and the profession of acting to explore how race is embodied and performed. Jimmy Stewart was an actor HYH saw on movie screens while living in the Philippines as a young man. Stewart embodied an ideal, white, American masculinity, and his performance inspired his fans to believe in the virtuous and heroic qualities of his characters. However, acting is also an illusion of reality and a performance of fiction. Acting has also been described as deception and actors as liars. Marcus, like Stewart, is an actor, and he lives a deceptive life as a fake Asian American. He is also a fictional character created by DHH, who, in turn, is a character created by David Henry Hwang. In other words, the characters wear multiple masks, and it is impossible to tell which mask is the 'real' one, or whether 'realness' exists at all. Themes of deception, performance and racial drag run throughout *Yellow Face*, and Hwang confronts them head-on. In the play, his characters address the audience directly, and he readily admits, 'in the end, everything's always all about me' (68). Despite the documentary approach of the play, *Yellow Face* is ultimately about Hwang's imaginative and philosophical musings about race, identity, family, life and death.

Rich, in his foreword to the published version of *Yellow Face*, notes, 'America's new and unlikely president [Barack Obama] has called himself a "mutt," and so are most of Hwang's American characters. Those mutts can speak for many of us in the audience – whatever the particular multi-identities we represent within the infinite mix that is the U.S. of A.'[18] Hwang is indeed dramatizing how the United States has moved beyond the phases of assimilation, isolation and multiculturalism. In the twenty-first century,

Americans may 'inexorably coalesce into an uncategorized but universal humanity', as Rich puts it.[19] Both Rich and Hwang point to a utopic world in which race, ethnicity and nationality will not matter and everyone will be recognized for their individual value. But the reality of American theatre continues to put demand on Hwang to represent Asian American culture. Despite the tremendous growth in Asian American theatre, Hwang remains the only playwright many think of when Asian American culture needs to be represented onstage. The anxiety that Hwang writes about in *Yellow Face* has not been alleviated by the election of President Obama or by the increasing diversity of the American population. Hwang represents the Asian American theatre community, but he is also successful in spite of it. With few exceptions, Asian American theatre continues to be perceived as less professional, while Hwang is lauded as one of the greatest American playwrights. Many in the Asian American theatre community celebrate his success, though many would also say privately that his plays are written for white audiences. With *Yellow Face*, Hwang reveals all of his many 'faces' with irony and humour. It is unclear, however, which 'face' he will wear in the future, and whether and how he will continue to represent the Asian American theatre community.

Chinglish

After *Yellow Face*, Hwang wanted to write about topics that extended beyond the United States and Asian American issues. He states in an interview: 'I'm less interested in the Asian-American thing at the moment. Thirty years ago when we were talking about Asian-American identity, identity politics, that was all fresh and exciting. And now it's like, we've already done that. And I am not that interested in it anymore. Been there, did that.'[20] Starting with *FOB*, Hwang has used his plays to question what it means to be an Asian American, and *Yellow Face* is the culmination of a journey that stretched more than thirty years. In writing *Yellow Face*, Hwang concluded that race is both a construct and real. When asked in an interview what he thinks about the concept of a post-racial society and racism, Hwang sums up the views he dramatizes in *Yellow Face*:

> We're at a point where you have to hold two contradictory ideas in your head at the same time: yeah, race is a construct, and ultimately we all want a post-race society. But racism is going to still happen and

when it does, you have to gear up and fight that stuff. And in some sense, these are two oppositional notions that you have to hold onto at the same time.[21]

As a dialectical thinker, Hwang is drawn to issues that are contradictory yet ironically related, and *Yellow Face* is his way of pushing both the logic and contradictions of race to the exhaustive end. As the first decade of the new millennium neared its end, Hwang became interested in international issues beyond American identity politics. In contemporary China, he found a new topic to dramatize.

Hwang wrote *Chinglish* after having visited China several times. He does not speak Chinese and knows little about contemporary Chinese culture, yet he is recognized in China as a celebrated Chinese American playwright. Paradoxically, *M. Butterfly* is yet to be produced in Mainland China because the government still denies its central spying incident, but Hwang has been invited to various functions and has provided his advice on arts-related programmes. With *Chinglish*, Hwang collaborated with other writers when creating his bilingual script. In her essay at the end of this book, Daphne Lei explains how this collaborative process was significant on many levels. As Lei acknowledges, the history of Chinese modernization is complex, and it is interpreted differently by those in Hong Kong, Taiwan and the Chinese diaspora. Lei's essay also addresses issues of translation and historical contexts. In this section, I focus on how *Chinglish* can be interpreted from an American audience's perspective. After all, Hwang chooses to tell the story of Chinese modernization through the perspective of an American in China. More specifically, China is seen through the eyes of a 'regular American' (the term he uses to describe Marcus in *Yellow Face*): a white, midwestern man from Cleveland, Ohio.

The play premiered at the Goodman Theatre in Chicago, Illinois, where it was directed by Leigh Silverman and starred Jennifer Lim and James Waterston. Since the success of *M. Butterfly*, his full-length plays have received mixed reviews from critics in New York City, in contrast to West Coast critics who have been more encouraging. Hwang had attributed this difference in reception partly to the cultural divide between the West Coast and the East Coast, and he had always wanted to debut a new play in Chicago, the 'second city' of American theatre. In the summer of 2011, the Goodman Theatre participated in what it called the 'Summer of David Henry Hwang: One Great Playwright, Three Great Plays', which was a citywide promotion of Hwang's work. When Robert Falls, the artistic director of the Goodman Theatre, decided to produce the world premiere of *Chinglish*, he learned that Silk Road Rising, a theatre company in Chicago, would be producing a revival of *Yellow Face*. Halcyon Theatre of Chicago then announced that it would revive *Family Devotions*. The production process of *Chinglish* moved quickly, and it was received warmly by the Chicagoan theatregoers. By the time *Yellow Face* opened at Silk Road Rising, *Chinglish* had moved to Broadway after receiving rave reviews in Chicago; Hwang's return to Broadway looked promising. The play won the prestigious Jeff Awards (Joseph Jefferson Awards) for Best Play and Scenic Design in 2011. While Chicago had given Hwang a warm welcome, recognizing him as one of the most important playwrights of contemporary America, reviews of the Broadway production by New York critics were not as glowing, and it closed much earlier than the production team expected.[22] The short run came as a surprise to many, including Hwang. The lack of a major star actor in the cast and the bilingual dialogue may have contributed to its short run.

Thematically, *Chinglish* is about the Midwest and its symbolic association with 'America's heartland'. The protagonist, Daniel Cavanaugh, is from Cleveland, and his grandfather founded the family-run company Ohio Signage. The multi-generation family business did well until the downturn in the American manufacturing industry and the economic recession that started in 2008. The Cleveland-based company represents the rise and fall of the manufacturing industry as a whole. Multi-national corporations, in search of higher profit margins, sought cheaper labour overseas, pulling jobs away from many midwestern cities. Daniel worked at Enron in Texas, and he was part of the financial scandal that erupted with the company's bankruptcy. Having barely avoided jail time, Daniel's role at Enron denied any future career in finance in the United States. He decides to seek business opportunities in the emerging economic superpower of China and sets his sights on the provincial capital of Guiyang. In the play, comparisons are made between Guiyang and Cleveland: both cities were traditionally rural but became industrial, and both regions are located at the geographical centre of their respective countries.

As a white man from the Midwest, Daniels is seen by the Chinese people as a 'real' American. Hwang does not include a Chinese American character like himself in the play, and he plays to the stereotypes of Americans that are pervasive in China. Daniel embodies all of the values the Chinese associate with American midwesterners: he is seen as honest, wholesome and trustworthy, while also being naive and easy to manipulate. Daniel, in turn, has his own set of assumptions about Guiyang, a city described by Cai, the city's cultural minister, as 'small', with a population of four million.[23] Daniel sees the Chinese as indecipherable and backward, but he also assumes them to be innocent, authentic and traditional. Without knowing a word of Mandarin, Daniel has the audacity to come to a 'small' town in China to supposedly rescue them from the potential embarrassment of mistranslation. To the eyes of the Chinese characters in the play, he is yet another arrogant white man who feels he can save the people of the third world with his expertise and intervention. However, as is typical of Hwang's plays, all of the assumptions made by both the white and Chinese characters in *Chinglish* are shown to be false and the reality far more complex.

The main story of the play is about Daniel's encounters and experiences in China as a novice businessman. The story is bookended by similarly structured opening and closing scenes (as with *FOB* and *Golden Child*). The bookend scenes take place in the 'present', while the main story takes place three years earlier. *Chinglish* opens with Daniel giving a presentation to the Commerce League of Ohio. As an 'expert' in US–China business relations, he gives a presentation about 'Chinglish', the mistranslation of Chinese into English. The first scene immediately signals to the audience that the play is a comedy about mistranslation, and Daniel provides numerous examples of Chinglish. He shows images of signs around China that make embarrassing and comical mistakes in translation. For example, the phrase 'Slippery Slopes Ahead' is translated as 'To Take Notice of Safe: The Slippery Are Very Crafty' (7). The first scene ends with Daniel's main warning to Americans interested in economic opportunities in China: 'When doing business in China, always bring your own translator' (8).

The second scene dramatizes Daniel's first visit to Guiyang and his meeting with Peter, a British man who has lived in China for nineteen years. Peter offers Daniel consulting services to help in business matters. Daniel wants to obtain a contract from the city of Guiyang to make English-language signs for the new Cultural Centre under construction. Peter advises Daniel that the most important aspect of doing business in China is *'guanxi'*, which can be translated as relationships or connections. Peter, having lived in China, has cultivated his *guanxi*, and he offers his help in exchange for a commission. Daniels trusts Peter, the only other white character in the play, and he hopes that their common racial background will benefit his business dealings. Peter, on the other hand, sees himself as more Chinese than British, and his incentive to help the American derives not from his sense of a common racial heritage but more from his desire to survive in a rapidly changing China. Peter is nostalgic for the past, when westerners were rare in China. When he was younger, he was a respected teacher of English and taller than most Chinese men, and he relished in standing out as different. In the twenty-first century, however, westerners are everywhere, and his special status in China has been diminished. The consulting service he offers to Daniel is his desperate attempt to stay relevant in a globalized economy.

In fact, all of the characters in *Chinglish* are motivated by the need to survive and get ahead in the new world order, where people are driven by the neoliberal logic of money and power, and deception is often essential if one is to best the competition. Every character in *Chinglish* has something to hide. Peter hides from Daniel the fact that he is a failed teacher and has no business experience; Daniel hides his past employment at Enron and the fact that his family business, Ohio Signage, is not successful; and Cai, the cultural minister, hides his nepotistic dealings while pretending to like Daniel's sales pitch. The character that is most successful at deceiving others and achieving what she wants is Xi, Guiyang's vice minister of culture. Xi is a beautiful woman, with whom Daniel foolishly has an affair and falls in love, but she is consumed by her desire to get ahead socially, politically and financially. At first, Daniel naively sees her as someone who is 'honest' and has a 'good face' and is only interested in helping a foreign man (59). But at the end of the play, he realizes that she 'helped' him in order to expose Cai's nepotism and help her husband (who is a judge) get promoted in the political party.

The first time Daniel asks her why she is helping him, she replies, 'Use at your own risk' (48). The second time he asks, she tells him his face is 'good', which in Chinese can also mean credible, trustworthy, honest and naive. Xi says in Chinese, 'And you still have your innocence', which Daniel does not understand (60). Daniel thinks Xi sees him as an honest and good man and believes that her cause is equally good and trustworthy, but in truth, Xi is able to use him for both sexual pleasure and political gain because he is gullible enough to fall for her schemes. Daniel thinks his relationship with Xi is built on genuine, shared feelings, but nothing can be further from the truth. In effect, the differences in connotation between 'good' and 'innocent' represent the distance between Daniel and Xi.

At the end of the first act, Xi discovers that Daniel has been lying about the financial health of his signage company, and when she realizes that her plan is in jeopardy, she tries to walk out. Daniel, in desperation, comes clean to Xi and tells the truth about why he is in Guiyang looking for new business deals. To Daniel's surprise, the news of his involvement with Enron is received by Xi not with contempt but with enthusiasm. Xi tells him, 'You. Good man, honest man' and changes her mind: 'Now, is possible' (62). Daniel's involvement with the Enron scandal immediately elevates him to the top of the business food chain, and Xi uses his confession to her advantage. Xi wants to frame Cai as a corrupt politician who insists on giving the signage contract to his sister-in-law, even though that requires rejecting an offer from an American who once worked at Enron, a world-famous company. Daniel's honest confession of dishonesty is, in turn, used for a corrupt cause, the purpose of which is to expose yet another case of corruption.

In this intricate chain of deception and corruption, both Daniel and Xi achieve what they want: Daniel gets the business contract to build English-language signs in Guiyang, while Xi can find satisfaction in gaining more political influence through her husband. More importantly, Daniel finds his *guanxi* by establishing a long-term working relationship with Xi's husband. Three years after arriving in China, Daniel succeeds in reviving his family business and establishing himself as a westerner who has gained the trust of the Chinese. At the end of the play, he continues his PowerPoint presentation to those who want to learn about doing business in China. Daniel is now the expert, one who understands how China deals with westerners.

The ending, however, is not necessarily a joyful one for Daniel. During one of his intimate moments with Xi, he reveals to her that his marriage is not a happy one, and that he is in love with Xi. For Xi, however, happiness and love are irrelevant to her marriage. For her, being her husband's political ally and working towards their mutual success defines her marriage. Daniel, for her, is an 'escape', a side benefit to her schemes. She enjoys feeling desired by a man, and she pursues the affair only for her pleasure. When she learns of Daniel's feelings towards her, she decides that her marriage is threatened and ends the relationship. 'Love', she tells Daniel, is 'your American religion', like Christianity, and she has faith in neither (110). Xi and Daniel understand the language of money and power, but they cannot overcome their mistranslation of human feelings. At the end of the play, Daniel is left with economic access to China and the profound sense that mistranslation is an inherent part of human relationships across cultures.

Three years after the break-up, Daniel is able to tell his audience that he has actually started liking Chinglish. He embodies the new transnational

American who can live in different cultures and find enjoyment in misunderstanding and mistranslations. This ending is an open and ambiguous one, as it is typical for all of Hwang's endings. *Chinglish* can be read as a celebration of globalization and the financial benefits that can come from a relationship between the United States and China. It can also be read as a warning against neoliberalism and the pursuit of the bottom line that is at its heart. Daniel learns the hard way that ambition and success are more important than love and honest communication in the world of global finance.

Hwang has described *Chinglish* as having similar themes as *M. Butterfly*. Both plays are about love and deception, and in each, a white man falls in love with his Chinese lover but finds himself heartbroken at the end. The Chinese woman (or someone thought to be a woman) hides her true motives in pursuing the man and comes out victorious at the end. Xi, like Song, does not reveal how much she knows, either of the English language or Western culture. She uses that apparent ignorance to manipulate the man to her own advantage. The woman embodies what the man sees as the cultural differences between the East and West, and she uses that perception to create a fantasy. For Gallimard, Song represents the 'vision of the Orient' and the Butterfly he desires. Daniel, on the other hand, mistakenly believes that he can renew himself as a good human being and that Xi sees who he really is beneath the label of a failed and corrupt Enron worker. He sees her as his saviour when, in fact, she is only taking an advantage of him. In Hwang's signature ironic style, Daniel seeks his American Dream through Xi, and he believes she can help him become the wholesome midwestern man. His fantasy of the perfect Chinese woman fails, however, just as it does for Gallimard.

The main difference between *M. Butterfly* and *Chinglish* is the degree of tragedy that befalls the white, male protagonist. Gallimard kills himself at the end, but Daniel, at least on the surface, is a successful businessman with a happy family. However, it is also possible to view the ending of *Chinglish* as a tragic one. *M. Butterfly* is a tragedy for one character, Gallimard, but the ending of *Chinglish* marks the death of the traditional midwestern values in both the United States and China. The play is about people in different cultures who seek salvation and an escape from the suffocating realities of their lives. Instead of finding their salvation in religion, political ideology or love, however, they find their most secure form of rescue in money and power. China, as a country, is no longer a purely communist nation, and the United States is no longer driven by moral values rooted in Christianity. As

Daniel discovers, money can buy anything; it is, in effect, the new religion of the globalized world.

Unlike Daniel, who wants to believe in love and the possibility of a happy marriage, Xi is focused on how she can get ahead in the new China. In one of her tense moments with Daniel, she declares, 'One day, China will be strong!' (78). Describing herself as a Chinese nationalist, she represents those Chinese people who believe their country has suffered too long under the influence of the West. From the Opium War to the Cold War, China has been unfairly suppressed and deceived by the West, but it will, according to Xi, once again become the dominant civilization it once was. Peter, as a British man, represents the diminished influence of European colonial powers in China as described by Xi. He was once an important man in China, but by the play's end, he loses all of his influence. His association with Cai proves to be detrimental, and both men face prosecution for corruption. When the police arrive at Cai's house, Peter willingly follows him out while singing a song from Peking Opera with him. The song, as performed by the two men, symbolizes traditional Chinese culture before it faced eradication during the Cultural Revolution and modernization. With the song, the two men from different cultures find a common bond and, in doing so, acknowledge their inability to adapt to changes in China. Cai is a failed minister of culture who has to witness the Chinese Acrobats, which he despises, selected by the new minister as the first show to be performed at the new Cultural Centre. In contrast to Cai, who faces prison time, Xi and her husband emerge as the 'perfect couple' of the new China. Standing next to her husband, she announces, 'We have all made sacrifices to bring progress to our city. Now, Guiyang is ready to join the New China!' (121–2).

Chinglish is a well-made comedy with a tight structure, and the play is meticulously crafted. It demonstrates Hwang's seasoned ability to write a plot-driven comedy without losing the seriousness of the topic. Compared to his earlier, less successful comedies, such as *Rich Relations* and *Face Value*, *Chinglish* showcases Hwang's sophisticated and nearly impeccable skills in writing comic scenes. As Hwang does with all of his plays, *Chinglish* is a serious comedy that has farcical elements as well as heartbreaks. Hwang modelled the play after David Mamet's *Glengarry Glen Ross*, which portrays how unethical people can become when the stakes for profit are high. *Chinglish* is lighter in tone, and the most unethical character in the play is a woman whose selfish plans are not revealed until the final curtain. Daniel shares some similarities with the male characters in Mamet's play, but unlike them he is ultimately a likeable character with whom the audience can sympathize. His genuine love for Xi redeems him, in some sense, from the corrupt pit of politics and profit.

Chinglish has been revived several times since it closed on Broadway: in 2012, it played at the Berkeley Repertory Theater, the South Coast Repertory and the Hong Kong Arts Festival. The play has also been produced at Portland Centre Stage and Syracuse Stage. The main difficulty in reviving it has been casting actors who can speak two languages. The character of Peter has been most challenging to cast because the actor who plays him must be an older, white, male actor who can speak both British English and Mandarin fluently. The production must also include supertitles that need to be managed by a bilingual staff. These and other production demands may have hampered the play's potential impact. However, the story of an American in China will be told beyond the theatre. Hwang plans to make a film version of *Chinglish*, and in 2014, he signed on to write the script for an original television series titled 'Shanghai', a drama about a group of Americans living in China, for Lionsgate and the Bravo Network.

Kung Fu

When David Henry Hwang announced that he would be writing a play about Bruce Lee, many wondered how he would tell the story of a man whose life and death have spawned a vast number of stories ranging from biographies to fantasy novels. Would Hwang dramatize his life in a documentary style? Would he focus on his death and the mythical status it has created? Or would he recreate Lee's martial arts movies for the theatre? The play, which came to be titled *Kung Fu*, was commissioned by Signature Theatre in New York City, which devoted its 2013–4 season to Hwang. Signature Theatre is known as a company that showcases the work of one playwright per year. According to its website, 'Signature is the first theatre company to devote an entire season to the work of a single playwright, including re-examinations of past writings as well as New York and world premieres. By championing in-depth explorations of a living playwright's body of work, the Company delivers an intimate and immersive journey into the playwright's singular vision.'[24] The Signature Theatre's selection of Hwang shined a spotlight on his career in playwriting and many took notice.

The Signature Theatre residency gave Hwang a rare opportunity to write a play that could showcase his 'singular vision'. His new play, *Kung Fu*, was thus written and produced in a context where he knew that his career and body of work would be scrutinized and celebrated. Why, then, did he choose to write about Bruce Lee? And why did he write in a style that requires music, dance, movement and an elaborate production? It is certainly possible that he wanted a 'big show', one that would have commercial appeal and turn a profit for the company that commissioned it. The name Bruce Lee certainly draws attention. He also wanted to experiment with a different form of theatre, however. Initially, he wanted to create a musical version of the play, but after numerous attempts, he decided against it. The official reason he has given is that he could not make Bruce Lee sing onstage. Instead of a musical, the form he decided on is a 'dancical' – a theatrical form in which a dialogue-based play incorporates dance numbers throughout for dramatic effect. Music is still an essential part of the show, but the characters do not sing. The result is a fast-paced, highly choreographed, theatricalized show, with actors moving in and out of dialogue-based scenes and intricately choreographed dance numbers.

Kung Fu is a biographical play about Bruce Lee, and it is based on Hwang's interaction with Lee's wife Linda Lee and daughter Sharon. Many scenes and passages of dialogue are based on actual events, and parts of the play can even be described as biographical documentary. But at the same time, the story Hwang tells moves fluidly through time and space, and the dance numbers are overtly theatrical and fantastical. An obvious approach when writing a bio-play about Bruce Lee would be to dramatize how he became a worldwide celebrity with the movies he made in Hong Kong. After all, his popular movies and his sudden death have made him a legend. Hwang, however, limits the setting of *Kung Fu* to 'Seattle, Los Angeles, Hong Kong and India. 1959–1971, with flashbacks to the 1940s'.[25] Lee was born in San Francisco in 1940. After being raised in Hong Kong, he attended the University of Washington, married Linda and tried to make himself known as a martial arts teacher and an actor. He left the United States to return to Hong Kong in 1971 after realizing that he would never land a lead role in Hollywood. What most people know about Lee took place after he arrived in Hong Kong. In other words, he was relatively unknown during the time period dramatized in *Kung Fu*.

The play opens with Lee, a student at the University of Washington, practising his martial arts at a gym and working as a waiter at Ruby Chow's restaurant in Seattle. In the first scene, he tries to impress a Japanese American girl with his martial arts moves. She rejects him after kissing him, saying, 'It feels like, I dunno, kissing one of my brothers' (5). Lee replies,

The Irony and Rhetoric of the Global Millennium

'Ssssh. I know what need. Man, so strong, so you are receiving protect-, protection. True Chinese man, as if to be, your hero' (5). Throughout the play, Lee speaks in a heavy Hong Kong accent just as Lee did in real life. This opening scene is interrupted by the appearance of Lee's father, who was an actor in Hong Kong. The father–son relationship is a major theme in the play, and Lee's father haunts and taunts him throughout, telling his son that he will never be a hero and that he should not try to become an actor. The main story line focuses on Lee's meeting and marrying Linda and his effort to play heroic characters in Hollywood. Lee teaches many Hollywood stars, most famously James Coburn and Steve McQueen. He is cast in the role of Kato in *The Green Hornet*, and although the show does not do well, Lee is recognized as a potential star. He pitches a television series called 'The Warrior', which would take place in the Old West and star Lee as a monk from the Shaolin Temple, the birthplace of kung fu. He would fight bad guys armed with guns using only his bare hands, and save young, white girls. Warner Brothers accepts the idea but rejects Lee, instead selecting David Carradine. Disillusioned, Lee leaves the United States, and the play ends with him visiting his father's grave. His last line is, 'It's time to come home', which contradicts what he had previously said throughout the play (98). In one of the earlier scenes, for example, he tells his ghostly father that America is his home because he has an American wife, and that he will never return to Hong Kong.

The play ends with the image of Lee becoming the heroic characters he would play in his later plays. The last stage direction reads:

> Music builds. Bruce rises to his feet. Breaks into a triumphant dance, more powerfully than before, anticipating the movies he will make in Hong Kong which will realize his dream. Ensemble members appear to fight him, and he defeats them all – with the electric joy which will secure his place as a film and martial arts legend. Bruce fights like a man who has just let a terrible weight fall from his back. (98–99)

The play ends on an optimistic note. Instead of showing the death of a hero, it concludes by showing how a hero was born.

Hwang makes Lee an Asian American hero, and he does so by telling an origin story. All legends need origin stories, and Hwang's investigation of Lee's time in the United States signals his wish to claim the martial arts star as an Asian American hero. At the same time, the way he tells Lee's story echoes many of his earlier plays, particularly his first, *FOB*. Bruce Lee in *Kung Fu* is similar to Steve in *FOB*: both are from Hong Kong, and both claim to be heroes, despite the fact that Americans see them as unwelcome foreigners. *Kung Fu* also returns to the style of playwriting Hwang started to develop early in his career.

As seen in *FOB* and his other early plays, the dramatization of 'real' situations is never stable, and Hwang allows the possibility of multiple interpretations of what is occurring onstage. Often in his plays, realism coexists with non-realism, and the balance between the two must be struck by those creating and watching the play. In this sense, the bio-play of Bruce Lee is not a 'real' documentation and should be approached as an unstable depiction of what many agree is 'real' about its subject's life. For instance, in one of the scenes in *Kung Fu*, Lee's father from the past invades his son's romantic dinner with Linda, reminding him how worthless he is. From the beginning of the play, there are many indications of the improbable lurking behind the mundane facade.

In *FOB*, Hwang added the fight sequence and the Chinese opera elements in a later version of the script at the encouragement of Robert Alan Ackerman, who directed the production at the Eugene O'Neill National Playwrights Conference in 1979. In *Kung Fu*, written thirty-five years later, fight sequences and Chinese opera elements become the main features of the play. The play is, after all, a dancical, which in many ways is the choreographer's genre, not the playwright's. Critics took notice of the choreography and the virtuosic bodies of the performers, and the script was seen as a vehicle to showcase the dance sequences. The chiselled body of the actor Cole Horibe, who played Bruce Lee in the Signature Theatre production, was used in publicity photos, and the choreography has been heralded as the best part of the play. In trailer videos produced by Signature Theatre, it is the dance and the choreography that are featured prominently. In a rare move, the name of the choreographer, Sonya Tayeh, was added in promotional materials next to the names of David Henry Hwang and Leigh Silverman (the play's director).

Indeed, most critics who disliked the play did praise the choreography. According to Charles Isherwood's mixed review in the *New York Times*:

> The writing often seems pitched at the level of an informative, morally instructive young-adult novel. As directed by Leigh Silverman, the play becomes truly animated only when the talky expositional scenes are interrupted by flaring action sequences that erupt like little bursts

of fireworks throughout. Mr Horibe, with a chiselled, lithe body that credibly evokes Lee's own, gives demonstrations of his highly personalized version of kung fu that are often breathtaking in their precision.[26]

As Isherwood notes, the story of *Kung Fu* is not complex and is already familiar to Bruce Lee fans. The importance of the play, however, is not in the story or how accurately it reflects real events. Rather, Hwang's innovation must be found in how he develops what might be called an Asian American choreography. According to Yutian Wong in her book *Choreographing Asian America*, the body in performance can be analysed to understand how identities are represented onstage. The choreographed body can also provide access to corporeal knowledge of how Asian Americans have been racialized throughout US history. She argues that 'Asian American performance artists "choreograph" selective identities in order to align or distance themselves from each other depending on political objectives related to race, gender, sexuality, ethnicity, and/or class identification'.[27] In other words, how we move our bodies signals and represents who we are. As Josephine Lee and Karen Shimakawa have noted, the very presence of the Asian American body onstage can be subversive and powerful.[28] Even in the twenty-first century, Asian characters continue to be played by white actors in yellowface make-up, and Asian American actors are vastly underrepresented on stage and screen. As Wong argues, how that body moves is critical because the 'physicality of the performer reveals complex relationships between the body and its environment'.[29]

According to Hwang, the dance in *Kung Fu* is a uniquely Chinese American form of theatre. This notion has been criticized by Frank Chin, James Moy and others, who accuse Hwang of essentializing and exoticizing the Asian body.[30] Bruce Lee used martial arts to challenge the Hollywood stereotype of Chinese men as weak and effeminate, but in doing so, he has himself become another stereotype. Asian American actors are often asked if they can do martial arts when they go to auditions. Hwang would insist that the choreography used in *Kung Fu* is a Chinese American form in which multiple genres of theatre – ranging from Chinese opera to American musicals – are integrated. Hwang presents his articulation of the Chinese American form as the 'singular vision' sought by Signature Theatre from their playwright in residence. Choreographing Bruce Lee's story allowed Hwang to showcase the most polished version of the Chinese American form of theatre he began to experiment with thirty-five years ago.

CHAPTER 6
OTHER CRITICAL PERSPECTIVES

'Something Beyond and Above': David Henry Hwang's Revision of *Flower Drum Song*
Josephine Lee

Flower Drum Song, the eighth musical by the celebrated duo Richard Rodgers and Oscar Hammerstein II, was originally inspired by Chinese American author C. Y. Lee's 1957 novel of the same title. The best seller attracted the attention of Hammerstein and Joseph Fields, who subsequently collaborated on the book with a score by Richard Rodgers. The stage version of *Flower Drum Song* originated in Boston on 23 October 1958 and subsequently moved to Broadway's St James Theatre, opening 1 December 1958, and closing 7 May 1960. The Broadway run was followed by a London production and a US tour, as well as a 1961 Hollywood film adaptation with a screenplay by Fields and directed by Henry Koster.

In October 2001, David Henry Hwang's revision of Rodgers and Hammerstein's *Flower Drum Song,* directed and choreographed by Robert Longbottom, premiered at the Mark Taper Forum in Los Angeles; a somewhat altered version of this 'revisical' ran at the Virginia Theater on Broadway from 17 October 2002 to 16 March 2003.[1] For his version, Hwang preserved the original songs but made drastic changes to the story and its characterizations, commenting that 'I wanted to write what Oscar Hammerstein might have wanted to write if he had been Chinese American'.[2] Hwang was drawn not only to the challenge of reworking Hammerstein and Fields' original book but also to the iconic significance of the musical's mostly Asian and Asian American cast. The original Broadway production in 1958 included Miyoshi Umeki as Mei Li, Pat Suzuki as Linda Low, Keye Luke as Wang Chi-Yang, Ed Kenney as Wang Ta, Patrick Adiarte as Wang San and Arabella Hong as Helen Chao. The film version featured James Shigeta as Wang Ta and Nancy Kwan as Linda Low, with Jack Soo as Sammy Fong.[3] Hwang called the 1961 film 'kind of a guilty pleasure', one of the very few mainstream representations of Asian Americans in film or television: 'One of the only big Hollywood films where you could see a lot of really good Asian actors onscreen, singing and dancing and cracking jokes'.[4]

Prior to *Flower Drum Song*, Hwang's work in opera and musical theatre included librettos for *1000 Airplanes on the Roof* (1988) and *The Voyage* (1992), both with music by Philip Glass; the chamber opera *The Silver River* (1997), with music by Bright Sheng; and the book (with Robert Falls and Linda Woolverton) for the Broadway musical *Aida* (2000), with music by Elton John and lyrics by Tim Rice. In terms of approach, however, Hwang's writing for *Flower Drum Song* seems more akin to his 1988 Tony Award-winning play, *M. Butterfly*, which deconstructs Puccini's opera *Madame Butterfly* and its accompanying fantasy of an erotic, submissive Oriental woman. *M. Butterfly* exposes this stereotype as a calculated performance by the spy Song Liling. Hwang incorporates a similar strategy into his *Flower Drum Song* by framing racial stereotypes as deliberate enactments rather than true revelations of character and by repurposing songs and themes in ways that highlight contemporary Asian American sensibilities.

Earlier versions of *Flower Drum Song* marked the important changes in mainstream attitudes towards Asians and Asian Americans that occurred after the Second World War. The anti-Chinese exclusion laws originating with the 1882 Chinese Exclusion Act were in the process of being dismantled by legislation such as the 1952 McCarran–Walter Act. Americans found a new interest in Asian countries and peoples during the Cold War as the United States expanded its military and political influence abroad.[5] Rodgers called *Flower Drum Song* 'the story of the confrontation of the Far Eastern and American civilizations', emphasizing a message of racial tolerance: 'The usual thing you hear, you know, is East is East, and West is West, and all that nonsense. We show that East and West can get together with a little adjustment.'[6] The musical's romantic plot and light-hearted tone reinforced more positive portrayals of Asian Americans that were in marked contrast to the hostility of an earlier period in which they were reviled as 'coolie' labour or the 'yellow peril'.

The light-hearted romantic tone and quaint ethnic characterizations of the 1958 Broadway production make this clear. Wang Chi-Yang lives in a luxurious Chinatown home with his sister-in-law, Madam Liang, and sons Wang Ta, a college student, and Wang San, a rebellious teenager. In the opening scenes, Ta discusses his romantic feelings with his aunt ('You Are Beautiful'). His father, Wang, enters after having been robbed and expresses his concern about life in America and finding a traditional Chinese wife for Ta. Madam Liang informs him that given the existing immigration quotas, finding a suitable bride might take years. Wang is presented with a possible solution by Sammy Fong, the wisecracking owner of a Chinatown nightclub, The Celestial Bar, who is looking to get out of his arranged marriage with Mei Li. He brings in Mei Li and her father, Dr Li, who have recently arrived illegally in the United States after a circuitous journey from China. Mei Li sings a flower drum song ('A Hundred Million Miracles'), and Wang is delighted with her; however, the match is complicated by Ta's infatuation with Linda Low, who, unbeknownst to Ta, is Sammy's longtime girlfriend as well as a stripper in his nightclub. On a date with Ta, Linda is surprised at his naivety but interested in his wealth; alone onstage, she sings of her interest in attracting a man who appreciates her beauty and will marry her ('I Enjoy Being a Girl'). A love-smitten Ta proposes to Linda.

The Wang family prepares for a double graduation: Ta from college and Madam Liang from citizenship school. Seamstress Helen Chao has made Ta a graduation gown, and Wang is forced to wear an uncomfortable, Western-style suit. Mei Li is introduced to Ta and is immediately taken with him ('I Am Going to Like It Here'). Wang gives Mei Li a new American-style gown, which she puts on; Ta is taken with her but preoccupied by his engagement with Linda. Mei Li and Ta chat about love and marriage ('Like a God'). In the garden of the Wang house, friends and family gather for the graduation party and celebrate America's amalgamation of cultures ('Chop Suey'). Linda and Frankie, a nightclub emcee pretending to be her naval officer brother, announce Ta's engagement to Linda. Sammy learns of Ta's engagement, and tells Mei Li that he will be stuck with the marriage contract unless Ta marries her ('Don't Marry Me'). Sammy confronts Linda about her engagement to Ta; Linda expresses her need for security but says that even after she is married she will stay in Chinatown ('Grant Avenue'). Helen, who overhears their conversation, praises Ta's character to Linda and then muses alone on her feelings for him ('Love, Look Away'). Sammy strategically invites the Wang family to his club, and they watch several show numbers ('Fan Tan Fanny' and 'Vagabond Sailor'/'Gliding Through My Memoree') before they see Linda's strip tease ('Grant Avenue' [reprise]), which breaks off the engagement between Ta and Linda. The distraught and drunken Ta then goes to Helen's apartment and falls asleep in her bed; a dream sequence expresses Helen's unrequited feelings for Ta. The next morning Mei Li comes to Helen's apartment bringing Wang's damaged suit and sees

Ta's dinner jacket with the boutonnière she gave him the night before. She leaves, having concluded that Ta has become intimate with Helen; however, Ta has no interest in Helen's romantic advances. Later that day, Wang and Madam Liang express their disappointment with young people ('The Other Generation'). A chastened Ta returns home and accepts his father's choice of Mei Li as a wife. Mei Li, however, refuses Ta, thinking that he is involved with Helen.

Meanwhile, Sammy has proposed marriage to Linda ('Sunday Sweet Sunday'); at the meeting of the Three Family Association, however, Mei Li holds Sammy to his initial marriage contract in spite of his protestations ('Don't Marry Me' [reprise]). Witnessing Linda's tears at Sammy's broken promises, Wang San and other children comment on their elders' peculiarities ('The Other Generation' [reprise]). As the arranged marriage between Sammy and Mei Li approaches, both Mei Li and Ta realize their feelings for one another and lament the contract that separates them. Mei Li ultimately finds a solution by declaring that she is an illegal immigrant ('My back is wet', she claims, riffing off a television movie in which a Mexican character declares herself unable to marry an American because she is 'a wetback'). The contract annulled, Mei Li and Ta are happily united ('A Hundred Million Miracles' [reprise]).

Both the 1958 stage musical and 1961 film of Rodgers and Hammerstein's *Flower Drum Song* present Chinatown as a safe tourist destination and its inhabitants as upstanding and attractive citizens-in-the-making. The only actual criminal is a white man who robs Master Wang; Mei Li's illegal entry into the United States becomes a fortuitous plot twist rather than a criminal act. Yet in making these characterizations palatable to mainstream white viewers, these versions of the musical relied on conventional presentations of Chinese Americans as exotic curiosities and erased the harder edges of immigrant life and racism in America. Asian American critics, in particular, have been troubled by the more stereotypical aspects of characters such as the old world patriarch Wang and the docile Mei Li (described by Sammy Fong as having 'skin like white jade' and being 'built like a Ming vase'[7]). Sammy Fong's nightclub upholds a tourist image of Chinatown as a place of escapist pleasures. 'Fan Tan Fanny', in which the original stage directions call for a backup chorus dressed in *idealized coolie costumes* (1959: 85), is Rodgers and Hammerstein's version of what is called *a Chinatown song*; with its cutesy rhymes and Tin Pan Alley melody, it is reminiscent of a century of earlier Broadway entertainments set in fantasy versions of Asian countries.

Like the oriental foods and domestic goods that added a touch of the exotic to white American culture, the racial difference of these Chinese American characters was mainly decorative in nature. Moreover, the 1958 *Flower Drum Song* staged characters who fit the prototype of the 'model minority', whereby successful assimilation is predicated on a wholehearted embrace of American values; they were, as Robert Lee describes, a '*racial* minority whose apparently successful *ethnic* assimilation was a result of stoic patience, political obedience, and self-improvement', and whose success stories 'sent a message to "Negroes and other minorities" that accommodation would be rewarded while militancy would be contained or crushed'.[8]

In his revision of *Flower Drum Song*, Hwang darkens the overall tone of the storyline in order to question these romanticized depictions of immigrant life and assimilation into white American culture. His version opens with Mei-Li (so spelled in Hwang's version) fleeing China after the persecution and death of her anti-communist father. She arrives in America with other new immigrants, carrying her only memento, her father's flower drum ('A Hundred Million Miracles'). She goes to The Golden Pearl Theatre, where Wang Chi-Yang and his son Ta are performing Peking Opera to a nearly empty house. Wang welcomes her as the daughter of his oldest friend from opera school. She successfully learns the woman's role for *The Flower Boat Maiden*, much to the relief of Ta, who has been unwillingly performing this female part ('I Am Going to Like It Here').

Hwang's *Flower Drum Song* juxtaposes traditional Peking Opera with the 'Oriental' nightclub acts that made Rodgers and Hammerstein's musical popular. Ta gives Mei-Li a job waiting tables on 'Nightclub Night', which features vigorous performances by Linda Low ('You Be the Rock'). Inspired by Mei-Li's opera performance, Ta suggests a new club number that combines traditional opera costumes and movement with striptease, and asks Mei-Li to coach Linda on the use of the costume's sleeves. Linda, who does not welcome Ta's romantic feelings towards her, offers to help Mei-Li attract him instead ('I Enjoy Being a Girl'). Wang, horrified by the goings-on during 'Nightclub Night', threatens to cancel Ta's show. Mei-Li encourages Ta to hold on to his dreams; after their duet ('You Are Beautiful'), he kisses her but is now confused by his attraction to Mei-Li as well as Linda. Madame Rita Liang, a theatrical agent specializing in 'Oriental talent', enters and expresses her hopes for marketing the nightclub acts ('Grant Avenue'). The Golden Pearl Theatre is transformed into Club Chop Suey, which becomes a commercial success. Ta and Mei-Li fall deeper in love ('Sunday'), yet Ta resists his attraction to her in favour of his unrequited feelings for Linda. Linda in turn gives Mei-Li lessons in dressing and dating, preparing her to surprise Ta after one of the club's performances. With growing audiences for Club Chop Suey ('Fan Tan Fannie'), even Wang is drawn into the nightclub scene, taking over a role formerly played by Harvard, the costume designer ('Vagabond Sailor'/'Gliding Through My Memoree'). The applause leads him to embrace the club's success wholeheartedly. Ta, on the other hand, is both irritated with his father's taking charge and disappointed that the 'surprise' promised to him by Linda was only Mei-Li. A dejected Mei-Li leaves Club Chop Suey at the end of the first act ('A Hundred Million Miracles' [reprise]).

Both Hwang's 'Club Chop Suey' and the 'Celestial Bar' of the earlier *Flower Drum Song* recall popular Chinatown establishments catering mainly to non-Asian tourists; these included Charlie Low's San Francisco-based Forbidden City, which promised spectacular and exotic pleasures including striptease, popular songs and dances and chorus girls.[9] The second act shows Wang's overly zealous embrace of the oriental kitsch beloved by Club Chop Suey audiences; he has taken on the stage name 'Sammy Fong' and he and the showgirls perform increasingly exaggerated numbers ('Chop Suey'). These hyperbolic performances upset Ta, as does the absence of Mei-Li. Ta is counselled by Uncle Chin ('My Best Love'), who reveals that Mei-Li is working at a fortune cookie factory. At the factory, the workers sing an ironic reprise of 'I Am Going to Like It Here' as they check in; Mei-Li is courted by Chao, another immigrant. While Mei-Li is reluctant to accept Chao's advances, after an emotional confrontation with Ta she agrees to go to Hong Kong with Chao, even giving him her flower drum to sell for passage money. Meanwhile, Madame Liang and Wang have dinner together and contemplate marriage ('Don't Marry Me'), while Linda announces her intention to go to Hollywood. Ta declares his intention to follow her but then learns from her that Mei-Li's flower drum is for sale in a pawnshop. Mei-Li is about to leave for the boat to Hong Kong ('Love Look Away') when Ta arrives to present her with the flower drum; he tells her that he missed Linda's bus to Los Angeles while waiting for the pawnshop to open. Mei-Li decides against leaving the United States with Chao, is reunited with Ta ('Like a God') and the two are married in the final scene ('A Hundred Million Miracles' [reprise]).

Hwang's new story reworks the musical's perspective on immigration. Rather than setting the play entirely in the United States, Hwang begins with a glimpse of a rapidly changing China; 'A Hundred Million Miracles' is no longer a quaint demonstration of cultural traditions but now reflects on how the cultural revolution prompted immigration to America. A chorus of immigrants articulate their hopes for 'the sweet breath of freedom': 'My child will be born in America, and will grow up without fear, for she will know neither famine nor war'; 'When I can do what I want, no man will ever be my master. When I can say what I wish, my lips will only speak the truth.'[10] Mei-Li, now a political refugee rather than an eager picture bride, comments more cautiously on her grief and uncertainty: 'Father, I carry your memory with me across the seas. I think I can survive whatever lies ahead – so long as I don't lose hope' (2003: 13). The flower drum that she carries is now less a sign of her affinity for traditional Chinese songs than a personal memento that will figure prominently in her decision to choose Ta over his rival Chao later in the play.

Hwang preserves the love story between Mei Li and Wang Ta at the centre of the earlier versions, yet fundamentally changes the ways that this romance comments on ethnic identity and assimilation. In earlier versions of *Flower Drum Song,* Ta's interest in both the brash Linda Low and the compliant Mei Li maps out a dichotomy of incompatible cultural values that differentiate the fully assimilated American from the recent immigrant. In those versions, Ta calls his father 'completely Chinese' and his brother San 'completely American' and says that he is trapped between these discordant worlds: 'But I am both, and sometimes the American half shocks the Oriental half, and sometimes the Oriental half keeps me from – showing a girl what is on my mind' (1959: 37). Hwang's *Flower Drum Song* at first seems to reference the same split between traditional Chinese culture and modern American values. Ta doggedly pursues Linda in spite of his developing feelings for Mei-Li, and Mei-Li angrily confronts his reservations: 'Then it's me you don't want, isn't it? Someone fresh off the boat, who doesn't know how to dress, or wear her hair' (2003: 60). Yet in Hwang's version, the choice between definitively 'Chinese' and 'American' characteristics is not so clearly defined. Hwang's *Flower Drum Song* pictures the Chinese American identity not as caught between worlds but as actively negotiating and reinventing what might be considered 'Chinese' or 'American'.

> **Mei-Li** Why not? Ta, sometimes you seem a hundred percent Chinese. Then a moment later, you become a hundred percent American.
> **Ta** So what does that make me? A hundred percent nothing?
> **Mei-Li** No. I think you are … a hundred percent both. (2003; 20)

Hwang's revision blurs clear distinctions between 'Chinese' and 'American' characterizations. Instead of picturing characters as stuck in different stages of an evolution from new immigrant to fully assimilated American, his characters perform culture less as the expression of their inherent natures and more as motivated by economic necessity or social pressure.

One such example can be found in Hwang's reframing of the song 'I Enjoy Being a Girl'. The lyrics of the song gleefully describe the labours and pleasure of 'being a girl', as Linda pictures herself carefully preparing for a competitive marriage market. She describes herself as 'a filly who is ready for the race', who makes herself ready for display by doing her hair, curling her eyelashes, and slathering a 'pound and a half of cream upon my face'; the prize for being 'strictly a female female' is to end up in the 'home of a brave and free male'. The 1958 version staged Linda Low as singing contemplatively to herself, at a moment when she is left alone during her initial date with Ta. The 1961 film sets this song in Linda's bedroom, after Ta telephones to ask her out; the camera then shows Linda (played memorably by Nancy Kwan) narcissistically singing to a series of her own mirror images.[11] In both the earlier stage and film versions, this song is portrayed as a private moment that seems consonant with Linda's real desire to give up her performances at the strip club in favour of marriage. As she tells Ta earlier: 'I want to be a success as a girl. Oh, it's nice to have outside accomplishments like singing, cooking or first aid. But the main thing is for a woman to be successful in her gender' (1959: 33). Hwang's *Flower Drum Song* does not make this song a solo number revealing Linda's true nature; in his version, Linda directs the song first to Mei-Li, turning it into a tutorial in assimilation as she, hoping to redirect Ta's affections, encourages Mei-Li to become Ta's 'American Dream'. If the earlier versions of Linda suggest a character whose actions are dictated by inherently feminine qualities, Hwang's version of Linda makes clear that she has more complex motivations for this mode of acting. Linda's overtly sexual demeanour is not evidence of some authentically 'girlish' identity but is prompted by an earlier rejection of Chinese patriarchy:

Mei-Li But my mother told me that a woman's life is filled with misery.

Linda Mine told me that same thing. Look at this picture. Me – at age fifteen, in Seattle. Low Lee-Fung. My friends called me 'Lowly'. Then one day I realized – we're not in China anymore. No more stuffing daughters down a well or selling us into slavery. And foot binding – what's *that* all about? No, this is the land of opportunity. (2003: 27)

Mei-Li then joins Linda in singing 'I Enjoy Being a Girl', underscoring how 'opportunity' for these female characters entails using gendered performances to win love or earn money, as Mei Li learns American dating customs and Linda pursues an acting career that relies on feminine display.

Linda wins both financial and romantic returns for her enactments of 'being a girl'. Despite Rodgers's comment that *Flower Drum Song* might 'show that East and West can get together with a little adjustment', interracial romance was never overtly referenced in the 1958 version, whereas in Hwang's revision Ta and Linda discuss the matter explicitly. In his version, Ta expresses his racial insecurity in his concern for Linda's preference for white boyfriends: 'How come you only date white guys, anyway?' Linda defends rather than denies this desire; the white boyfriend becomes an accessory for the convincing performance of assimilation: 'We all wanna be Americans – like everyone else. (*Pause.*) When I'm out with my boyfriends, no one ever says to me, "Go back to where you came from." Is that so terrible? To feel now and then like I actually belong here?' (2003: 86). Hwang's *Flower Drum Song* thus foregrounds an ongoing tension between Linda's enactment of these aggressively 'American' feminine behaviours and her inability to ever be truly seen as white. This is reinforced when 'I Enjoy Being a Girl' is subsequently turned into a rousing nightclub number; Linda's striptease performance – featuring Linda stripping from an elaborate Chinese opera costume into a bikini, with a chorus of Asian American women posing as *reflections in her mirror* (a nod to a famous scene from the 1961 film) – exploits the contrast between what is seen as an indelibly 'Chinese' appearance and an 'American' role.

Hwang's framing of Rodgers and Hammerstein's nightclub numbers openly mocks the exotic allure of Asian Americans performing as perpetual foreigners for white patrons; the Club Chop Suey performance of 'I Enjoy Being a Girl' is announced as 'that "all-American Chinese Dream" – Linda Low and the "Fresh Off the Boat Dancers."' Like its predecessors, Hwang's musical preserves the way such novelty acts stage Asian bodies as comically incompatible with American song and dance. Songs such as 'Gliding Through My Memoree' present Chinese American chorus girls as inadequate representations of European females, with the song's humour relying on an assumed difference between an Asian racial type and the many varieties of desirable white women described by the 'vagabond sailor'. Hwang maintains the racialized comedy of this song (although thankfully in his version of 'Gliding Through My Memoree' the 'Irish Girl' is not asked to say 'Ellin go blah' as she is in the 1958 musical [1959: 88]). Yet Hwang does not simply generate amusement at the presumed incongruity of seeing Asian bodies performing characterizations such as the 'stately Scandinavian type/a buxom, blue-eyed blonde' (1959: 88), but rather highlights how these campy performances are motivated by economic pragmatism. In the earlier versions of *Flower Drum Song*, the Wang family's money makes them immune from the financial pressures faced by most immigrants. Though Ta mentions discrimination to Linda, telling her that 'it is difficult for a Chinese, even with a college degree, to find employment' (1959: 36), his casual remark is quickly passed over as he then tells her that his father is quite wealthy. In contrast, Hwang makes his versions of Master Wang and Ta impoverished artists, who constantly stress the need to market themselves to white American consumers as a form of survival. Hwang's Madam Liang argues for the conversion of 'The Golden Pearl' to 'Club Chop Suey' as a necessary part of reforming the image of Chinatown from its association with 'Opium dens, Tong wars, female slavery and questionable cuts of meat' to a more appealing set of associations: 'We've got to show the Americans who we really are. No more inscrutable Orientals, but smiling all-American faces. Polite men, beautiful women, the finest cuisine in the world' (2003: 36). As part of this, Hwang reimagines 'Grant Avenue' (a musical tribute to the tourist delights of Chinatown) as a fantasy of ethnic re-invention, in which Madame Liang leads other cast members in describing the transformation of San Francisco's Chinatown from ethnic ghetto to prime real estate.

Thus the exaggerated racial stereotypes, such as Master Wang's proposed 'Master Confucius, Ancient Oriental Wiseguy', appear as calculated performances catering to white audiences rather than characterizations that reveal the true nature of individuals. Similarly, Hwang exemplifies traditional Chinese culture through the performance of Peking Opera rather than with the demonstrations of everyday behaviour that appeared in the earlier stage and film versions, which include quaint expressions, exotic customs and strange foods such as those ordered by Madam Liang: 'two pounds of sea horse, one pound of dried snake meat and a box of longevity noodles ... and a dozen two thousand year eggs' [1959: 9–10]). Thus Hwang's *Flower Drum Song* stresses that both 'American' and 'Chinese' are cultural performances rather than innate identities. Peking Opera can never be mistaken for a natural state of being; that it involves years of disciplined practice is emphasized by Ta's inability to learn his female role properly.

At first, Master Wang champions Peking Opera as a defence against the vacuity of American popular culture: 'So long as we draw breath, the Peking

Opera lives. Especially here, in this land of white devils and fake Chinese. If we give up the fight, then who? Who will remain, to keep our world from being washed away by Coca-Cola and Mickey Mouse?' (2003: 17). But by the end of the play, Master Wang has embraced the success of the nightclub, staging the song 'Chop Suey' as the most exaggerated of the glitzy nightclub numbers, in which the female chorus parades around in giant, light-up take-out containers, while the male chorus dances with giant chopsticks. His conversion to nightclub impresario prompts Ta's consternation that the club has now become 'some kind of weird Oriental minstrel show' (2003: 72). In a reversal of attitudes, it is Ta who no longer finds satisfaction in the nightclub and who returns to what he previously thought obsolete. The discipline and practice of Peking Opera turns out to be the most generative aspect of the musical, inspiring close personal connections that bind people across time, space and culture. This is suggested both by the familial connections between Mei-Li's father and Master Wang and by the developing love between Mei-Li and Ta, which is played out in opera rehearsals. Hwang resituates the song 'You are Beautiful' into this context, providing an opportunity for a genuine connection between Mei-Li and Ta. Under Mei-Li's tutelage in operatic relationships (including her gentle reminder that 'to create something new, we must first love what is old' [2003: 33]) Ta gains pride in his ethnic roots and respect for traditional culture.

Unlike its predecessors, Hwang's version of *Flower Drum Song* teaches that respect for aspects of Chinese culture, such as Peking Opera, does not signal a natural affinity for traditional values. Rather, characters find in the preservation of culture a necessary refuge against the self-hatred born from living in the United States. Hwang emphasizes the bitter realities masked by the American Dream; his second act includes an ironic reprise of 'I am Going to Like It Here' sung by workers at the fortune cookie factory. Prefacing Mei-Li's heartbroken rendition of 'Love, Look Away' are testimonials of loneliness, broken promises and dashed hopes in America ('Can someone take my child back to Hong Kong? I cannot make enough to support us both. I will send for him one day, I promise'; and 'I am a physicist! And they made me scrub floors, like a coolie!' [2003: 88]). Instead of the lovelorn Helen Chao, Hwang gives Ta a male rival in a young and virile Chao (who, in one of the changes from the Mark Taper production, was given much more romantic potential on Broadway). Chao actively protests his lot, creatively subverting both the robotic labour of the factory and the orientalist kitsch of the fortune cookie by loading his cookies with comments such as 'Stop eating now, you're already too darn fat' (2003: 75). Chao offers Mei-Li a new life in Hong Kong, telling her that 'Chinese should live where they can be proud to be Chinese' (2003: 90). Chao articulates the impossibility of being accepted as 'Asian American'; though the Chinese in the United States might be lauded for assimilation, they remain excluded as non-white. Chao's sentiments suggest that for Asian Americans, social performances will continue to be circumscribed in the United States; they remain exotic spectacles, invisible labour or model minorities.

Despite highlighting the hardships of immigrant life, Hwang chooses to end the play on an optimistic note, asserting that the United States can nonetheless also be a home for Asian Americans. Mei-Li responds to Chao by asserting her faith not only in Ta but also in a viable Chinese American identity, telling Chao that pride in being Chinese is 'possible here' (2003: 90). Hwang stresses the importance of the performing arts in fostering this possibility: to thrive in America is not only to prosper economically but also to be able to express oneself with artistic integrity. The ending of the play affirms not only the romantic union of Mei-Li and Ta but also their creation of a new form of intercultural theatre based on Peking Opera, which Master Wang describes as using 'the traditions of my old opera days to tell new stories – of life in America' (2003: 96). This unprofitable but satisfying artistic enterprise is contrasted with the continued racism in Hollywood film and television, expressed through the careers of Madame Liang and Linda Low. Madame Liang recalls her former career as a Hollywood starlet: 'They called me "The Queen of the Oriental Crowd Scenes." Whenever a Japanese village got bombed, that was me, screaming' (2003: 80). Linda's announcement of her first movie role serves as a reminder that such stereotyping has not ended: 'I play this peasant girl in the Korean War, and when my village gets bombed, I scream' (2003: 96).

The ending thus suggests the continued necessity of countering persistent racial typecasting with new kinds of Asian American performance; in these references, Hwang nods towards the history of Asian American theatre companies (beginning with Los Angeles's East West Players in 1965) that will nurture racial pride, create a sense of community and generate exciting new art.[12] Significantly, the play ends not only with the marriage of Mei-Li and Ta but also with a recognition of Asian American actors past and present. With the final reprise of 'A Hundred Million Miracles', Mei-Li and Ta speak in honour of their parents and ancestors, 'whose legacy was passed down to me the day I was born' (2003: 96). After they and the other leads state the birthplaces of their characters, cast members, speaking directly to the audience, individually state their actual place of birth.[13] In this final tableau, Hwang breaks the fourth wall of the stage, acknowledging the labour and artistry of those who have just performed. In doing so, he connects them to the Asian Americans who performed in the original Broadway and film casts. For Hwang, the true heroes of *Flower Drum Song* are not just the famous composer and lyricist who gave the play name recognition, but the Asian American actors who inspired a later generation to recreate a new version of *Flower Drum Song*. The legacy celebrated here thus moves from the familial to the theatrical, as those who now perform the musical are imagined as following in the footsteps of earlier Asian American performers who worked in nightclubs, preserved traditional Asian arts, established Asian American theatre companies and appeared on Broadway. Throughout his version of *Flower Drum Song*, Hwang highlights the accomplishments of those who, in singing and dancing their way to mainstream recognition, continue to face both the pressures of racial representation and the demands of their art; his closing number caps this tribute by designating their achievements part of the 'hundred million miracles' happening every day.[14]

David Henry Hwang's *Golden* Opportunities
Dan Bacalzo

When he was ten years old, David Henry Hwang embarked upon a journey that would, in many ways, define his life. Travelling from Los Angeles, where he lived, to the Philippines, where his maternal grandmother resided, he spent the summer interviewing her about his ancestors, documenting the stories that he feared would be forever lost after his ailing grandmother passed on. This included the tale of his great-grandfather, Tiong-Yee, who converted to Christianity in 1918. The trip resulted in Hwang's first major writing endeavour, a ninety-page novel entitled *Only Three Generations*, after a Chinese proverb relating to wealth. 'My tome was duly Xeroxed and distributed to relatives, who showered it with excellent reviews', he relates.[15]

Years later, Hwang – now a Tony Award-winning playwright for his seminal work *M. Butterfly* – returned to the tales his grandmother told him to create *Golden Child*. The show debuted Off-Broadway at the Public Theater in 1996, received a Tony Award nomination for Best Play for its Broadway run at the Longacre Theatre in 1998 and was revived in 2012 by the New York-based Signature Theatre as the company's first production in a Signature One residency devoted to the works of the playwright. I attended all three productions and have also drawn evidence from a video recording of the Public performance, the published script of the Broadway version and an unpublished script provided by Signature of the latest incarnation. This part of the chapter examines all three New York productions and some of the differences between them and considers how Hwang deals with issues of legacy and nostalgia while reimagining his family history and the turbulent time and place in which his play is set.[16]

Golden Frames

In each iteration of the play, the plot centres on Eng Tieng-Bin, who is modelled after Hwang's great-grandfather. Tieng-Bin is a Chinese businessman in early-twentieth-century China with three wives and many children, including Ahn, his 'golden child'. After meeting Reverend Baines, a white Christian missionary from England, Tieng-Bin resolves to convert. This throws his household into chaos as Tieng-Bin's actions threaten the power dynamics among his three wives. Of particular concern to them is the fact that while polygamy is allowed within the Chinese Confucian tradition, it is not an accepted practice of the Christian Church.

Golden Child is a bittersweet drama about a time of transition. It is by no means a simplistic portrait of East versus West or tradition versus modernity. As a result of his decision, Tieng-Bin loses the love of his life: his third wife, Eling, whose death in childbirth is in part triggered by angry ghosts unhappy with the abandonment of the ancestral worship practice. At the same time, the progressive changes wrought by Tieng-Bin's new way of thinking include abolishing the foot-binding practice of the women in his household, beginning with his daughter, Ahn. However, while the arc of the story (set in the early twentieth century) remains the same in the three different New York productions, the framing sequence differs significantly. The alterations to the script demonstrate Hwang's ongoing desire to reinvent the past, mixing facts and fiction as he looks back on events inspired by his family's history.

In the Public Theater production (1996), Stan Egi, a young actor close to the age of Hwang at the time *Golden Child* was written, played the role of Andrew, a direct descendant of Eng Tieng-Bin (whom he also played). The show begins with Andrew riding in a taxicab, ruminating on his impending fatherhood. He is visited by the ghostly figure of his grandmother, Ahn, who comes to offer advice. At the time of the play's premiere, Hwang had recently had a son, Noah, with his wife, Kathryn Layng, and this event in the playwright's own life informed the way he crafted his drama. In an interview regarding the Public Theater production, Hwang notes that he began the play prior to his wife's pregnancy, but as his work on it continued after his son's birth, it took on 'more of the viewpoint of putting your heritage or your family history in some sort of perspective, and finding a way to own it as a prerequisite for raising a child'.[17] In this quote, Hwang aligns himself with the Andrew character, who becomes a fictional stand-in for the playwright.

This incarnation of the script even includes an allusion to its source material, as the ghost of Ahn reminds Andrew that as a ten-year-old boy, he visited her in the Philippines and she regaled him with tales from the past. She wants to make sure such stories are not forgotten, asking him, 'What will you tell new baby about your ancestors?'[18] Andrew is reluctant to tell the child anything, associating his forebears with a brand of fundamentalist Christianity from which he feels that he has escaped. Andrew even sees signs that tell him that he 'must be born again' just prior to Ahn's ghostly visit. But through his grandmother's retelling of the story of Eng Tieng-Bin, Andrew discovers a different meaning in her chronicles than the one she has intended and that there is more to his family's history – even the story of his grandfather's conversion to Christianity – than he had thought.

In the Broadway mounting of *Golden Child* (1998), veteran actor Randall Duk Kim played the dual roles of Andrew and Tieng-Bin and the part was reworked so that Andrew was an older character. Consequently, his relationship with his ancestors shifted an entire generation, with Andrew now receiving a ghostly visitation from his mother, rather than his grandmother. In a sense, this distances the play from the playwright's own life without sacrificing the autobiographical component. Played by an older actor, impending fatherhood has a different resonance. Indeed, the ghost of Ahn complains that she has had to wait far too long to become a grandmother, prompting Andrew to declare that he 'never wanted to become a father'.[19] Andrew is on his third marriage, an ironic parallel to the three wives of his ancestor, Tieng-Bin. Whereas the Andrew in the Public script was anxious yet still happy about his new role as a father, the Broadway Andrew initially seems more conflicted about his wife Elizabeth's unplanned pregnancy.

In revising the script, Hwang also shifted the framing sequence from a moving taxicab to the more sedate setting of a bedroom where Andrew – revealed to be a writer – decides to write down his family's history at the end of the play. He tells Elizabeth, 'I want to preserve this. For our child. Like my mother did for me' (51). Andrew's attitude towards his past has been transformed by Ahn's ghostly visitation. There is no more mention of his desire to avoid becoming a father. Instead, he wants to ensure that he passes on the stories that were so important to him when he was younger and which he finds value in once again.

For the 2012 Signature production, Hwang once again made changes to the framing sequence. Here, the action begins in the late 1960s as a teenage grandson – not identified by name – visits his still-living grandmother, Ahn, in the Philippines to record stories about their family's history. This scene is played more for laughs than the openings of the previous two versions, particularly as Greg Watanabe – who doubled as the grandson and Tieng-Bin – has a strong comic presence. The lighter mood at the beginning of the play impacts the tone of the production as a whole, which seems to emphasize the comedic elements of the piece. It is also worth noting that here it is the grandson who seeks his grandmother out, taking a more active role in the way the main narrative is introduced. This scenario is also the closest to the way Hwang describes his own childhood experience of documenting his grandmother's tales.

The first two versions of the script emphasize ideas of legacy and lineage, with the doubts Andrew feels about becoming a father placed at the forefront of the narrative. After hearing the ghost of Ahn tell the story of Eng Tieng-Bin's conversion to Christianity and the sacrifices he made to try and create a better life for those he loved, Andrew gains a new understanding of how history can and should be passed on. In the Broadway script, the final passage is Andrew's address to his unborn child, in which he says:

> I watch your mother sleeping, knowing you are growing inside her. And suddenly the room is filled with spirits – so many faces, looking down on me. And on each face, a story, some I have been told, some I can only imagine, and some I will never know at all. But many of them, people not so different from myself, who struggled with what to keep, and what to change – for the next generation. (52)

Andrew's ancestors were flawed human beings who made imperfect decisions and had to live with the consequences. But what they did helped to pave the way for a better future for their descendants. Eng Tieng-Bin's bold conversion to Christianity caused so much pain for himself and his family, yet his daughter Ahn pays him respect because, as she puts it, 'he is the one ... who take the binding from my feet' (51). This is a lasting, positive change that was worth more to her than what she endured as a result.

Ahn's devotion to her father can be read as a variation on the ancestor worship that is a recurring theme within the play. On several occasions, characters pray directly to their deceased parents with the belief that burning offerings to them will let their spirits intercede on their children's behalf in the living world. Eventually, Tieng-Bin forbids this practice in order to conform to the principles of Christianity that Reverend Baines has taught him. The decision does not sit well with many, particularly his first wife, Siu-Yong. However, Ahn agrees with this break with tradition, saying, 'Mama believed in our ancestors, she did everything for them. But when she called on them for help, there was nothing they could do' (50). Ahn instead embraces her newfound Christianity, even if Andrew notes, 'Whenever you opened a Bible, or said a prayer to Jesus, you were actually making an offering ... to your father' (51). This does not mean that Ahn's conversion was false, however. She simply folded the Confucian idea of ancestor worship into her Christian practice, much like people all over the world have incorporated elements of former belief systems into newly acquired religions.

In the most recent incarnation of *Golden Child*, the teenage grandson does not immediately understand the lessons to be learned from hearing about his great-grandfather. He thinks the story terrible because Tieng-Bin's conversion to Christianity coincided with Siu-Yong's suicide and Eling's death during childbirth – with both fatalities resulting from a chain of events that might not have occurred if Tieng-Bin had never met with Reverend Baines. The grandson does not make a declaration about legacy like Andrew did in the earlier script. Instead, the play ends with grandson and grandmother listening to the tape recording of the story that has just been told. There is greater ambiguity in this ending, with the emphasis placed on preserving history, rather than necessarily learning a lesson from it. It is unclear what the grandson takes away from his grandmother's story. However, we are keenly aware of the young man's desire to document his family's past, with the onstage prop of a large, 1960s-style tape recorder a clear reminder of his project.

In her study of Asian American performance, Josephine Lee considers the impulse for many Asian American playwrights to pen works that recreate histories of their communities. She remarks, 'The eagerness to write history points to the desire for an authenticating past that will support a communal future.'[20] While the character of the grandson may not immediately recognize what he has gained from hearing the story of his great-grandfather, he does explain what he wanted to find out. He hoped that discovering details of his family's past would help him understand his place in the world. He tells his grandmother:

> You don't know what it's like. To be the only Chinese kid in my school. People are always going, 'Oh, you speak really good English!' But when other kids say weird stuff, I always think, 'You guys don't know anything. You're just ignorant jerks. Cuz my family, back where they came from – originally? – they were like these amazing leaders, they were rich, they were awesome!' (beat) Maybe I was wrong. Maybe I'm the ignorant jerk.[21]

The grandson's desire to uncover the past stems from his need for self-validation. He makes note of his racial difference from his peers and the way that it has caused them to make assumptions about him. He is not attempting to distance himself from his racial heritage, however. In fact, he embraces it by nostalgically imagining a lineage that he can be proud of.

In the late seventeenth century, a Swiss physician coined the term 'nostalgia' as a way of describing the experience of Swiss mercenaries who were fighting battles far from their homeland. Nostalgia is derived from the Greek *nostos* (a return home) and *algos* (a painful condition) and was considered a pathological medical condition of homesickness.[22] In more recent years, the term has come to indicate sentimentality rather than pathology. But I suggest that we might also view the word as productive. Svetlana Boym talks about how nostalgia 'can be retrospective but also prospective'.[23] In other words, nostalgia can be used to re-envision home – or in the case of Andrew and the grandson, an ancestral homeland – in order to construct an identity that can help to mitigate present-day difficulties and suggest a future worth living.

Boym further theorizes that there are two different kinds of nostalgia: restorative and reflective. The first is tied to nationalism and concerned with reconstructions of rigidly defined notions of truth.[24] In bringing early-twentieth-century China to the stage, it might appear that Hwang's play is restoratively trying to reconstruct this past. However, the playwright often employs an ironic point of view that is out of keeping with Boym's definition. For example, while *Golden Child* is written in English, the characters are presumably speaking Mandarin throughout. When the English-speaking character Reverend Baines enters, he speaks in pidgin English, a theatrical convention used to indicate that he has a different access to the Chinese language than the rest of the characters. The writing strategy is a direct commentary on how Asian characters are often represented in American popular culture, which has often served to make them appear comically ignorant.

Moreover, Hwang's Asian characters speak in late-twentieth-century American slang, with Siu-Yong's line 'What are you – retarded?' a clear indication of anachronistic phrasing (14). The playwright used a similar tactic in his previous *M. Butterfly*. In an interview about that play, he lambasts existing representations of the East by non-Asian writers as often being rendered in 'inscrutable poetic fashion' and remarks that what he intends to do is 'go to the other extreme and make it so slangy and contemporary that it is jarring'.[25] Hwang does not set out to imitate conversational language. There is still a heightened quality to his phrasing. But he makes it clear that his characters are not linguistically limited by some preconceived notion of a mysterious Orient.

Since there is a focus on the past, nostalgia still seems involved in *Golden Child*'s playful use of language, but Hwang's writing style better fits Boym's definition of reflective nostalgia. She claims that this type 'is more about individual and cultural memory [where] the past opens up a multitude of potentialities'.[26] Reflective nostalgia is dislocated from a fixed meaning, recognizing that truth is illusory or, at the very least, open to interpretation. The past exists as something that we can project present, and possibly future, desire upon. We can imagine things not as they were but how we might like them to be.

Hwang's 2012 script for *Golden Child* acknowledges nostalgic desire while also embedding a cautionary note. After the grandson hears Ahn's story, he wonders if he is mistaken about what it should mean for him. He fears that his classmates were right and that there is nothing from his family's past that he can be proud of. His grandmother's express reason for telling him the story is so that he can learn how she became a Christian and to relate her hope that her grandson will become a pastor. He unequivocally rejects this outcome, yet he still places value on her story, punching out the tabs on the cassette tape it has been recorded on so that it cannot be erased. There appears to be a limit to the uses of nostalgia, as it is subject to multiple narrative interpretations. In this case, those of the grandmother and grandson do not coincide and a coherent meaning that can apply to both the characters remains elusive.

However, the Signature production of *Golden Child* demonstrates the importance of family legacy in one other crucial way. A programme note inserted into the *Playbill* identifies the voice of the grandson heard on a pre-recorded audio playback as Noah D. Hwang, the real-life son of playwright David Henry Hwang. When I viewed this production, I initially failed to notice the insert and did not realize that actor Greg Watanabe was not the voice heard on the recording, even though he played the grandson onstage. I would venture that many other patrons similarly did not make this subtle connection. And yet, the very fact of David Henry Hwang's son – now a 16-year-old – speaking as the voice of the grandson in the play seems a fitting way to acknowledge the script's grounding in the Hwang family legacy.

Changing History

The majority of *Golden Child* is set in China, during the winter of 1918 and spring of 1919. This period falls squarely within what historian Daniel H. Bays refers to as 'the high point of the foreign missionary age in China [when] China seemed to be modernizing and Christianizing at the same time'.[27] This era, which Bays identifies as lasting from 1902 to 1927, immediately follows the Boxer Rebellion, a military conflict that attempted to oust foreigners from China and stem the tide of missionary evangelism. Instead, it resulted in the capture of China's capital by the Eight-Nation Alliance (consisting of Austria–Hungary, France, Germany, Italy, Japan, Russia, the United Kingdom and the United States) and ultimately in accelerating foreign involvement in China.

Golden Child is also set after the 1911 Revolution, which ended imperial rule and established the Republic of China. Hwang makes reference to this historical shift within the play when Eng Tieng-Bin tells his wives that he has invited Reverend Baines to their household. 'After all, the founder of our Chinese republic, Dr Sun Yat-Sen – he studied both Western medicine and Christianity', he informs them (15). More than that, Sun Yat-Sen was a Protestant, and several members of China's National Assembly were also Christians.[28]

In an interview, Hwang elaborates on the changes in the sociopolitical landscape of early-twentieth-century China, saying, 'A lot of the progressive and educated Chinese at the time … started to realize that the Chinese model, the tradition established for the last five thousand years, was no longer working. They had been exposed to the West. So many people looked to the West for models – how China might be transformed.'[29] The political reality that existed during the time of the play provides a necessary context to understanding why Eng Tieng-Bin is willing to risk so much in order to progress with the changing times.

However, Hwang makes clear it is not merely political expedience that prompts Tieng-Bin to convert. He is attracted to the ideas that Baines espouses and is particularly fond of the Western notion of individualism. He hopes that Christianity can give him the strength to break from the confines of tradition. At Baines's urging, he declares, 'I should be able to make my own way, live my own life, choose the woman I love' (37). Speaking aloud these desires – which run counter to what he claims his ancestors' voices are telling him – is both shameful and liberating for Tieng-Bin.

It also heralds his tragic downfall. When he informs Eling of his plan to tear down the family altars and bring her with him to the Philippines as his only wife, she balks at the notion. She tells him that she could not possibly abandon her dedication to her parents and that going away with him would cause First Wife to lose face. Up to this point in the play, Eling has seemed quite open to modernization, wearing western lingerie for her husband and enjoying the recordings of Italian opera that she listens to on the phonograph player he has given her as a gift. When Tieng-Bin reminds her of this desire to be 'modern', she responds by saying, 'But does that mean I can no longer be Chinese?' (39). There are traditional values that Eling wants to preserve, and she fears that modernization – which seems to increasingly be associated with westernization – will cause her to lose her sense of identity.

Eling also tells her husband that he is the only one in the household who actually believes in Christianity, even though Ahn and Luan (a.k.a. 'Second Wife') have been attending the reverend's lessons. She backs this declaration by revealing that Luan has been casting aspersions on the sincerity of Ahn's motives, 'telling anyone who'll listen that Ahn is only pretending to be interested … so she can spy for First Wife' (39). When Tieng-Bin confronts Siu-Yong about this charge, he finds her doped-up on opium and their bitter conflict is what leads her to take her own life. Soon after, Siu-Yong's ghost pays a visit to Eling, admonishing her for her behaviour and saying that her deceased parents, whom Eling is no longer honouring, are now impoverished spirits. This confirms Eling's worst fears about the perils of abandoning her previous belief system in favour of converting to Christianity to appease her husband. It also contributes to her going into labour, which she does not survive.[30]

The deaths of Siu-Yong and Eling leave Tieng-Bin with only one wife, Luan, who throughout the play has been characterized as a manipulative schemer. Despairing after Eling's death, Tieng-Bin briefly returns to the practice of ancestor worship in order to communicate with his deceased parents. 'Is this how you punish a disobedient son?' he asks them. 'Take from me the wife I love, even the wife I respect, leaving me with the one for whom I feel … nothing' (49). Tieng-Bin expresses regret regarding his decision to convert to Christianity, but it is too little, too late. Ahn, however, has no doubts about her new religion and sees her father's travails as necessary to secure a better future for his family.

Still, Ahn's very presence as a ghost who visits Andrew acknowledges that there is more than one valid belief system. When Andrew admonishes this ghostly visitation, saying, 'Christians don't come back from the dead', Ahn's sly response is 'You forget – I am *Chinese* Christian. Best of east, best of west' (7). By visiting Andrew, the ghost of Ahn is perhaps suggesting that it is unwise to ignore the voices of your ancestors – with Tieng-Bin's loss as a cautionary tale. However, this interpretation only holds true for the first two versions of *Golden Child*, as Ahn remains alive in the Signature production. Indeed, the supernatural elements are downplayed in Hwang's most recent incarnation of the script, although Siu-Yong still makes an appearance from beyond the grave to take revenge against Eling for betraying her.

It should be evident that, while inspired by stories of Hwang's ancestors, *Golden Child* is not a factual retelling of events. In any conversion of real-life history to fictional narrative, it is important to keep in mind the artistic process that requires the alteration of certain details. Indeed, in a 1997 interview about the play, Hwang states, 'My mother had a few quibbles about some things I either invented or presumed in *Golden Child*, since it was based on her family'.[31] Here, the playwright identifies a dilemma facing several writers who use their lives as raw material: the ones whose histories are somehow represented in the piece recognize the changes and possible misrepresentations, while those who view the play knowing only that it is based upon autobiography are more likely to accept it as factual.

In a way, Hwang's assertion that the play has an autobiographical component invites critics and audience members to speculate on the fidelity of the work. In his *New York Times* review of the Broadway production, theatre critic Peter Marks notes, 'Mr. Hwang has said in interviews that the play is based on his own family history in China in the early twentieth century, and for those unfamiliar with Chinese culture, "Golden Child" possesses what feels like authentic and exotic detail'.[32] Note how the phrase 'what feels like' is used to modify the words 'authentic' and 'exotic' within this sentence. Marks seems to imply that he recognizes the way Hwang manipulates discourses of truth and authenticity, partially through claims of autobiography and possibly also a production design that suggests a kind of Orientalism.

It should be noted that as playwright, Hwang is not responsible for the design work. In the first two New York productions, set designer Tony Straiges created the atmosphere of turn-of-the-century China using three separate pavilions to represent the living spaces of Eng Tieng-Bin's wives. For the Signature production, Neil Patel collapsed the space into one pavilion, with the understanding that the action shifted between multiple rooms in the household. The original Off-Broadway and Broadway productions were lavishly costumed by Martin Pakladinez, and Anita Yavich's colourful period clothing for the Signature production could also be seen as a marker of exoticism.

However, while charges of Orientalism might certainly be levelled, I would like to suggest that there is something different at work here. It is possible to interpret the visual representation of early twentieth-century China, as well as the in-script theatrical devices that the playwright employs, as a manifestation of Hwang's nostalgic desire to make a literary return to a homeland that he feels is essential to his present-day identity. The familiar markers of a China that both playwright and audience members can recognize – even if they have never personally experienced it – function as a kind of theatrical shorthand.

In a 2000 conversation with former *New York Times* lead critic Frank Rich, Hwang spoke about his incorporation of Asian stage devices in his plays as a means of 'consciously trying to find an Asian American form'.[33] This desire to reference Asia through such visual devices is tied directly to Hwang's ambition to find a theatrical vocabulary that can serve as a direct tribute to his Asian heritage. It is also a clear example of what Boym calls reflective nostalgia, using a cultural past to open up the possibilities for meaning in the present.

Hwang's use of these cultural markers can furthermore be seen as an example of what Dorinne Kondo refers to as 'counter-Orientalisms', defined as 'sites for the production and performance of contestatory wish-images in the form of racial, gender, national, and transnational identities'.[34] In other words, the use of exotic imagery is not in and of itself associated with negative political value. There may be a subversive intervention at play, and the meaning attached to the images is not quite as fixed as it initially appears, as when Andrew decides that Ahn's stories can have a value beyond her wish to reconvert him to Christianity. Considered within the context of the play – in all three of the incarnations discussed here – the representational strategy of showing China as an exotic locale is not so much Orientalist as it is nostalgic. It is a China seen through layers of memory – that of the older Ahn reminiscing about her childhood as well as the older David Henry Hwang looking back at his ten-year-old self's dedication to preserving his family history.

Marita Sturken describes memory as 'a narrative rather than a replica of an experience that can be retrieved and relived'.[35] As such, it may be idealized, distorted and even fictionalized – the very approach that Hwang has taken in converting his grandmother's stories into dramatic material. The play pays homage to family members whose decisions and experiences not only altered their own lives, but also those of all their descendants – including Hwang. In regards to *Golden Child*, the playwright says in an interview:

> I sometimes think of this play as another form of ancestor worship. I'm conjuring up the ghosts of my ancestors in my own mind and trying to reconcile myself to them. I don't know if anything I've written is true. But it allows me to feel that I have a connection to my ancestors, and to try to understand their motivations, so that I feel more able to deal with the next generation.[36]

In this statement, Hwang makes clear that his representations are inextricably bound to his cultural heritage – even if he, himself, is unsure if what he writes is in the most literal sense 'true'. The idea of legacy comes up again, and the wish-image (to borrow Kondo's terminology) that is *Golden Child* attempts to bridge the past and present and move from the specific circumstances of one family's history to a larger cultural representation that invites us to consider our own genealogies and the ways that the choices made by our ancestors continue to shape our futures.

Butterfly and Locust: *Chinglish* and Asian American Theatre in the Transnational Context
Daphne Lei

One of the most historic events in the recent history of Asian American theatre is the success of David Henry Hwang's *Chinglish*. *Chinglish* defies all the bilingual conventions of Asian American theatre and thoroughly integrates a Chinese language into the play.[37] It is a daring attempt whose success depends on a few major assumptions: a new, bilingual (Chinese–English) audience; a sufficient bilingual talent pool for casting; and finally, the competence of a non-Chinese speaker to write a convincing bilingual play. Is the American theatre market ready for such a new adventure? Despite rising Chinese economic power worldwide and a dramatic increase in Chinese immigration to the United States, Chinese Americans constitute slightly over one per cent of the entire US population according to the 2010 US Census.[38] What an audacious undertaking this Tony Award winner committed himself to!

Chinglish premiered at the Goodman Theatre in Chicago in 2011 and soon moved to Broadway before travelling to other cities in the United States. It even crossed the Pacific and participated in the Hong Kong Arts Festival in 2013 after its California performances, with the same cast and set. English and Mandarin Chinese are both spoken interchangeably throughout the play, with translations projected above the stage in supertitle. The bilingual script was published in 2012, which I will discuss in detail below. The play's reception has been generally positive and many audiences cannot stop laughing at the hilarious mistranslations occurring throughout the play.[39]

Asian American theatre represents a relatively small branch of contemporary American theatre, presumably sharing the non-mainstream 'ethnic' space with African American theatre and Latino theatre. However, the general language (spoken and written) for Asian American theatre is standard English or what is generally considered 'white' English. In the history of Asian American theatre, issues of bilingualism and translation are rarely addressed. The most extensive use of an Asian language in the genre is probably seen in the Genny Lim classic, *Paper Angels*, in which the plight of Chinese immigrants at Angel Island in the early twentieth century is dramatized with bilingual dialogue, especially in the scenes where interviews/interrogations take place. A Chinese immigrant (Cantonese speaker), an American immigration officer (English speaker) and a translator (speaker of both Cantonese and English) together create memorable scenes of Cantonese–English interaction and translation. However, one of the most theatrical moments is when the sad news about a protagonist's suicide is delivered, which is done entirely in Cantonese, without any English translation. The ingenious use of an alien language without translation at a moment of desperation demonstrates that humanity needs no translation onstage.[40] However, this bilingual trend has not continued as Asian American theatre further develops and matures. In most cases, while a small number of Asian words or Asian accents may be incorporated into a play, they symbolize a more general Asian heritage or represent bilingualism or biculturalism in a broader sense; they usually function in a decorative manner and do not alter the syntax or grammar of the play as Suzan-Lori Parks's writing does.

Moreover, such Asian languages are often adopted by non-native Asian language writers, and delivered by non-native speaking actors for audiences of non-native speakers. In the history of Asian American literature and theatre, this usage of Asian languages has helped construct an imagined 'Asia' and an 'Asianness' with a *nisei* vision.[41] In other words, before the age of globalization, such an imagined Asia could exist without having to prove its authenticity against changing standards from the other side of the Pacific Ocean. In such theatre, Asian authenticity does not matter because it is the unique, hybridized, Asian Americanness that is being celebrated. However, as American readers and audiences increasingly come into contact with Asian cultures and languages, and when 'global citizens' constitute part of the readership and audienceship of Asian American literature and theatre, is this Asian American nation with specific aesthetics and language in jeopardy? What is the path of development for Asian American theatre as it becomes more transnational?

In this chapter, I will analyse *Chinglish* on three levels: first, I situate it in the context of Asian American theatre, especially in the tradition of 'East versus West' or 'Asian versus American'. Second, by paying specific attention to language, I uncover a hidden, post-colonial Hong Kong voice in Hwang's play, one which addresses the complexity of 'Chineseness' at a transnational level. As China increasingly dominates the world's economy, voices from the Chinese periphery are often ignored or even silenced. My reading demonstrates how a bilingual play can function on different levels depending on an audience's linguistic cognition. Finally, on a meta-theatrical level, I analyse the binary of 'Asian American theatre versus mainstream theatre' in American multicultural discourse, which I compare with the 'Chinese periphery versus Chinese centre' binary in the irreversible trend of globalization. How does Asian American theatre maintain its local and cultural distinctiveness without being either consumed by the mainstream or tokenized as a permanent, underrepresented minority? As the provincial city in *Chinglish* daringly engages an American business without the central government's approval, Asian American theatre might also bypass American mainstream theatre and institutional multiculturalism by connecting at the transnational level. Although *Chinglish* did have its shining moment on Broadway and in major regional theatres, it is its overseas adventures that have given the play a new significance. These transnational connections represent a new direction that Asian American theatre might consider taking in order to make the genre more sustainable in an increasingly globalized world: instead of the vertical 'local to national' or 'minority to mainstream' approach, Asian American theatre might consider a horizontal 'local to transnational' approach. The vertical approach for Asian American theatre is less likely to be successful because of the relatively small Asian American population; an alternative survival tactic would be surrendering to the static rhetoric of institutionalized multiculturalism, of 'separate but equal'. On the other hand, the horizontal approach to create transnational alliances would ensure a continuous and vibrant supply of 'Asianness' for the genre.

A New Butterfly Syndrome

The story of *Chinglish* centres on the intercultural and international adventures of an American businessman from Ohio named Daniel Cavanaugh. In order to save his family business, a signage company in Cleveland, he hopes to land a contract with a provincial Chinese government to translate the signs of the new cultural centre into English. In attempting to do so, he must communicate with Chinese communist officials with the aid of a translator, and when translators are not available, he has to rely on his own 'Chinglish'. After some backdoor wheeling and dealing, political scandals and illicit extramarital affairs, the American businessman learns to manipulate the system and discovers a perfect niche for developing his business in China.

The play begins with a PowerPoint presentation. Daniel, after his success in China, is invited by the Commerce League of Ohio to give a lecture to American businessmen who are interested in opportunities in China. The slides show examples of mistranslated signs. For example: when the Chinese on a sign shows 注意安全坡道路滑, the English translation reads: 'To Take Notice of Safe: The Slippery Are Very Crafty'. Daniel explains: 'The proper translation should be: "Slippery Slopes Ahead"'.

While the translation is not perfect, it nevertheless captures its central message, expressing safety concerns about a slippery road. The next slide provides an even more hilarious example of mistranslation. The sign, '干货计价处', is translated into 'Fuck the Certain Price of Goods'.

Daniel explains the confusion between 'Fuck the Certain Price of Goods' (mistranslation) and 'Dry Goods Pricing Department' (original meaning):

> You see, after the Communist government came to power, Chairman Mao ordered that the centuries-old system of writing Chinese characters – beautiful, arcane, devilishly complicated – be simplified for the 'masses' – or, as we would call them today, 'consumers'. In so doing, the ideographs for 'dry' and 'to do' were merged. And 'to do' is also slang for, well, to 'do' someone. Once you know that, it all makes sense. (7–8)

Two minutes into the play, the arrogant and successful American businessman has given the audience an in-your-face criticism of the Chinese communist system. He also lays down the golden rule:

> The first rule of doing business in China is also the last. Assuming you are an American. Because, if you are American, it is also safe to assume that you do not speak a single fucking foreign language. If you take away nothing else from our talk today, remember this. Write it down.
> (*Pause.*)
> When doing business in China, always bring your own translator. (8)

After the brief scene, which helps frame the play, *Chinglish* is told through flashbacks, moving from Daniel's first meeting with a bilingual British expatriate named Peter Timms (scene 2) and his awkward meeting with Chinese officials and translators (scene 3), through an illicit affair with Xi (the vice minister of culture) to his eventual understanding of the Chinese system (scenes 4, 6, 8, 10, 11). Daniel grows from a naive, 'honest', 'good man' to Xi's crafty accomplice and a very successful businessman (59).[42] The entire play – except for the brief beginning and ending slide presentations at the business meeting – takes place in Guiyang, a southern provincial city that is trying to establish its local identity with a newly built cultural centre. A few types of Chinese are presented in the play: government officials who are either loud and vulgar (minister) or cold and arrogant (judge and vice minister), awkward and clumsy translators and cartoon-like passers-by (ill-mannered waitress, American-pop-music-inflicted youngster, spy-on-your-neighbour type of hotel manager). The Chinese protagonist – the Vice Minister Xi, who seduces Daniel for her own romantic 'escape' but refuses his love – helps the American with the business deal that eventually leads to political gain for her husband. In other words, most Chinese in this play are not very pleasant characters: their mannerisms are cold, awkward or vulgar; their personalities are crafty, manipulative and power-thirsty.

The beautiful, cunning and powerful Xi can be seen as a reincarnation of Song Liling from *M. Butterfly*, Hwang's Tony Award-winning classic. In *M. Butterfly*, the disguised diva Song successfully seduces the French diplomat Gallimard, mainly because of Song's excellent 'performance', playing into and against the old butterfly stereotype. Song is both a demure, beautiful Oriental woman who always submits to her Western man and a defiant nationalist from the new China who accuses the West of an 'international rape mentality towards the East': 'Her mouth says no, but her eyes say yes.'[43] We see similar dynamics in *Chinglish*. In scene 3, Daniel lays out all the examples of ridiculous English mistranslations he has encountered in China to demonstrate an urgent need for Western intervention. Xi then levels the playing field by pointing out some equally stupid Western mistakes in using Chinese and reminds the two westerners who the real boss is in this transnational business transaction: 'My point is, we must not be so quick to turn to foreigners to solve our nation's problems' (28–32). Later in the play, she also expresses her ultimate distrust for westerners: 'Westerners have always fed us lies. That's why I'm a Chinese Nationalist. … But soon, it will be our turn to use you! What come around, go around! … One day, China will be strong!' (78). Daniel, initially as duped as the butterfly-seeking French diplomat Gallimard, wises up by the play's end and becomes a successful global businessman.

If this is a play that marks a significant transition from the traditional Asian American family drama to a transnational level by setting the location in China and by using a Chinese language extensively, one might ask: why are most Chinese characters in this play *not* portrayed in a more sympathetic light, given *Chinglish* regularly critiques both the Chinese government and the Chinese themselves? In addition to Daniel's direct criticism of the communist reforms in the beginning of the play, Peter, an English teacher from the United Kingdom, also expresses critical views of the Chinese government:

> Business in China is built on relationships [*guanxi*]. … Western economists have held that a fair and consistent legal system – with predictable outcomes – is necessary for solid economic growth. … But, here in China, the legal system is a joke. No one expects justice.

> And yet, Chinese have maintained consistent growth over decades, at levels the West can only dream about. ... People here know roughly what to expect. The trick is to understand that all these outcomes take place *outside* the formal justice system. (9)

The *guanxi* (personal relationships) Peter references, as well as the practice of 'entering through the back door' (pulling strings or using personal connection to make a deal), are presented as the only keys to success in this lawless China. Business success, even when achieved by illegal means, is highly valued. When Daniel mentions that he has worked at Enron, it surprisingly impresses everyone: 'He's among the masterminds of the world-famous scandal!' Daniel explains he was only a salesman selling security, but through a mistranslation, Daniel 'sold customers the belief that they were secure'. Xi takes this opportunity to further exaggerate his connection with Enron: 'He was a top salesman! Responsible for eleven billion dollars of stock', and 'a chief architect of the disaster!' Finally, it is the anti-American Chinese nationalism that ultimately puts Daniel on the throne: 'The biggest financial collapse in American history! There have been many larger ones since', Daniel proudly claims, 'But we were the first!' (93–99).

Perhaps the negative portrayal of the Chinese represents a new view from the West in an age of Chinese economic dominance. The West, represented by a single American and a single Briton, is the minority in the play. The paths these two travel are opposite: Peter starts as a Chinese expert favoured by high officials but becomes disillusioned about the system after finding out that Daniel has excluded him from his 'back door' deal with Xi. Daniel, on the other hand, starts as a desperate businessman clueless about the Chinese system and learns to climb the social ladder through Xi. Peter's social descent crosses paths with Daniel's ascent as the former rants about the behaviour of Xi and Daniel:

> That's a lie! Like all the other lies in the country! 'Socialism with Chinese characteristics'. What does that even mean? And here is the biggest lie of all! China is a socialist state, run for the benefit of the people? What a load of crap! Party officials are criminals, who should all be in jail! (87–88)

Peter's and Daniel's opposite paths also parallel the political destinies of the minister and vice minister. By employing Daniel, the vice minister successfully secures her own and her husband's political career by seizing power from the minister, who is condemned as a 'corrupt official' and sentenced to jail time (115). After this public rant, along with the minister's fall, Peter no longer has a chance in China, a country he has lived in for nineteen years and loves as his own. The opposite outcomes for the two westerners seems to suggest that in a country where 'everything now has to make money' (*xiang qian kan*) integrity and honesty have no value at all (55).[44] It also indicates a change in the East/West power relation over the past twenty years: Westerners have lost the inherent advantage of simply being Western; they now have to play by Chinese rules if they want to succeed in China. Although both Peter and Daniel come to China voluntarily, an 'evil' and irresistible vortex seems to consume the integrity of its Western visitors. In order to survive and thrive in China, one has to be contaminated (although it is admittedly a voluntary contamination).

Despite all the negative portrayals, China nevertheless is presented as the ultimate winner in the East/West interaction. With the East/West conflict of *M. Butterfly* in mind, one can easily read *Chinglish* as a statement on the triumph of Chinese nationalism over the old Western imperialism, a 'revenge' that is long overdue after the Opium Wars. Gallimard is duped but Daniel is an accomplice; Gallimard starts in a privileged position (and falls), while Daniel is willing to submit almost unconditionally (and succeeds) – the transformation of the western characters in the history of Asian American theatre over the past two decades not only corresponds to a change in the global economic and political climate but also indicates the rising significance of Asian populations within the United States. However, today's 'Chinese' situation is much more complicated than a simple 'East versus West' binary. With deeper analysis of the specific languages and political situations in Chinese regions, I propose to take a transnational approach and to read the play as an allegory of today's Hong Kong/China situation.

Post-colonial, Anti-Locust Rhetoric

The literary tradition of Frank Chin and Maxine Hong Kingston, a tradition that has bred many Asian American playwrights like David Henry Hwang, is hardly a bilingual one. Hwang never hides his incompetence in speaking Chinese and he jokingly compares learning Chinese to quitting smoking: after a few tries, he finally gave up.[45] Working with a translator, a Hong Kong native and writer named Candace Mui Ngam Chong (莊梅岩), Hwang was able to 'write a little more deeply about China without actually knowing Chinese. And to write a bilingual play without being bilingual'.[46] *Chinglish* is not only a bilingual play about Chinese–English translation; it tackles much more complex *Chinese* problems by using translation both as a metaphor and a dramatic device, and my focus here is on the post-colonial Hong Kong perspective.

The award-winning playwright Candace Mui Ngam Chong, who received her theatre training both in Hong Kong and in the United Kingdom and has lived in New York for a year, is one of the most respected young Hong Kong playwrights today. Her works often focus on social justice issues, such as media censorship (*Wild Boar*, 2012) and religion and morality (*The French Kiss*, 2006).[47] Much more than a language translator, in creating the script of *Chinglish*, Chong also functioned as a cultural interpreter with a specific post-colonial sensibility unique to Hong Kong. Having examined *Chinglish* in the context of Asian American theatre (particularly with regard to themes of Asian versus American and Chinese versus English), I will now investigate the intricacy and complexity of the Chinese languages (both spoken and written) presented in the play. By doing so, my analysis of *Chinglish* engages both the local Hong Kong and transnational contexts in the new millennium.

In the play's opening scene, Daniel explains the two types of Chinese writing systems: 'the centuries-old system of writing Chinese characters – beautiful, arcane, devilishly complicated' was 'simplified for the "masses"' under the new communist regime (8). There is an undertone of resentment, mockery and cynicism in this statement. While this political act significantly increased the literacy rate in the rural population in the new China, the 'dry goods/fuck goods' joke nevertheless reveals an elitist view of the 'peasant' China. Why is it necessary to explain the differences between the old and new writing systems since the act took place over half a century ago? Indeed, among the numerous mistranslation jokes in the play, this 'dry goods/fuck goods' confusion is the only one concerning the writing system and the only one giving a reason for mistranslation. It is very unlikely that Daniel (and certainly not Hwang) has extensive knowledge about Chinese writing systems; it is equally unthinkable that a majority of American audiences would care about the intricate differences between two Chinese writing systems. If Hwang, then, lacked knowledge and had little motivation to include such a discussion, why was it in the play?

I propose to read this vulgar joke as representative of Candace Chong's intervention in the pan-Chinese situation today. A little contemporary history of the Chinese nations is necessary here. 'Chinese nations' refer to several 'Chinese' regions: Mainland China (PRC: People's Republic of China, the communist nation established in 1949), Taiwan (ROC: Republic of China, whose democratic regime was first established in China in 1912 and moved to Taiwan in 1949; it is a nation not recognized by the United Nations), Hong Kong (a post-colonial state from the United Kingdom and special administrative region [SAR] under the PRC since 1997), and Macau (a post-colonial state from Portugal and an SAR under the PRC since 1999). While the inhabitants of these regions are largely of the Han ethnicity, their culture, politics, economics and languages are very different. While the English word 'Chinese' refers to a vague pan-Chinese ethnicity and language, or rather, an imagined unity of Chineseness, it does not correspond to local identities such as Hong Konger (*xianggang ren*) or Taiwanese (*Taiwan ren*), both of which are aligned with particular political, cultural, linguistic and ideological identities. Similarly, the notion of 'Asianness' and 'Americanness' evoked by the early Asian American playwrights often implies fixed and uniform identities. By investigating the complexity of 'Chinese', 'Chineseness' and 'Chinese language', I hope to offer an alternative reading of *Chinglish* that indicates a new strategy in creating Asian American plays in the age of globalization.

Hong Kong, a small Chinese nation of about seven million, has a complicated political history. The small fishing village became part of the British colonial empire after the first Opium War (1842).[48] During the century-long colonization that followed, Hong Kong became one of the most westernized and affluent Chinese cities and a very important centre for world finance and the entertainment industry in Asia. Except for the period of Japanese occupation (1941–5) during the Second World War, Hong Kong was able to grow in peace and prosperity for over a century. Meanwhile, the Chinese mainland was going through political turmoil as it changed from the imperial Qing dynasty (1644–1911), went through a brief era as a republic (1912–49) and finally became a communist nation (1949). One can imagine the anxiety of Hong Kongers, who had been breathing the air of freedom and capitalism until 1997, when Hong Kong was 'returned' to China, an unfamiliar 'motherland' for most Hong Kongers. Even though the Basic Law stipulated that the status quo of Hong Kong would be maintained for fifty years after the transfer, large emigration expressed Hong Kongers' 'vote of no confidence' for the communist regime.[49] Language was another important issue during the transition: since Hong Kong was under British control when the new China was established, Hong Kongers retained (and still maintain) their local Cantonese spoken language and traditional Chinese writing system.

Hong Kong's economic superiority, along with its anxiety over the prospect of being ruled by an authoritarian regime after the Basic Law expires, defines the complex Hong Kong identity today. Hong Kong's dissatisfaction with censorship, corruption and the backdoor policy of the Chinese government is commented on by the westerners in *Chinglish*, as referenced above. The uncouth behaviour of minor Chinese characters and the loudness of the minister are a contrast to the civilized westerners and the cold but elegant vice minister, who has received a little bit of English education abroad (in Sri Lanka, another former British colony). One can easily draw an analogy between Sri Lanka, an island located near the southeastern tip of the Indian subcontinent and nicknamed the 'Pearl of the Indian Ocean', and Hong Kong, located at the southeastern tip of Mainland China and known as the 'Pearl of the East'. Hong Kong's superiority is subtly referenced in Xi's Sri Lanka experience. While the westerners seem to inevitably become corrupt in China, certain Chinese are more refined than the mass because of their English education abroad.

Recent anti-Chinese sentiment in Hong Kong can be traced back to the Tiananmen Incident in 1989. The government's violent crackdown on student protesters aggravated the anxiety of Hong Kongers about the impending 1997 takeover. Ever since the incident, on every 4 June (the date of the Tiananmen crackdown), tens of thousands of Hong Kongers take to the streets to protest against the authoritarian regime in Beijing and advocate for autonomy and democracy in Hong Kong. The most recent 'Umbrella Revolution' (or Umbrella Movement), a protest and occupy movement by Hong Kong students in a number of business regions in Hong Kong, was a loud and clear statement and an appeal to the Chinese government for universal suffrage. Although the revolution was unfortunately short-lived (September to December 2014), and like Tiananmen did not result in any concrete political change, it nevertheless represented a significant and unique contemporary Hong Kong voice.[50] As the world watched young people passionately and peacefully express their longing for liberty and democracy on the Hong Kong streets, everyone was reminded of the bloodshed in the Tiananmen Square in 1989.

In addition, a new rhetoric, adopting the derogatory term 'locust' to refer to mainland Chinese, has recently become another anti-Chinese force in Hong Kong. In 2013, studies showed that anti-Chinese (mainland Chinese) sentiment had reached a record high in Hong Kong, about 35.6 per cent,

Other Critical Perspectives

whereas the sentiment against the Japanese (the traditional 'enemy') was only 14.9 per cent.[51] While the tanks in Tiananmen Square are more than a thousand miles and two decades distant, the ubiquitous 'locusts' have made a serious impact on daily life here and now.[52]

Moreover, Hong Kong, along with Taiwan and Macau, is one of the only Chinese nations in the world today where traditional Chinese characters are used as the standard writing system. Due to the comparatively small number of traditional Chinese character users and the decreasing emphasis on handwriting skills in the digital age, there is a fear among Sinologists that one of the oldest writing systems in the world will be replaced completely by the easier and faster simplified writing system. The effect of such a total elimination of the knowledge of traditional Chinese characters could be devastating since all the ancient texts, as well as modern publications before the 1950s, are in traditional characters. The precarious future of the old writing system has caused the Taiwanese government to set up a taskforce to preserve the writing system, with the intention of applying for UNESCO 'world heritage' status. However, Taiwan, which has the largest population of traditional Chinese character users, is unfortunately *not* recognized by the United Nation as a nation-state.[53] Hong Kong and Macau, on the other hand, will not be able to defend their writing system once the Basic Law expires (in 2047 and 2049, respectively). Perhaps the urgent mission of convincing UNESCO to preserve the endangered ancient writing system can only be successful as a joint venture of Hong Kong and American writers, so that the 'beautiful, arcane, devilishly complicated' writing system can be saved. And perhaps, with enough understanding of both writing systems among all Chinese speakers, such 'fuck/dry' type of misunderstanding can be largely avoided.

The bilingual script of *Chinglish* – published by Theatre Communications Group (TCG), one of the most important companies for script publication in the United States – contains English, traditional Chinese characters and romanization of the Chinese characters in *pinyin* (the current standard romanization system in China). When Mandarin Chinese is spoken, the script shows the *pinyin*, which indicates the sound of the Chinese line, the traditional Chinese characters and then the English translation. Below is an example, taken from the scene when Xi points out the westerners' misuse of Chinese on their clothing:

Xi: Hàn shān shàng xǐe zhe 「wǒ biàn tài」．
汗衫上寫著「我變態」。
T-shirts reading: 'I am pervert'. (29)

163

Examples like this appear throughout the script, making it nearly impossible to read all three types of writing and to fully enjoy the flow of the script. Indeed, I would argue that the inclusion of the Chinese characters and *pinyin* are not for the sake of reading, particularly since the targeted readers for TCG publication are not Hong Kongers or Taiwanese. Rather, it is a gesture of support for the struggle of Hong Kongers and the Taiwanese to preserve their linguistic heritage and functions to literally preserve in print the traditional Chinese writing system.[54]

On stage, translation happens both in dialogue and in supertitles. Other than providing translation for non-Chinese speaking audiences, the supertitles have an additional function, according to Hwang. Many aspects of Chinese official lives, like the obsession of *guanxi* and entering through the backdoor, have made truth less transparent. The translated supertitles, along with the language both spoken and mistranslated by the characters, provide different aspects of the same 'truth'. In Hwang's mind, this is intended 'to make transparent what is normally hidden to outsiders'.[55] Translations and mistranslations can both function as subtext for the main text that is spoken by the characters.

Meta-theatrical Parallelism

The collaboration of a Hong Kong and an Asian American writer provides an opportunity to read *Chinglish* at a meta-theatrical level. Even though the play takes place in China and contains no Hong Kong characters, Hwang claims that 'Hong Kongers are the best audience for *Chinglish*' because 'Hong Kongers understand best the absurdity of Chinese society and the difficulties of foreign businessmen'.[56] Indeed, the performance was very well received in Hong Kong: audiences smiled at Peter's observation that 'the legal system is a joke', and when he finished ranting – 'And here is the biggest lie of all! China is a socialist state, run for the benefit of the people? What a load of crap!' – the audience gave a very enthusiastic ovation. Hwang says: 'This could not have happened in New York, because they had no idea of the absurdity of the sentence; the applause in Hong Kong audience is full of resonance.'[57]

Candace Chong speaks of an incident in 2010, when a small theatre company received threatening phone calls about their performance dealing with the Tiananmen Incident. She was troubled by the news but also glad to know that China's Great Firewall had not intervened much locally. In 2012, she wrote *Wild Boar* to comment on media censorship.[58] Hwang, referencing *Chinglish*, has also spoken on censorship: 'The fact that this play can be staged here is the best proof of Hong Kong's freedom of speech! Why is Hong Kong important? At least up till now, Hong Kong still have [sic] the freedom of news media, and creative arts are not under censorship.'[59] Despite his reputation as the best-known Chinese American playwright, Hwang has not been able to bring his signature piece, *M. Butterfly*, to China because China has completely denied the spying incident that forms the play's central narrative. The political situation in *Chinglish* also makes it impossible to perform in China.[60] Ultimately, Hwang believes that Hong Kong plays an important cultural role for China: 'China has been working very hard to raise the cultural soft power, but it also executes severe censorship. These two (cultural soft power and censorship) are exactly the opposite.'[61]

The producer Lily Fan, who was born in Hong Kong, has expressed hope that the Hong Kong performance would serve as a 'launch pad', and more production partners would be willing to take the play to other free Chinese regions. Future touring destinations under consideration include Taiwan, Singapore, Southeast Asian countries, Australia and Canada. Additionally, the West End, Boston and Houston are possibilities, given they are places where many ethnic Chinese reside in different political and cultural systems and where laughing at the ridiculous *guanxi* and backdoor policy is possible. Leigh Silverman, the director of the California and Hong Kong productions, acknowledges the slim possibility of *Chinglish* being performed in China, but observes that 'there remain places like Macau and Singapore'.[62]

Lily Fan and Leigh Silverman's hopes speak to a discourse that is largely unknown to the non-Chinese world: the Chinese centre versus Chinese periphery. While the China centre holds the political, economic and military power, the Chinese periphery (Taiwan, Hong Kong and many other 'free Chinese regions', including the worldwide Chinese diaspora), which possesses rich cultural and artistic soft power, sometimes forms alliances among the different regions to both counterbalance the central power and to assert local 'Chinese' identities that are often in danger.[63] This 'centre versus periphery' situation parallels the 'mainstream versus ethnic' theatre culture in the United States. Asian American theatre is under constant threat of either being consumed by the commercialism of American mainstream theatre or tokenized as a cultural or ethnic icon on the margin. By working closely with Chong, Hwang was able to start a new chapter in his writing career with the prospect of a comprehensive international tour to 'free Chinese regions'; their transnational collaboration has also pointed to a possible strategy for future Asian American writers coping with the irreversible forces of globalization.

Conclusion

Through Candace Chong, David Henry Hwang has written a play that goes beyond the traditional Asian American context and explores the complexity of multi-layered Chineseness; through David Henry Hwang, Candace Chong has made a marginalized Hong Kong voice heard on the American stage. Similar to *M. Butterfly*, *Chinglish* deals with cultural conflict and the negotiation of power in East/West interactions. For general American audiences, and Asian American audiences in particular, this old theme, along with the new jokes, is sufficient for American box-office success. The sharp-tongued vice minister and the dramatic Chinese 'victory' are the new Butterfly syndrome that breaks the Asian American stereotype of the complacent, model minority. The descent of Peter and the ascent of Daniel in *Chinglish* also reflect the changing role of China as an increasingly important political and economic global player. By analysing the Chinese writing system, Candace Chong's intervention and the Hong Kong tour, readings of *Chinglish* may function on a much more complex transnational level. Such readings also suggest a transnational alliance among Chinese peripheral regions to counterbalance the Chinese central power and to preserve distinctive local 'Chinese' identities.

In an increasingly borderless world, it would be hypocritical to insist that Asian American theatre remains an ethnic theatre within American institutionalized multiculturalism; on the other hand, by taking a non-ethnic road, this small genre could easily be swallowed by the neoliberal market forces of commercialized theatres. The vice minister engages the American to win her political struggle; Hwang transcends the borders of American multiculturalism by creating a bilingual play with a Hong Kong connection; Chong stages a protest from the Chinese periphery against the centre. All these transnational tactics show that the dramaturgy of Hwang and Chong simultaneously targets both domestic and transnational audiences and proposes a new direction for Asian American playwrights, as well as a new way that contemporary Asian voices can be heard in non-diasporic contexts. From the Orientalized butterfly to anti-locust rhetoric, Asian American theatre has gone beyond small ethnic community theatre and expanded the scope of traditional ethnic theatre, functioning as a global player on the international stage.

CHRONOLOGY

1957 David Henry Hwang is born on 11 August in Los Angeles, California to Henry Yuan Hwang, a banker, and Dorothy Hwang, a pianist. He is the oldest of three children and has two sisters. He grows up in San Gabriel, a suburb of Los Angeles.

1975 Hwang graduates from the Harvard School, an elite preparatory academy in Los Angeles. He is recognized for his oratory skills in the debate team. (He attended San Gabriel High School for three years and was recruited by Harvard School for his senior year to join their debate team.)

Hwang enrols as a freshman at Stanford University.

1976 During his freshman year at Stanford, Hwang watches Thornton Wilder's *The Matchmaker* at the American Conservatory Theatre and decides to pursue playwriting. He studies with John L'Heureux, a professor of creative writing at Stanford, and the two design a playwriting major within the Creative Writing Department.

1977 In the summer, Hwang interns at the East West Players in Los Angeles and watches a workshop of Frank Chin's *Gee Pop!*.

1978 Hwang attends the Padua Hills Playwriting Festival workshop where he works with Sam Shepard and María Irene Fornés.

1979 *FOB* is produced at the Junipero House (later renamed Okada House) dormitory at Stanford University.

Hwang graduates from Stanford University with a bachelor's degree in English.

In June, *FOB* is selected for the Eugene O'Neill Playwriting Festival and is produced at the National Playwrights Conference. The production is directed by Robert Alan Ackerman who encourages Hwang to include fight choreography from traditional Chinese opera.

Chronology

1980   Hwang teaches writing at Menlo Atherton High School.

FOB is produced at the Joseph Papp Public Theater/New York Shakespeare Festival (hereafter Public Theater). The production is directed by Mako (who was at the time artistic director of the East West Players).

From fall of 1980 to spring of 1981, Hwang attends the Yale School of Drama to study theatre history. He leaves the programme without graduating.

1981   Hwang receives his first Obie Award for Best Play for *FOB*.

The Dance and the Railroad commissioned by the New Federal Theatre under a grant from the U.S. Department of Education and opens in March at the New Federal Theatre. In July, the play opens at the Public Theater.

On 18 October, *Family Devotions* opens at the Public Theater.

1983   *The House of Sleeping Beauties* and *The Sound of a Voice* are produced together as 'Sound and Beauty', which opens on 6 November at the Public Theater.

Hwang receives a Rockefeller Fellowship.

1984   Hwang receives a Guggenheim Fellowship.

1985   In September, Hwang marries Ophelia Chong, a Chinese Canadian artist.

Hwang receives a National Endowment for the Arts Fellowship.

The television movie 'Blind Alleys', co-written by Hwang and Frederic Kimball and starring Cloris Leachman and Pat Morita, airs on Metromedia in Boston.

1986   On 16 February, *As the Crow Flies* opens on a double bill with *The Sound of a Voice* at the Los Angeles Theatre Centre.

On 21 April, *Rich Relations* opens at The Second Stage in New York City.

1988   On 10 February, *M. Butterfly* has a world premiere at the National Theatre in Washington D.C.

On 20 March, *M. Butterfly* opens at the Eugene O'Neill Theatre on Broadway and runs for 777 performances; the play receives the

Tony Award for Best Play, the Drama Desk Award and the Outer Critics Circle Award for Best Play; it is also nominated for the Pulitzer Prize in Drama.

On 15 July, *1000 Airplanes on the Roof,* a science fiction music drama composed by Phillip Glass with libretto by Hwang opens in at the Hangar #3 of the Vienna Airport in Austria.

1989 Hwang's marriage with Ophelia Chong is dissolved.

On 10 February, *M. Butterfly* opens at the Shaftsbury Theatre on the West End in London.

1990 In May, *FOB*, directed by Hwang, opens at Pan Asian Repertory in New York City.

1992 On 1 March, *Bondage* opens at the Actors Theatre of Louisville as part of the 16th Annual Humana Festival of New American Plays in Louisville, Kentucky.

On 12 October, *The Voyage*, an opera composed by Philip Glass with libretto by Hwang opens at the Metropolitan Opera House in New York, which commissioned it.

1993 In February, *Face Value* opens as a pre-Broadway tryout at the Colonial Theatre in Boston. Previews are presented at the Cort Theatre on Broadway in March and closes after eight performances.

On 1 October, the film version of *M. Butterfly* directed by David Cronenberg with the screenplay by Hwang and starring Jeremy Irons and John Lone is released.

Hwang marries Kathryn A. Layng, an actress.

1994 The film *Golden Gate* with the original screenplay written by Hwang is released.

'Solo', a song written by Prince with Hwang, is released on Prince's album *Come*.

1996 Hwang's son, Noah, is born.

On 29 March, *Trying to Find Chinatown*, a one-act play, premieres as part of the Actors Theatre of Louisville's Humana Festival.

Hwang writes *Bang Kok*, a one-act play, as part of *Pieces of the Quilt*, a show conceived by Sean San Jose.

Chronology

On 17 November, *Golden Child*, premieres at the Public Theater. Hwang receives his second Obie Award for the play.

1997 On 11 January, *Golden Child* has its West Coast premiere at the South Coast Repertory, which commissioned the play, in co-production with the John F. Kenney Centre for the Performing Arts. The play opens at the Kennedy Centre on 1 March.

Hwang writes the libretto for *The Silver River*, an American chamber opera composed by Bright Sheng. On 27 July, the opera premieres at the Santa Fe, New Mexico Chamber Music Festival.

1998 Hwang is commissioned to write an adaptation of Henrik Ibsen's *Peer Gynt* by Trinity Repertory Company in Providence, Rhode Island. The play opens at the company on 3 February.

On 2 April, *Golden Child* opens at the Longacre Theatre on Broadway. The production receives the Tony Award nomination for Best Play.

1999 Hwang writes *Merchandising* for the Actors Theatre of Louisville's Humana Festival as part of its 'T(ext) Shirt Plays'.

2000 On 23 March, *Aida*, a musical by Elton John and Tim Rice with the book co-written by Hwang opens at the Palace Theater on Broadway. It has 1852 performances and receives four Tony Awards (including actress Heather Headley and John and Rice for Best Original Score).

2000 Hwang's daughter, Eva, is born.

In March, 'The Lost Empire', a television mini-series written by Hwang airs on NBC.

On 14 October, Hwang's adaptation of *Flower Drum Song* by Richard Rodgers and Oscar Hammerstein II opens at the Mark Taper Forum in Los Angeles.

In November, *Jade Flowerpots and Bound Feet* premieres at the Public Theater as part of *The Square*, a set of plays conceived by Lisa Peterson and Chay Yew.

2002 The film *Possession*, co-written by Hwang, is released.

On 17 October, Hwang's adaptation of *Flower Drum Song* opens at the Virginia Theatre on Broadway. He receives his third Tony nomination for Best Book of a Musical.

2003 On 24 May, *The Sound of a Voice*, an opera composed by Philip Glass and libretto by Hwang, opens at the American Repertory Theatre.

2004 Hwang adapts Peter Sis' *Tibet Through the Red Box* for the Seattle Children's Theatre, where it premieres on 30 January.

2005 Hwang writes the Spanish-language libretto for *Ainadamar* (*Fountain of Tears* in Arabic), an opera composed by Osvaldo Golijov. It opens on 30 July. In 2007, it receives two 2007 Grammy Awards for Best Opera Recording and Best Classical Composition.

In October, Hwang's father, Henry Y. Hwang, dies of colon cancer.

2006 Hwang writes the book for Disney's *Tarzan* with music and lyrics by Phil Collins. On 10 May, the musical opens at the Richard Rodgers Theatre on Broadway.

2007 Hwang writes *The Great Helmsman* as part of *Ten*, a production of short plays directed by Lloyd Suh. The play premieres on 30 April at the Public Theatre.

In May, *Yellow Face* premieres at the Centre Theatre Group/Mark Taper Forum in co-production with the East West Players in Los Angeles.

On 30 June, *Alice in Wonderland*, an opera by the composer Unsuk Chin with the English libretto by Hwang, premieres at the Bavarian State opera as part of the 2007 Munich Opera Festival.

In December, *Yellow Face* transfers to the Public Theatre. Hwang receives his third Obie Award for the play. The play is selected as a finalist for the Pulitzer Prize in 2008 and becomes Hwang's second play to receive the honour.

2008 On 2 July, *The Fly*, an opera by the composer Howard Shore with a libretto by Hwang premieres at the Théâtre du Châtelet in Paris, France.

Chronology

2010 On 8 March, *A Very DNA Reunion* premieres as part of *The DNA Trail: A Genealogy of Short Plays About Ancestry, Identity, and Confusions*, a production of short plays produced by the Silk Road Theatre Project (later renamed Silk Road Rising).

On 6 June, *Icarus at the Edge of Time*, a multi-media presentation composed by Philip Glass and co-written by Hwang, premieres at the World Science Festival.

2011 On 18 June, *Chinglish* premieres at the Goodman Theatre in Chicago. Hwang receives the Joseph Jefferson Award for Best New Work.

Hwang wins the PEN/Laura Pels Award for a Master American Dramatist.

On 28 October, *Chinglish* opens at the Longacre Theatre on Broadway.

2012 Signature Theatre announces Hwang as the playwright in residence for the 2013–14 season.

Hwang wins the Inge Award for Distinguished Achievement in the American Theatre.

Hwang wins the Steinberg Distinguished Playwright Award (the 'Mimi').

On 13 November, a revival of *Golden Child* opens at the Signature Theatre.

2013 On 24 March, a revival of *The Dance and the Railroad* opens at the Signature Theatre.

On 9 May, the Signature Theatre revival of *The Dance and the Railroad* opens at the Wuzhen Theatre Festival near Shanghai, marking Hwang's debut in the People's Republic of China.

In June, a film version of *Yellow Face* premieres on YouTube. It is directed and adapted by Jeff Liu and produced by the YOMYOMF Network. It is recognized as the first theatrical play to be produced specifically for YouTube.

On 21 May, *Yellow Face* makes its UK premiere at Park Theatre in Finsbury Park, London.

2014	Hwang receives a Doris Duke Performing Artist Award.
	On 24 February, *Kung Fu*, a play about the life of Bruce Lee, premieres at the Signature Theatre. The choreographer of the show, Sonya Tayeh and Emanuel Brown, the fight director, receive Obie Awards.
	On 5 May, *Yellow Face* transfers to the Royal National Theatre in London.
	On 13 June, *An American Soldier,* a one-act opera by the composer Huang Ruo with libretto by Hwang, opens at the Washington National Opera.
	Hwang is appointed Head of the Playwriting Concentration of the Columbia University School of the Arts Theatre Program.
2015	On 14 January, Hwang receives the Distinguished Artist Award from the International Society of Performing Arts at the New York 2015 Congress.
	Hwang becomes a writer/producer for the Showtime television series, *The Affair*.

NOTES

Introduction

1. Alex Witchel, 'The Man Who Can Make Bruce Lee Talk', *New York Times Magazine* (7 November 2012), http://www.nytimes.com/2012/11/11/magazine/david-henry-hwang-the-man-who-can-make-bruce-lee-talk.html?emc=eta1 (accessed 8 February 2015).
2. William A. Henry III, 'David Henry Hwang: When East and West Collide', *Time* 134, no. 7 (14 August 1989): 62.
3. David Henry Hwang, unpublished interview with Esther Kim Lee, New York City, 15 January 2015.
4. David Henry Hwang, introduction to *FOB and Other Plays* (New York: Plume, 1990), x–xv, xi.
5. Hwang, *FOB and Other Plays*, xv.
6. Hwang, *FOB and Other Plays*, xiii.
7. Hwang, unpublished interview with Esther Kim Lee, New York City, 15 January 2015.
8. Hwang made this observation during our recent interview.
9. For an early history of Asian Americans' protest against the practices of yellowface make-up in the American theatre, see Chapter 1 of Esther Kim Lee, *A History of Asian American Theatre* (New York: Cambridge University Press, 2006), 7–22.
10. W. E. B. Du Bois, *The Souls of Black Folk* (New York: Dover Publications, 1994), 2.
11. Hwang, unpublished interview with Esther Kim Lee, New York City, 15 January 2015.

Chapter 1

1. David Savran, 'David Hwang', in *In Their Own Words: Contemporary American Playwrights* (New York: Theatre Communications Group, 1988), 123.
2. Hwang has made the comment about his inability to get 'lost in the woods' on several occasions. I heard the statement during his answer to a question that followed his keynote address at the Comparative Drama Conference in Baltimore, MD, 5 April 2014.

Notes

3. Josephine Lee, *Performing Asian America: Race and Ethnicity on the Contemporary Stage* (Philadelphia: Temple University Press, 1997), 34.
4. See Maggie Ann Bowers, *Magic(al) Realism* (London: Routledge, 2004) for a historical and theoretical study of magical realism.
5. Salman Rushdie, *Midnight's Children* (London: Picador, 1982), 9, quoted in Bowers, *Magic(al) Realism*, 3.
6. Toby Silverman Zinman, 'Sam Shepard and Super-Realism', *Modern Drama* 29, no. 3 (1986): 423.
7. Savran, 'David Hwang', 122.
8. Hwang, *FOB and Other Plays*, xi.
9. Henry David Hwang, *Trying to Find Chinatown: The Selected Plays* (New York: Theatre Communications Group, 2000), 6.
10. Frank Chin's *Chickencoop Chinaman* premiered in 1972 at the American Place Theatre, and it was the first Asian American play to be produced professionally in New York City. His second play, *Year of the Dragon*, was developed at the Asian American Theatre Workshop, which he founded in San Francisco. For the history of the plays and the Workshop, see my *A History of Asian American Theatre*.
11. Frank Chin, 'The Most Popular Book in China', in *Maxine Hong Kingston's The Woman Warrior: A Casebook*, ed. Sau-Ling Cynthia Wong (New York: Oxford University Press, 1999), 28. The controversy between Kingston and Chin has been extensively documented. See, for example, King-Kok Cheung's essay 'The Woman Warrior versus the Chinaman Pacific: Must a Chinese American Critic Choose between Feminism and Heroism?', in Wong, *Maxine Hong Kingston's The Woman Warrior*, 113–34.
12. Hwang remembers watching a rehearsal, not a fully finished production, of Chin's play in 1977. David Henry Hwang, unpublished interview with Esther Kim Lee, 15 January 2015, New York City.
13. Jennifer 8. Lee, *The Fortune Cookie Chronicles: Adventures in the World of Chinese Food* (New York: Twelve, 2009), 9.
14. Hwang, *FOB and Other Plays*, 8. Subsequent references to this play are given in parentheses.
15. David Henry Hwang, unpublished interview with Esther Kim Lee, 16 March 2000, New York City. Also quoted in Lee, *A History of Asian American Theatre*, 134.
16. Frank Rich, 'Theater: *FOB*, Rites of Immigrant Passage', *New York Times* (10 June 1980): C6.
17. Rich, 'Theater: *FOB*, Rites of Immigrant Passage', C6.
18. See the fifth chapter of Esther Kim Lee, *A History of Asian American Theatre*, 129–37.
19. Josephine Lee, *Performing Asian America*, 178.

Notes

20. Rich, 'Theater: "FOB," Rites of Immigrant Passage', C6.
21. 'David Henry Hwang on *The Dance and the Railroad*', Vimeo video: 25, posted by 'Signature Theatre', 7 January 2013, http://vimeo.com/57018823.
22. Frank Rich, 'Stage: "Dance, Railroad" by David Henry Hwang', *New York Times* (31 March 1981), C5.
23. Hwang, *FOB and Other Plays*, xi–xii.
24. Hwang, *FOB and Other Plays*, xi.
25. In a video recording of the play, the hyper-theatrical scenes are portrayed using different cinematic techniques. The rest of the play takes place on a theatrical stage with cameras filming the action as written in the play, but in the hyper-theatrical scenes, the two characters are in full Cantonese opera costumes and makeup, and appear in what can best be described as an abstract and nondescript film set with a white background. The video was recorded at the Anspacher Theatre on 6 December 1981. See *The Dance and the Railroad*, Emile Ardolino (dir.), ABC Video Enterprises, 1981 (VHS).
26. Savran, 'David Hwang', 120.
27. Hwang, *Trying to Find Chinatown*, 104. Subsequent references to this play are given in parentheses.

Chapter 2

1. Hwang, *FOB and Other Plays*, xii.
2. Savran, *In their Own Words*, 122.
3. Savran, *In their Own Words*, 122.
4. Savran, *In their Own Words*, 21.
5. Frank Rich, '"Sound and Beauty": Two One-Act Plays', *New York Times* (7 November 1983): C13.
6. Yasunari Kawabata, *House of the Sleeping Beauties and Other Stories*, trans. Edward Seidensticker (Tokyo: Kodansha International, 1969), 98.
7. Rich, '"Sound and Beauty": Two One-Act Plays', C13.
8. Hwang, *Trying to Find Chinatown*, 199. Subsequent references to this play are given in parentheses.
9. David Henry Hwang, *The Sound of a Voice*, in *Between Two Worlds: Contemporary Asian American Plays*, ed. Misha Berson (New York: Theatre Communications Group, 1990), 155. Subsequent references to this play are given in parentheses.
10. William C. Boles, *Understanding David Henry Hwang* (Columbia: University of South Carolina Press, 2013), Kindle edition, Kindle location, 884–6.
11. Boles, *Understanding David Henry Hwang*, Kindle location, 892.

Notes

12. David Henry Hwang, *As the Crow Flies*, in *Between Two Worlds: Contemporary Asian American Plays*, ed. Misha Berson (New York: Theatre Communications Group, 1990), 94.
13. Hwang, *As the Crow Flies*, 94.
14. Hwang, *As the Crow Flies*, 100. Subsequent references to this play are given in parentheses.
15. Frank Rich, 'Stage: "Rich Relations," From David Hwang', *New York Times* (22 April 1986): C15.
16. Hwang, *FOB and Other Plays*, xiv.
17. Hwang, *FOB and Other Plays*, xiii.
18. Alexis Soloski, 'David Henry Hwang, Amy Herzog, and Thomas Bradshaw Talk Art, Cash, and Duping Joe Papp: A Playwrights Roundtable', *Village Voice* (19 September 2012), http://www.villagevoice.com/2012-09-19/theater/david-henry-hwang-amy-herzog-and-thomas-bradshaw/ (accessed 8 February 2014). In the full quote, Hwang states, 'It's not that great a play, really. Sometimes you write them and they're not so great and you still need to do them'.
19. Hwang, *FOB and Other Plays*, xiii.
20. Soloski, 'David Henry Hwang'.
21. Hwang, *FOB and Other Plays*, 214. Subsequent references to this play are given in parentheses.

Chapter 3

1. Richard Bernstein, 'France Jails 2 in Odd Case of Espionage', *New York Times* (11 May 1986).
2. For further details on the history of *Madame Butterfly*, see Maria Degabriele, 'From *Madame Butterfly* to *Miss Saigon*: One Hundred Years of Popular Orientalism', *Critical Arts* 10, no. 2 (1996): 105–118.
3. David Henry Hwang, *M. Butterfly* (New York: Plume, 1989), n.p. All subsequent references to this play are given in parentheses.
4. I use the feminine pronoun for Song when Gallimard and the audience see her as a woman. When Song is revealed to be a man, I use the masculine pronoun.
5. James S. Moy, 'David Henry Hwang's *M. Butterfly* and Philip Kan Gotanda's *Yankee Dawg You Die*: Repositioning Chinese American Marginality on the American Stages', *Theatre Journal* 42, no. 1 (1990): 54.
6. David Richards, 'Chinese Puzzle: At the National, a Curious "M. Butterfly"', *Washington Post* (11 February 1988): C1.
7. Bryer, 'David Henry Hwang', 143.
8. Bryer, 'David Henry Hwang', 143.

9. David Henry Hwang, 'My Worst Career Mistakes: Part Three (My Lunch with Neil)', You Offend Me You Offend My Family, 22 April 2010, http://youoffendmeyouoffendmyfamily.com/my-worst-career-mistakes-part-three-my-lunch-with-neil/ (accessed 13 January 2015).
10. Frank Rich, '*M. Butterfly*: A Story of a Strange Love, Conflict and Betrayal', *New York Times* (21 March 1988): C13.
11. Rich, '*M. Butterfly*: A Story of a Strange Love', C13.
12. Michael Finegold, 'Transformational Glamour', *Village Voice* (29 March 1988): 118. Quoted in Karen Shimakawa, 'Who's to say? Or, Making Space for Gender and Ethnicity in *M. Butterfly*', *Theatre Journal* 45, no. 3 (1993): 354.
13. Moy, 'David Henry Hwang's *M. Butterfly*', 53.
14. Moy, 'David Henry Hwang's *M. Butterfly*', 53.
15. Moy, 'David Henry Hwang's *M. Butterfly*', 54.
16. Hwang, *M. Butterfly*, 95.
17. Quoted in Moy, 'David Henry Hwang's *M. Butterfly*', 54. The original quote is from Gerard Raymond, 'Smashing Stereotypes', *Theatre Week* 3, no. 2 (11 April 1988): 8.
18. David Henry Hwang, 'Are Movies Ready for Real Orientals?' *New York Times* (11 August 1985), section 2, p. 1.
19. Hwang, 'Are Movies Ready for Real Orientals?' section 2, p. 1.
20. In Frank Chin's *Year of the Dragon*, the protagonist, Fred Eng, pretends to be a pidgin-speaking 'Chinaman' tour guide in order to cater to white tourists. Philip Kan Gotanda addresses issues of stereotypes in *Yankee Dawg You Die* and *Natalie Wood is Dead*. As for Diana Son, Asian female stereotypes are represented in various forms in *R. A. W. ('Cause I'm a Woman)*.
21. Josephine Lee, *Performing Asian America*, 109.
22. Josephine Lee, *Performing Asian America*, 109.
23. Dorinne Kondo, '*M. Butterfly*: Orientalism, Gender, and a Critique of Essentialist Identity', *Cultural Critique* 16 (1990): 26.
24. Karen Shimakawa, 'Who's to say? Or, Making Space for Gender and Ethnicity in *M. Butterfly*', *Theatre Journal* 45, no. 3 (1993): 362.
25. Gabrielle Cody, 'David Hwang's M. Butterfly: Perpetuating the Misogynist Myth', *Theater* 20, no. 2 (1989): 27.
26. For a review of the London production, see Matt Wolf, 'From Broadway to London, With Some Surprises', *New York Times* (28 May 1989), http://www.nytimes.com/1989/05/28/theater/theater-from-broadway-to-london-with-some-surprises.html (accessed 20 January 2014).
27. For Hwang's recollection of his interaction with David Geffen, see Hwang, 'My Worst Career Mistakes'.
28. Patti Hartigan, 'Hwang's Political Stage; Writer Wonders How Much to Stir the Melting Pot', *Boston Globe* (15 April 1994): 91.

Notes

Chapter 4

1. See Esther Kim Lee's, *A History of Asian American Theatre* for the history of both the beginning of Asian American theatre and the controversy surrounding *Miss Saigon*.
2. Kevin Kelly, 'M. Butterfly, Miss Saigon and Mr. Hwang', *Boston Globe* (9 September 1990): B89.
3. See Dinitia Smith, 'Face Values: The Sexual and Racial Obsessions of Playwright David Henry Hwang', *New York Magazine* (11 January 1993): 45; and Tracie Rozhon, 'Habitats/45 West 67th Street: Exit Actor and Actress, Enter Author and Actress', *New York Times* (24 November 1996), section 9, p. 4.
4. Hwang, *Trying to Find Chinatown*, 253. Subsequent references to this play are given in parentheses.
5. Jon D. Rossini, 'From *M. Butterfly* to *Bondage*: David Henry Hwang's Fantasies of Sexuality, Ethnicity, and Gender', *Journal of American Drama and Theatre* 18, no. 3 (2006): 70.
6. Rossini, 'From *M. Butterfly* to *Bondage*', 71.
7. Michael Grossberg, 'Humana Playwrights Take Relevant Risks', *Columbus Dispatch* (25 March 1992): 8E.
8. *Jungle Fever* is an American film released in 1991. Directed by Spike Lee, it explores interracial relationships between New Yorkers in the 1990s.
9. Bruce Weber, 'On Stage, and Off', *New York Times* (23 October 1992): C2.
10. Boles, *Understanding David Henry Hwang*, Kindle location, 1655–1662.
11. 'Hwang Play Closes After 8 Previews', *New York Times* (16 March 1993), C14.
12. Kevin Kelly, 'Hwang Looks Beyond "Face Value"', *Boston Globe* (17 February 1993): 25.
13. Kelly, 'Hwang Looks Beyond "Face Value"', 25.
14. Boles, *Understanding David Henry Hwang*, Kindle location, 1632–1633.
15. Kelly, 'Hwang Looks Beyond "Face Value"', 25.
16. David Henry Hwang, *Face Value* (unpublished play script, pre-Broadway Boston version), 1. Subsequent references to this play are given in parentheses. This is the version used for the pre-Broadway previews in Boston.
17. Ronald Ebens and Michael Nitz, both white, worked in the Chrysler plant. Vincent Chin was a Chinese American man living in the Detroit area. After a scuffle at a bar, Ebens and Nitz beat Chin with a baseball bat, and Chin died four days later. There was evidence that the incident was a racially motivated hate crime, and the two white men blamed Chin for the Japanese automobiles they believed were causing layoffs in the American auto industry. Despite the gravity of the crime, Ebens and Nitz were sentenced to only three years of probation. The murder of Vincent Chin has since become a rallying point for the Asian American movement. The name Ebens has a particular resonance in the Asian American community, and the murder of Chin is a central part

Notes

of courses offered by Asian American studies departments and programmes on college campuses around the country. Finally, Vincent Chin is mentioned later in the play by Linda. For details of this history, see Chapter 3 in Helen Zia's *Asian American Dreams: The Emergence of an American People* (New York: Farrar, Straus, and Giroux, 2001), 55–81.

18. Kevin Kelly, 'Hwang's "Face Value" Flops on Its Farce', *Boston Globe* (15 February 1993): 31.
19. Hwang, *Trying to Find Chinatown*, 285. Subsequent references to this play are given in parentheses.
20. Holly Harrison, 'Exploring Identity', *Business Times* (Singapore) (26 April 1996): 11.
21. David Henry Hwang, 'Bringing Up "Child"', in *Golden Child* (New York: Theatre Communications Group, 1998), v.
22. Smith, 'Face Values', 45.
23. Smith, 'Face Values', 45.
24. Jan Herman, 'Calendar Section', *Los Angeles Times* (3 November 1996): 6.
25. Hwang, 'Bringing Up "Child"', vi.
26. Hwang, 'Bringing Up "Child"', vi.
27. Laurie Winer, 'Tracing a Family's Past, Future Through Eyes of *Golden Child*', *Los Angeles Times* (10 November 1996): F1.
28. Ben Brantley, 'Extending a hand to Ancestral Ghosts in China', *New York Times* (10 November 1996): C20.
29. Hwang, 'Bringing Up "Child"', viii.
30. Brantley, 'Extending a hand', C20. The Public Theater version has not been published.
31. Steven Drukman, 'Taking Bittersweet Journeys into the past', *New York Times* (10 November 1996), section 2, p. 5.
32. Drukman, 'Taking Bittersweet Journeys into the past', section 2, p. 5.
33. Hwang, *Golden Child*, 20. Subsequent references to this play are given in parentheses.
34. The quote is taken from an interview posted on Signature Theater's website and used for promotional purposes. See 'David Henry Hwang on *Golden Child*', Vimeo video, 2:40-3:10, posted by 'Signature Theater', 3 October 2012, http://vimeo.com/50701816.

Chapter 5

1. Robert Simonson, 'David Henry Hwang to Work on Book for Disney's *Aida*', *Playbill* (7 May 1999), http://www.playbill.com/news/article/david-henry-hwang-to-work-on-book-for-disneys-aida-81767 (accessed 17 March 2015).

Notes

2. Pat Craig, 'Aida Experience: Playwright Hwang Has Newfound Interest in Musicals', Contra Costa Times (2 August 2001): D01.
3. Craig, 'Aida Experience: Playwright Hwang Has Newfound Interest in Musicals', D01.
4. Chris Jones, Variety (13 December 1999): 117.
5. Ben Brantley, 'Broadway And Vine: Ape-Man Hits Town', New York Times (11 May 2006): 11.
6. David Rooney, 'Tarzan', Daily Variety (11 May 2006): 6.
7. Brantley, 'Broadway And Vine: Ape-Man Hits Town', 11.
8. For a descriptive review of The Square, see Dan Bacalzo, 'The Square', Theatre Journal 54, no. 3 (2002): 489–91.
9. David Henry Hwang, Jade Flowerpots and Bound Feet, in Version 3.0: Contemporary Asian American Plays, ed. Chay Yew (New York: Theatre Communications Group, 2011), 574. Subsequent references to this play are given in parentheses.
10. The play and several related videos may be found here: https://www.youtube.com/playlist?list=PLamdUEW_ElS744V7uZY8yqsQCTAa0u0g2.
11. Linda Winer, 'Theater Review', Newsday (10 December 2007), http://www.newsday.com/lifestyle/theater-review-1.532846 (accessed 8 February 2015).
12. Jack Viertel, 'Fun with Race and the Media: An Interview with the Playwright', American Theatre 25, no. 4 (April 2008): 60.
13. 'Yellow peril' is an old but lasting stereotype of Asians as gravely dangerous to the West. For studies on yellow peril, see John Kuo Wei Tchen and Dylan Yeats, Yellow Peril!: An Archive of Anti-Asian Fear (London: Verso, 2014) and Christopher Frayling, The Yellow Peril: Dr. Fu Manchu and the Rise of Chinaphobia (London: Thames & Hudson, 2014).
14. For details regarding how actual names are used, see Dan Bacalzo, 'Yellow Face by David Henry Hwang', in The Best Plays Theater Yearbook: 2007-2008, ed. Jeffrey Eric Jenkins (New York: Limelight Editions, 2009), 139–48. As Bacalzo points out, Hwang's wife, actress Kathryn Layng, was part of the acting ensemble, but she is not represented as a character in the play.
15. David Henry Hwang, Yellow Face (New York: Theatre Communications Group, 2009), 8. Subsequent references to this play are given in parentheses.
16. It is worth noting that supposition can be made as to the identity of NWOAOC. Here, I quote the entirety of a note by Jeffrey Eric Jenkins, who edited Dan Bacalzo's essay on Yellow Face: 'A lengthy, front-page investigative article by Tim Golden and Jeff Gerth titled "China Sent Cash to US Bank, With Suspicions Slow to Rise" appeared on 12 May 1999, in the New York Times. In it David Henry Hwang's playwriting success and former bank directorship are mentioned. The article appeared alongside two other page-one pieces that detail campaign contributions made by Chinese nationals and chart rising nationalism among the Chinese young. It is unknown if Golden's and Gerth's

Notes

were the names withheld from *Yellow Face*'. See Bacalzo, '*Yellow Face* by David Henry Hwang', 145n1.

17. Frank Rich, foreword, in Hwang, *Yellow Face*, viii.
18. Rich, in Hwang, *Yellow Face*, vii.
19. Rich, in Hwang, *Yellow Face*, vii.
20. Dennis Polkow, 'Chinglish Lessons: The Playwright on the Chicago Summer of David Hwang', *New City Stage* (15 June 2011), http://newcitystage.com/2011/06/15/chinglish-lessons-the-playwright-on-the-chicago-summer-of-david-henry-hwang/(accessed 8 February 2015).
21. Polkow, 'Chinglish Lessons'.
22. See Boles's section on *Chinglish* in *Understanding David Henry Hwang* for a summary of both the Chicago and New York City reviews.
23. David Henry Hwang, *Chinglish* (New York: Theatre Communications Group, 2012), 33. Subsequent references to this play are given in parentheses.
24. 'Signature Theatre–About', Signature Theatre, http://www.signaturetheatre.org/about/index.aspx (accessed 8 February 2015).
25. David Henry Hwang, *Kung Fu* (unpublished play script, opening night draft, Signature Theatre, 24 February 2014), ii. Subsequent references to this play are given in parentheses.
26. Charles Isherwood, 'A Dragon Returns, This Time Onstage: David Henry Hwang's "Kung Fu" Opens at Signature Theatre', *New York Times* (24 February 2014), http://www.nytimes.com/2014/02/25/theater/david-henry-hwangs-kung-fu-opens-at-signature-theater.html?_r=0 (accessed 8 February 2015).
27. Yutian Wong, *Choreographing Asian America* (Middletown, CT: Wesleyan University Press, 2010), 21.
28. See Josephine Lee's, *Performing Asian America* and Karen Shimakawa's *National Abjection: The Asian American Body Onstage* (Durham: Duke University Press, 2002).
29. Wong, *Choreographing Asian America*, 40.
30. See, for example: Moy, 'David Henry Hwang's *M. Butterfly*', 54.

Chapter 6

1. For a useful comparison of the Mark Taper and Broadway versions, see Dan Bacalzo, 'A Different Drum: David Henry Hwang's Musical "Revisal" of Flower Drum Song', *Journal of American Drama and Theatre* 15, no. 2 (2003): 71–83; also see David H. Lewis, *Flower Drum Songs: The Story of Two Musicals* (Jefferson, NC: McFarland and Company, 2006).
2. Quoted in Karen Wada, afterword to *Flower Drum Song*, by David Henry Hwang (New York: Theatre Communications Group, 2003), 100.

Notes

3. Soo had appeared in the Broadway cast as well, taking over the role from white actors Larry Storch and Larry Blyden. Another non-Asian American lead in both the Broadway and film versions was the African American actress Juanita Hall as Madam (Auntie) Liang.
4. Quoted in Misha Berson, 'A Drum with a Difference', *American Theatre* 19, no. 2 (February 2002): 14–18, 76.
5. See Christina Klein, *Cold War Orientalism: Asia in the Middlebrow Imagination* (Berkeley: University of California Press, 2003).
6. Quoted in Robert Berry White, 'Back in Lights', *Newsweek* (1 December 1958): 53.
7. Richard Rodgers, Oscar Hammerstein II and Joseph Fields, *Flower Drum Song* (New York: Farrar, Straus, and Cudahy, 1959), 20. Subsequent references to this play are given in parentheses.
8. Robert E. Lee, *Orientals: Asian American in Popular Culture* (Philadelphia: Temple University Press 1999), 145, 146.
9. See Arthur Dong's documentary, *Forbidden City U.S.A.*, VHS, directed by Arthur Dong (PBS Video, 1989), as well as SanSan Kwan's 'Performing a Geography of Asian American: The Chop Suey Circuit', *TDR: The Drama Review* 55, no. 1 (2011): 120–36.
10. Hwang, *Flower Drum Song*, 12–13. Subsequent references to this play are given in parentheses.
11. For an excellent analysis of this film scene, see Anne Anlin Cheng, *The Melancholy of Race: Psychoanalysis, Assimilation, and Hidden Grief* (Oxford: Oxford University Press 2001).
12. See Esther Kim Lee's, *A History of Asian American Theatre* (Cambridge: Cambridge University Press 2006).
13. The Broadway 2002 cast included performers from Ottawa, Seoul, Okinawa and Hong Kong, as well as different locales in the United States, highlighting the pan-ethnic and international nature of the cast.
14. The two are sometimes related: in the publicity surrounding the Mark Taper and Broadway production of Hwang's *Flower Drum Song*, much was made of the casting of Jodi Long as Madame Liang, whose father Larry Leung was in the original Broadway cast.
15. David Henry Hwang, 'Collaborating With Myself', *Theater Week* (9 December 1996): 68.
16. It is also worth noting that the play was originally commissioned by South Coast Repertory. Between its premiere at the Public and its run on Broadway, it was developed further at South Coast Repertory, the Kennedy Centre, Singapore Repertory Theatre and the American Conservatory Theatre.
17. Quoted in Gerard Raymond, 'Full Circle', *Public Access Stagebill* (November 1996): 14.

18. Dialogue from the 1996 Public Theater incarnation of *Golden Child* is taken from a video recording of the production by the New York Public Library's Theatre on Film and Tape Archive.
19. David Henry Hwang, *Golden Child* (New York: Dramatists Play Service, 1999), 7. It is worth noting that this version – used in the Broadway production – is the only published edition of the script currently available. Subsequent references to this play are in parentheses.
20. Lee, *Performing Asian America*, 137.
21. David Henry Hwang, 'Golden Child' (unpublished play script, Signature Theatre, New York, 2012), 76.
22. Renato Rosaldo, *Culture and Truth: The Remaking of Social Analysis* (Boston: Beacon Press, 1989), 71.
23. Svetlana Boym, *The Future of Nostalgia* (New York: Basic Books, 2001), xvi.
24. Boym, *The Future of Nostalgia*, 41.
25. Quoted in Gerard Raymond, 'Smashing Stereotypes', *Theater Week* (11 April 1988): 8.
26. Boym, *The Future of Nostalgia*, 49–50.
27. Daniel H. Bays, *A New History of Christianity in China* (Malden, MA: Wiley-Blackwell, 2012), 92.
28. Bays, *A New History of Christianity in China*, 95.
29. Quoted in Bill Jacobson, 'Golden Child: Playwright David Henry Hwang Explores America's Attitudes Towards HIV and the Asian Community', *A&U* (May 1998): 44.
30. Interestingly, while Eling's child is said to live in the Public and Signature versions of the play, he perishes in the Broadway script.
31. Quoted in Terry Hong, 'Born Again: David Henry Hwang, Broadway's Golden Boy, Returns to the Stage with *Golden Child*', *A. Magazine* (February/March 1997): 80.
32. Peter Marks, 'The Unbinding of Traditions', *New York Times* (3 April 1998): E1.
33. Hwang made this remark on 14 November 2000, at an evening entitled 'David Henry Hwang: 20 Year Retrospective' at The Violet Café at New York University, when he was Artist-in-Residence at NYU's A/P/A Studies Program & Institute.
34. Dorinne Kondo, *About Face: Performing Race in Fashion and Theater* (London: Routledge, 1997), 11.
35. Marita Sturken, *Tangled Memories: The Vietnam War, the AIDS Epidemic, and the Politics of Remembering* (Berkeley: University of California Press, 1997), 7.
36. Quoted in Misha Berson, 'The Demon in David Henry Hwang', *American Theatre* 15, no. 4 (April 1998): 18.
37. There are many different languages that fall under the term 'Chinese'. Some scholars prefer to use 'Sinophone' as an umbrella term for different types of

Notes

Chinese languages. In the context of this chapter and the play, Chinese (as a language) refers to Mandarin Chinese, the official language of China and Taiwan and one of the most-spoken languages in the world. Chinese writing systems will be addressed later.

38. 'Chinese' in the US Census is broadly defined. This group includes people who identify themselves as Chinese, Taiwanese, or 'in combination with one or more other races'. See Elizabeth M. Hoeffel, Sonya Rastogi, Myoung Ouk Kim and Hasan Shahid, 'The Asian Population: 2010', United States Census Bureau (3 March 2012), http://www.census.gov/prod/cen2010/briefs/c2010br-11.pdf.

39. I saw two performances of *Chinglish*, both at the South Coast Repertory in Costa Mesa, California (30 January and 22 February 2013).

40. Genny Lim, '*Paper Angel*', in *Unbroken Thread: An Anthology of Plays by Asian American Women*, ed. Roberta Uno (Amherst: University of Massachusetts Press, 1993), 45–6.

41. *Nisei*, a Japanese term, which means 'second generation', is used by Asian Americans to indicate American-born Asians of immigrant parents.

42. This is Xi's description of Daniel.

43. Hwang, '*M. Butterfly*', in *Modern and Contemporary Drama*, ed. Miriam Gilbert, Carl H. Klaus, and Bradford S. Field, Jr. (New York: St. Martin's Press, 1994), 836.

44. *Xiang qian kan* (everyone's eyes on money) is a pun for 'looking forward' or 'progress'. Forward and money share the same sound, *qian*.

45. The comments were made at a post-show discussion following a performance of *Chinglish* at the South Coast Repertory on 30 January 2013.

46. Hwang's words are from an interview with Neena Arndt before the premiere of *Chinglish* at the Goodman Theatre in Chicago, 2011. This interview is reprinted in the production programme for *Chinglish*, South Coast Repertory January 2013, 8–9.

47. Candace Mui Ngam Chong is a four-time winner of the Best Script of the Hong Kong Drama Awards. Her winning works include *Alive in the Mortuary* (2003), *Shall We Go to Mars?* (2005), *The French Kiss* (2006) and *Murder in San José* (2010). *Murder in San José* and *Wild Boar* (2012) have been translated into English. She also wrote the libretto for the three-act opera *Dr. Sun Yat-sen*, which premiered in Hong Kong in 2011. A good introduction to Chong's works is Sharon Lee, 'A Playwright of Our Time: Candace Chong Mui-ngam captures the social and political issues facing Hong Kong for the stage', *Varsity.com* (6 December 2013), http://varsity.com.cuhk.edu.hk/index.php/2013/12/candace-chong-mui-ngam/(accessed 8 February 2015).

48. The British colonial acquisition of Hong Kong took several decades, from 1842 to 1898.

49. The Basic Law, which serves as the constitutional document of the Hong Kong SAR, was signed by the Chinese and British governments in 1984. One

Notes

basic principle of the Basic Law is 'One Country, Two Systems': Hong Kong is allowed to maintain its status quo and not to adopt the Chinese communist or socialist system for fifty years after the 1997 takeover.

50. The name 'umbrella' references both a local characteristic and a protest strategy. The tropical island climate makes umbrellas a necessity for Hong Kong daily life (both for sun and rain), and they are also essential to protect oneself from the tear gas or pepper spray used by police forces. Moreover, the verb for using an umbrella, *cheng*, has the double meaning of standing and enduring. Opening an umbrella hence shows the solidarity of 'united we stand' for Hong Kong suffrage.

51. Wu Yu, 'Mainland Visitors, Hong Kongers Don't Welcome You!', *Deutsche Welle* (12 June 2013), http://www.dw.de/内地游客香港人不欢迎你/a-17275533 (accessed 8 February 2015).

52. There is a long history of the Chinese populace being compared with locusts because of their sheer numbers. Hong Kongers also use the term to refer to the large number of Chinese visitors in recent years: tourists overcrowd public spaces and transportation, traders clear store shelves of goods, buyers push up real estate prices and many pregnant women travel to Hong Kong to give birth so their children can enjoy certain privileges unavailable in China. The large number of visitors with unfamiliar behaviour and languages are not welcomed by local citizens, who fear their very limited resources are being unjustly 'shared'. For an article discussing this recent locust rhetoric, see Michelle FlorCruz, 'Anti-Locust Protest in Hong Kong Call for Restrictions on Chinese Mainland Tourists', *International Business Times* (19 February 2014), http://www.ibtimes.com/anti-locust-protests-hong-kong-call-restrictions-chinese-mainland-tourists-1556457 (accessed 8 February 2015).

53. See Joseph Yeh, 'Preserving Traditional Chinese Characters in Taiwan, a valuable asset of Chinese culture', *Culture.TW* (22 January 2010), http://www.culture.tw/index.php?option=com_content&task=view&id=1610&Itemid=157 (accessed 8 February 2015). Estimates place traditional Chinese character users at approximately thirty million. The population in Taiwan is about twenty-three million.

54. As I write, another aspect of the Hong Kong language is being threatened. Cantonese, the mother tongue of the locals, is gradually being replaced by Mandarin, the official 'Chinese' for China, in the education system. At least 70 per cent of the primary schools in Hong Kong are now taught in Mandarin. See Vivienne Chow, 'Speaking up in Cantonese, a Tongue in Peril', *South China Morning Post* (23 December 2014), http://www.scmp.com/news/hong-kong/article/1603994/speaking-cantonese-tongue-peril (accessed 8 February 2015).

55. David Henry Hwang, 'Stranger Than Fiction: A British businessman's death mirrors a Broadway hit', production program for *Chinglish*, South Coast Repertory January 2013, 4–5.

56. 'The Chinese American Broadway Playwright Discusses the Absurd Chinese Nationalism in *Chinglish*', *etnet* (4 May 2013), http://www.etnet.com.hk/

57. 'The Chinese American Broadway Playwright Discusses the Absurd Chinese Nationalism in *Chinglish*'.
58. Lee, 'A Playwright of Our Time'.
59. 'The Chinese American Broadway Playwright Discusses the Absurd Chinese Nationalism in *Chinglish*'.
60. The plot of *Chinglish* is similar to a recent news story about a high ranking official, Bo Xilai. The corruption, connection with foreign businessmen, illicit extramarital affair and favouritism that allowed Bo's son to study abroad likely make it impossible for *Chinglish* to go to China. See 'The Surprising "Stage Version" of Bo Xilai Incident on Broadway', *Deutsche Welle* (19 May 2012), http://www.dw.de/薄熙来事件在百老汇惊现舞台版/a-15958758 (accessed 8 February 2015).
61. 'The Chinese American Broadway Playwright Discusses the Absurd Chinese Nationalism in *Chinglish*'.
62. Kavita Daswani, 'Found in translation: David Henry Hwang mines linguistic mix-ups to hilarious effect in his hit play', *South China Morning Post* (24 February 2013), http://www.scmp.com/lifestyle/arts-culture/article/1156186/found-translation (accessed 24 May 2015).
63. To understand more about the concept of the 'Chinese centre vs. periphery' and transnational alliances among Chinese peripheries in the context of theatre as identity performance, see Daphne Lei, *Alternative Chinese Opera in the Age of Globalization: Performing Zero* (New York: Palgrave Macmillan, 2011).

BIBLIOGRAPHY

I. Primary sources on David Henry Hwang

Published works

As the Crow Flies. Between Worlds: Contemporary Asian American Plays, edited by Misha Berson, 91–108. New York: Theatre Communications Group, 1990.

Chinglish. New York: Theatre Communications Group, 2012.

Flower Drum Song. New York: Theatre Communications Group, 2003.

FOB and Other Plays. New York: Plume, 1990. Comprises *FOB*; *The Dance and the Railroad*; *Family Devotions*; *The House of Sleeping Beauties*; *The Sound of a Voice*; *Rich Relations*; *1000 Airplanes on the Roof*.

'From Come'. *On a Bed of Rice: An Asian American Erotic Feast*, edited by Geraldine Kudaka, 456–61. New York: Anchor, 1995.

Golden Child. New York: Dramatists Play Service, 1999.

Golden Child. New York: Theatre Communications Group, 1998.

Golden Child. videotaped at the Joseph Papp Public Theater, New York Public Library's Theatre on Film and Tape Archive, Billy Rose Theatre Collection, New York Public Library for the Performing Arts, New York: 1996, 3 videocassettes.

The Great Helmsman. 2007: The Best Ten-Minute Plays for Three or More Actors, edited by Lawrence Harbison, 31–7. Hanover, NH: Smith and Kraus, 2008.

Jade Flowerpots and Bound Feet. Version 3.0: Contemporary Asian American Plays, edited by Chay Yew, 574–9. New York: Theatre Communications Group, 2001.

Jade Flowerpots and Bound Feet. 2004: The Best Ten-Minute plays for Two Actors, edited by Michael Bigelow Dixon and Liz Engleman, 179–85. Hanover, NH: Smith and Kraus, 2004.

M. Butterfly. New York: Plume, 1989.

Merchandising. Humana Festival '99: The Complete Plays, edited by Michael Bigelow Dixon and Amy Wegener, 299–303. Hanover, NH: Smith and Kraus, 1999.

1000 Airplanes on the Roof: A Science Fiction Music-Drama, realized with Philip Glass and Jerome Sirlin. Layton, UT: Gibbs Smith, 1989.

Trying to Find Chinatown: The Selected Plays. New York: Theatre Communications Group, 2000. Comprises *FOB*; *The Dance and the Railroad*; *Family Devotions*; *The Sound of a Voice*; *The House of Sleeping Beauties*; *The Voyage*; *Bondage*; *Trying to Find Chinatown*.

Yellow Face. New York: Theatre Communications Group, 2009.

Bibliography

Unpublished works

Hwang, David Henry. 'Ainadamar' (libretto), Osvaldo Golijov (composer), Tanglewood Musical Centre, Lenox, MA, 2003.

Hwang, David Henry. 'Bank Kok', unproduced short-play commissioned for *Pieces of the Quilt*, San Francisco Magic Theatre, 1995.

Hwang, David Henry. 'Face Value', Colonial Theatre, Boston, 1993.

Hwang, David Henry. 'The Fly' (libretto), Howard Shore (composer), Théâtre du Châtelet, Paris, 2008.

Hwang, David Henry, 'Golden Child', unpublished play script, Signature Theatre, New York, 2012.

Hwang, David Henry. 'Hushed Tones', *America: Now and Here Tour*. Kansas City, MO, March 2011.

Hwang, David Henry. 'Kung Fu', unpublished play script, Signature Theatre, opening night draft, 24 February 2014.

Hwang, David Henry. 'Odysseus on 43rd Street', Lark Play Development Centre, 26 April 2012.

Hwang, David Henry. 'The Silver River' (libretto), Bright Sheng (composer), Sante Fe Chamber Musical Festival, 1998.

Hwang, David Henry. 'Sound and Beauty' (libretto), Philip Glass (composer), American Repertory Theatre, Cambridge, MA, 2003.

Hwang, David Henry. 'Tarzan' (book), music by Phil Collins, Richard Rodgers Theatre, New York City, 2006.

Hwang, David Henry. 'Venus Voodoo' (libretto), Lucia Hwong (composer), Lincoln Center, New York City, 1989.

'A Very DNA Reunion'. *The DNA Trail: A Genealogy of Short Plays about Ancestry, Identity, and Confusions*, Silk Road Theatre Project, Chicago, 2010.

Hwang, David Henry, and Brian Greene. 'Icarus at the Edge of Time' (libretto), Philip Glass (composer), Alice Tully Hall, New York City, 2010.

Hwang, David Henry, Robert Falls, and Linda Woolverton. 'Aida' (book), music by Elton John and Tim Rice, directed by Robert Falls, Palace Theatre, New York City, 2000.

Hwang, David Henry, and Unsuk Chin. 'Alice in Wonderland' (libretto), Unsuk Chin (composer), Bavarian State Opera, Munich Opera Festival, 2007.

Adaptations

Hwang, David Henry. *Tibet through the Red Box*, by Peter Sis. New York: Playscripts, 2006.

Hwang, David Henry, and Stephen Müller (adapters), *Peer Gynt*, by Henrik Ibsen. New York: Playscripts, 2006.

Screenplays and television plays

Hwang, David Henry. *The Dance and the Railroad*, directed by Emile Ardolino, ABC Video Enterprises, 1981, VHS.

Hwang, David Henry. 'Dances in Exile', episode for *Alive from Off-Centre*, directed by Howard Silver, KTCA Minneapolis, 1991, television.

Hwang, David Henry (story). *Forbidden Nights*, directed by Waris Hussein, Warner Brothers, 1990, film.

Hwang, David Henry. *Golden Gate*, directed by John Madden, Samuel Goldwyn, 1994, film.

Hwang, David Henry. *Korea: Homes Apart*, directed by Christine Choy and J. T. Takagi, Third World Newsreel, 1991, film.

Hwang, David Henry. *M. Butterfly*, directed by David Cronenberg, Geffen Pictures, 1993, film.

Hwang, David Henry. *The Monkey King* [also known as *The Lost Empire*], directed by Peter Macdonald, Hallmark Entertainment, 2001, television.

Hwang, David Henry, and Frederic Kimball. *Blind Alleys*, directed by William Cosel and David F. Wheeler, Metromedia Playhouse, 1985, television.

Hwang, David Henry, Neil LaBute, and Laura Jones. *Possession*, directed by Neil LaBute, USA Films/Warner Bros., 2002, film.

Speeches, interviews with David Henry Hwang

Chai, Barbara. 'Speakeasy: Letting the Writer Write'. *Wall Street Journal* (31 October 2012): A.29.

'A Conversation with David Henry Hwang'. *Bearing Dream, Shaping Visions: Asian Pacific American Perspectives*, edited by Linda A. Revilla, Gail M. Nomura, and Shirley Hune, 185–9. Pullman: Washington State University Press, 1993.

'A Conversation with David Henry Hwang'. *Yolk* (March 2001): 29.

Cooperman, Robert. 'Across the Boundaries of Cultural Identity: An Interview with David Henry Hwang'. In *Staging Difference: Cultural Pluralism in American Theatre and Drama*, edited by Marc Maufort, 365–73. New York: Peter Lang, 1995.

'David Henry Hwang on *Golden Child*'. Vimeo video, posted by 'Signature Theatre', 3 October 2012, http://vimeo.com/50701816.

'David Henry Hwang on *The Dance and the Railroad*'. Vimeo video, posted by 'Signature Theatre', 7 January 2013, http://vimeo.com/57018823.

DiGaetani, John L. 'An interview with David Henry Hwang'. In *A Search for a Postmodern Theater: Interviews with Contemporary Playwrights*, 161–74. New York: Greenwood Press, 1991.

DiGaetani, John L. '"M. Butterfly": An Interview with David Henry Hwang'. *Drama Review* 33, no. 3 (1989): 141–53.

Frockt, Deborah. 'David Henry Hwang'. In *The Playwright's Art: Conversations with Contemporary American Dramatists*, edited by Jackson R. Bryer, 123–46. New Brunswick: Rutgers University Press, 1995.

Hong, Terry. 'Born Again: David Henry Hwang, Broadway's Golden Boy, Returns to the Stage with *Golden Child*'. *A. Magazine: Inside Asian America* (February/March 1997): 80.

Hong, Terry. 'The Great Hwang Way: Terry Hong Coaxes a Few Secrets Out of Playwright David Henry Hwang'. *A. Magazine: Inside Asian America* (February/March 2001): 67.

Bibliography

Hong, Terry. 'Through the Looking Glass: Leading Asian-American Theatre Artists Reflect on the Past Four Decades'. *American Theatre* (January 2003): 73–85.

Hwang, David Henry. 'Keynote Address'. Comparative Drama Conference, Baltimore, Maryland, 4 April 2014.

Hwang, David Henry. unpublished interview with Esther Kim Lee, 16 March 2000, New York City.

Hwang, David Henry. unpublished interview with Esther Kim Lee, 15 January 2015, New York City.

Hwang, David Henry, and Tzi Ma. 'One on One'. *Yolk* (December 1994): 34.

Kondo, Dorinne. 'Interview with David Henry Hwang'. In Kondo, *About Face*, 211–25.

Lyons, Bonnie. '"Making His Muscles Work for Himself": An Interview with David Henry Hwang'. *Literary Review* 42, no. 2 (1999): 230–44.

Moss-Coane, Marty, and John Timpane. 'David Henry Hwang'. In *Speaking on Stage: Interviews with Contemporary American Playwrights*, edited by Phillip C. Kolin and Colby H. Kullman, 277–90. Tuscaloosa: University of Alabama Press, 1996.

Piepenburg, Erik. 'He Writes About What He Knows'. *New York Times* (2 December 2007): A.6.

Rich, Frank. 'A Conversation with David Henry Hwang', remarks delivered at 'David Henry Hwang: 20 Year Retrospective', The Violet Café, New York University, 14 November 2000.

Savran, David. 'David Hwang'. In *In Their Own Words: Contemporary American Playwrights*, 117–31. New York: Theatre Communications Group, 1988.

Soloski, Alexis. 'David Henry Hwang, Amy Herzog, and Thomas Bradshaw Talk Art, Cash, and Duping Joe Papp'. *Village Voice* (September 2012), http://www.villagevoice.com/2012-09-19/theater/david-henry-hwang-amy-herzog-and-thomas-bradshaw/ (accessed 8 February 2015).

Tichler, Rosemarie, and Barry J. Kaplan. 'David Henry Hwang'. In *The Playwright at Work: Conversations*, 28–48. Evanston, IL: Northwestern University Press, 2012.

Viertel, Jack. 'Fun with Race and the Media, an Interview with the Playwright'. *American Theatre* (April 2008): 60–1.

Miscellaneous publications by Hwang

Afterword to *M. Butterfly*. New York: Plume, 1989, 94–100.

'Are Movies Ready for Orientals?' *New York Times* (11 August 1985): A1.

'Bringing Up "Child"'. In *Golden Child*, v–ix. New York: Theatre Communications Group, 1998.

'Collaborating With Myself'. *Theater Week* (9 December 1996).

'David Henry Hwang'. In *Between Worlds: Contemporary Asian-American Plays*, edited by Misha Berson, 16–19. New York: Theatre Communications Group, 1990.

'Evolving a Multicultural Tradition'. *MELUS* 16, no. 3 (1989–90): 16–19.

'Foreword: The Myth of Immutable Culture Identity'. In *Asian American Drama: 9 Plays from the Multiethnic Landscape*, edited by Brian Nelson, vii–viii. New York: Applause, 1997.

'Fractures, Large and Small'. *American Theatre* (December 2009): 62–3.
'In Today's World, Who Represents the "Real" China?' *New York Times* (1 April 2001): A2, A32.
Introduction to *FOB and Other Plays*. New York: Plume, 1990, x–xv.
Introduction to *Flower Drum Song*, by C. Y. Lee. New York: Penguin, 2002, xiii–xxi.
Introduction to *Flower Drum Song*, New York: Theatre Communications Group, 2003, ix–xiv.
'Islands in the Mainstream'. *The American Theatre Reader*, 123–7. New York: Theatre Communications Group, 2009.
'My Worst Career Mistakes: Part Three (My Lunch With Neil)'. You Offend Me You Offend My Family (22 April 2010), http://youoffendmeyouoffendmyfamily.com/my-worst-career-mistakes-part-three-my-lunch-with-neil/ (accessed 8 February 2015).
'A New Musical by Rodgers and Hwang'. *New York Times* (13 October 2002): 2: 1.
'People Like Us'. *Guardian* (April 1989): 21.
'Philip Kan Gotanda'. *BOMB* 62 (1998): 20–6.
'Response'. In *Yellow Light: The Flowering of Asian American Arts*, edited by Amy Ling, 222–7. Philadelphia: Temple University Press, 1999.
'Stranger Than Fiction: A British businessman's death mirrors a Broadway hit'. *Chinglish* production program, South Coast Repertory theatre, January 2013, 4–5.
'Worlds Apart'. *American Theatre* (January 2000): 50–6.
Hwang, David Henry and Prince. 'Solo', *Come*, Warner Bros, 1994, compact disc.

II. Secondary sources: Newspapers, magazines, production program and websites

Bernstein, Richard. 'France Jails 2 in Odd Case of Espionage'. *New York Times* (11 May 1986).
Berson, Misha. 'A Drum with a Difference: David Henry Hwang Repaves Rodgers and Hammerstein's Musical Road to Chinatown'. *American Theatre* (February 2002): 14–18, 76.
Berson, Misha. 'The Demon in David Henry Hwang'. *American Theatre* (April 1998): 14–18, 50–1.
Brantley, Ben. 'Broadway And Vine: Ape-Man Hits Town'. *New York Times* (11 May 2006): 11.
Brantley, Ben. 'Extending a hand to Ancestral Ghosts in China'. *New York Times* (10 November 1996): C20.
Campbell, Karen. 'In the Realm of the Voices'. *American Theatre* (October 2003): 103–6.
Chow, Vivienne. 'Speaking up in Cantonese, a Tongue in Peril'. *South China Morning Post* (23 December 2014), http://www.scmp.com/news/hong-kong/article/1603994/speaking-cantonese-tongue-peril (accessed 8 February 2015).
Craig, Pat. '*Aida* Experience: Playwright Hwang Has Newfound Interest in Musicals'. *Contra Cost Times* (2 August 2001): D01.

Bibliography

Daswani, Kavita. 'Found in translation: David Henry Hwang mines linguistic mix-ups to hilarious effect in his hit play'. *South China Morning Post* (24 February 2013).

Drukman, Steven. 'Taking Bittersweet Journeys into the past'. *New York Times* (10 November 1996), section 2, p. 5.

FlorCruz, Michelle. 'Anti-Locust Protest in Hong Kong Call for Restrictions on Chinese Mainland Tourists'. *International Business Times* (19 February 2014), http://www.ibtimes.com/anti-locust-protests-hong-kong-call-restrictions-chinese-mainland-tourists-1556457 (accessed 8 February 2015).

Grossberg, Michael. 'Humana Playwrights Take Relevant Risks'. *Columbus Dispatch* (25 March 1992): 8E.

Harrison, Holly. 'Exploring Identity'. *Business Times* (Singapore) (26 April 1996): 11.

Hartigan, Patti. 'Hwang's Political Stage; Writer Wonders How Much to Stir the Melting Pot'. *Boston Globe* (15 April 1994): 91.

Henry, William A., III. 'David Henry Hwang: When East and West Collide'. *Time* (14 August 1989).

Herman, Jan. 'Calendar Section'. *Los Angeles Times* (3 November 1996): 6.

'Hwang Play Closes After 8 Previews'. *New York Times* (16 March 1993): C14.

Isherwood, Charles. 'A Dragon Returns, This Time Onstage: David Henry Hwang's "Kung Fu" Opens at Signature Theater'. *New York Times* (24 February 2014), http://www.nytimes.com/2014/02/25/theater/david-henry-hwangs-kung-fu-opens-at-signature-theater.html?_r=0 (accessed 8 February 2015).

Jones, Chris. *Variety* (13 December 1999): 117.

Kelly, Kevin. 'Hwang Looks Beyond "Face Value"'. *Boston Globe* (17 February 1993): 25.

Kelly, Kevin. 'Hwang's "Face Value" Flops on Its Farce'. *Boston Globe* (15 February 1993): 31.

Kelly, Kevin. 'M. Butterfly, Miss Saigon and Mr. Hwang'. *Boston Globe* (9 September 1990): B89.

Lee, Sharon. 'A Playwright of Our Time: Candace Chong Mui-ngam captures the social and political issues facing Hong Kong for the stage'. *Varsity.com* (6 December 2013), http://varsity.com.cuhk.edu.hk/index.php/2013/12/candace-chong-mui-ngam/ (accessed 8 February 2015).

Marks, Peter. 'The Unbinding of Traditions'. *New York Times* (3 April 1998): E1.

Polkow, Dennis. 'Chinglish Lessons: The Playwright on the Chicago Summer of David Hwang'. *New City Stage* (15 June 2011), http://newcitystage.com/2011/06/15/chinglish-lessons-the-playwright-on-the-chicago-summer-of-david-henry-hwang/ (accessed 8 February 2015).

Production program for *Chinglish*. South Coast Repertory theatre, January 2013.

Raymond, Gerard. 'Full Circle'. *Public Access Stagebill* (November 1996).

Raymond, Gerard. 'Smashing Stereotypes'. *Theater Week* (11 April 1988).

Rich, Frank. '*M. Butterfly*: A Story of a Strange Love, Conflict and Betrayal'. *New York Times* (21 March 1988): C13.

Rich, Frank. '"Sound and Beauty": Two One-Act Plays'. *New York Times* (7 November 1983): C13.

Rich, Frank. 'Stage: "Dance, Railroad" by David Henry Hwang'. *New York Times* (31 March 1981): C5.

Rich, Frank. 'Stage: "Rich Relations," From David Hwang'. *New York Times* (22 April 1986): C15.

Rich, Frank. 'Theater: *FOB*, Rites of Immigrant Passage'. *New York Times* (10 June 1980): C6.

Richards, David. 'Chinese Puzzle: At the National, a Curious "M. Butterfly"'. *Washington Post* (11 February 1988): C1.

Rooney, David. 'Tarzan'. *Daily Variety* (11 May 2006): 6.

Rozhon, Tracie. 'Habitats/45 West 67th Street: Exit Actor and Actress, Enter Author and Actress'. *New York Times* (24 November 1996), section 9, p. 4.

'Signature Theatre–About'. Signature Theatre, http://www.signaturetheatre.org/about/index.aspx (accessed 8 February 2015).

Simonson, Robert. 'David Henry Hwang to Work on Book for Disney's *Aida*'. *Playbill* (7 May 1999), http://www.playbill.com/news/article/david-henry-hwang-to-work-on-book-for-disneys-aida-81767 (accessed 17 March 2015).

Smith, Dinitia. 'Face Values: The Sexual and Racial Obsessions of Playwright David Henry Hwang'. *New York Magazine* (11 January 1993): 41–5.

'The Surprising "Stage Version" of Bo Xilai Incident on Broadway'. *Deutsche Welle* (19 May 2012), http://www.dw.de/薄熙来事件在百老汇惊现舞台版/a-15958758 (accessed 8 February 2015).

Weber, Bruce. 'On Stage, and Off'. *New York Times* (23 October 1992): C2.

White, Robert Berry. 'Back in Lights'. *Newsweek* (1 December 1958): 53.

Winer, Laurie. 'Tracing a Family's Past, Future Through Eyes of *Golden Child*'. *Los Angeles Times* (10 November 1996): F1.

Winer, Linda. 'Theater Review'. *Newsday* (10 December 2007), http://www.newsday.com/lifestyle/theater-review-1.532846 (accessed 8 February 2015).

Witchel, Alex. 'The Man Who Can Make Bruce Lee Talk'. *New York Times Magazine* (7 November 2012), http://www.nytimes.com/2012/11/11/magazine/david-henry-hwang-the-man-who-can-make-bruce-lee-talk.html?emc=eta1 (accessed 8 February 2015).

Wolf, Matt. 'From Broadway to London, With Some Surprises'. *New York Times* (28 May 1989), http://www.nytimes.com/1989/05/28/theater/theater-from-broadway-to-london-with-some-surprises.html (accessed 20 January 2014).

Yeh, Joseph. 'Preserving Traditional Chinese Characters in Taiwan, a valuable asset of Chinese culture'. *Culture.TW* (22 January 2010), http://www.culture.tw/index.php?option=com_content&task=view&id=1610&Itemid=157 (accessed 8 February 2015).

Yu, Wu. 'Mainland Visitors, Hong Kongers Don't Welcome You!' *Deutsche Welle* (12 June 2013), http://www.dw.de/内地游客香港人不欢迎你/a-17275533 (accessed 8 February 2015).

III. Secondary sources: Critical studies

Bacalzo, Dan. 'A Different Drum: David Henry Hwang's Musical "Revisal" of *Flower Drum Song*'. *Journal of American Drama and Theatre* 15, no. 2 (2003): 71–83.

Bibliography

Bacalzo, Dan. 'The Square'. *Theatre Journal* 54, no. 3 (2002): 489–91.

Bacalzo, Dan. '*Yellow Face* by David Henry Hwang'. In *The Best Plays Theater Yearbook: 2007-2008*, edited by Jeffrey Eric Jenkins, 139–48. New York: Limelight Editions, 2009.

Bak, John S. 'Vestis Virum Reddit: the Gender Politics of Drag in Tennessee Williams's *A Streetcar Named Desire* and David Henry Hwang's *M. Butterfly*'. *South Atlantic Review: The Publication of the South Atlantic Modern Language Association* 70, no. 4 (2005): 94–118.

Bays, Daniel H. *A New History of Christianity in China*. Malden, MA: Wiley-Blackwell, 2012.

Boles, William C. *Understanding David Henry Hwang*. Columbia: University of South Carolina Press, 2013, Kindle edition.

Botelho, Teresa. 'Redefining the Dramatic Canon'. In *Positioning the New: Chinese American Literature and the Changing Image of the American Literary Canon*, edited by Tanfer Emin Tunc and Elisabetta Marino, 182–42. Newcastle upon Tyne: Cambridge Scholars, 2010.

Bowers, Maggie Ann. *Magic(al) Realism*. London: Routledge, 2004.

Boym, Svetlana. *The Future of Nostalgia*. New York: Basic Books, 2001.

Chang, Williamson B. C. '*M. Butterfly*: Passivity, Deviousness, and the Invisibility of the Asian-American Male'. In *Bearing Dream, Shaping Visions: Asian Pacific American Perspectives*, edited by Linda A. Revilla, Gail M. Nomura, and Shirley Hune, 181–4. Pullman: Washington State University Press, 1993.

Chen, Tina. 'Betrayed into Motion: The Seduction of Narrative Desire in *M. Butterfly*'. *Critical Mass: A Journal of Asian American Cultural Criticism* 1, no. 2 (1994): 129–54.

Cheng, Anne Anlin. *The Melancholy of Race: Psychoanalysis, Assimilation, and Hidden Grief*. Oxford: Oxford University Press, 2001.

Cheng, Anne Anlin. 'Race and Fantasy in Modern American: Subjective Dissimulation/Racial Assimilation'. In *Multiculturalism and Representation: Selected Essays*, edited by John Rieder and Larry E. Smith, 175–97. Honolulu: University of Hawaii Press, 1996.

Cheung, King-Kok. 'The Woman Warrior Versus the Chinaman Pacific: Must a Chinese American Critic Choose between Feminism and Heroism?' In *Maxine Hong Kingston's The Woman Warrior: A Casebook*, edited by Sau-ling Cynthia Wong, 113–34. New York: Oxford University Press, 1999.

Chin, Frank. 'The Most Popular Book in China'. In Wong, *Maxine Hong Kingston's The Woman Warrior: A Casebook*, edited by Sau-ling Cynthia Wong, 23–8. New York: Oxford University Press, 1999.

'The Chinese American Broadway Playwright Discusses the Absurd Chinese Nationalism in *Chinglish*'. *Etnet* (4 May 2013), http://www.etnet.com.hk/www/tc/news/topic_news_detail.php?category=china&newsid=817 (accessed 8 February 2015).

Cody, Gabrielle. 'David Henry Hwang's *M. Butterfly*: Perpetuating the Misogynist Myth'. *Theater* 20, no. 2 (1989): 24–7.

Cooperman, Robert. 'New Theatrical Statements: Asian-Western Mergers in the Early Plays of David Henry Hwang'. In *Staging Difference: Cultural Pluralism in*

American Theatre and Drama, edited by Marc Maufort, 201–13. New York, Peter Lang, 1995.

Craig, Pat. '*Aida* Experience: Playwright Hwang Has Newfound Interest in Musicals'. *Contra Cost Times* (2 August 2001): D01.

Davis, Rocio. 'Desperately Seeking Stereotypes: David Henry Hwang and *M. Butterfly*'. *Revista de Estudios Norteamericanos* 2, no. 3 (1994): 53–64.

Davis, Rocio. '"Just a Man": Subverting Stereotypes in David Henry Hwang's *M. Butterfly*'. *Hitting Critical Mass* 6, no. 2 (2000): 59–74.

Deeney, John J. 'Of Monkeys and Butterflies: Transformation in MH Kingston's *Tripmaster Monkey* and DH Hwang's *M. Butterfly*'. *MELUS* 18, no. 4 (1993): 21–39.

Degabriele, Maria. 'From *Madame Butterfly* to *Miss Saigon*: One Hundred Years of Popular Orientalism'. *Critical Arts* 10, no. 2 (1996): 105–18.

Dickey, Jerry. '"Myths of the East, Myths of the West": Shattering Racial and Gender Stereotypes in the Plays of David Henry Hwang'. In *Old West-New West: Centennial Essays*, edited by Barbara Howard Meldrum, 272–80. Moscow: University of Idaho Press, 1993.

Du Bois, W. E. B. *The Souls of Black Folk*. New York: Dover Publications, 1994.

Eng, David L. 'In the Shadows of a Diva: Committing Homosexuality in David Henry Hwang's *M. Butterfly*'. In *Asian Sexualities: Dimensions of the Gay and Lesbian Experience*, edited by Russell Leong, 131–52. New York: Routledge, 1996.

Frayling, Christopher. *The Yellow Peril: Dr. Fu Manchu and the Rise of Chinaphobia*. London: Thames & Hudson, 2014.

Garber, Marjorie. 'The Occidental Tourist: *M. Butterfly* and the Scandal of Transvestism'. In *Nationalisms and Sexualities*, edited by Andrew Parker, Mary Russo, Doris Sommer, and Patricia Yaeger, 121–46. New York: Routledge, 1992.

Garber, Marjorie. *Vested Interests: Cross-Dressing and Cultural Anxiety*. New York: Routledge, 1992.

Grace, Sherrill. 'Playing Butterfly with David Henry Hwang and Robert Lepage'. In *A Vision of the Orient: Texts, Intertexts, and Contexts of* Madame Butterfly, edited by Jonathan Wisenthal, Sherrill Grace, and Melinda Boyd, 136–51. Toronto: University of Toronto Press, 2006.

Haedicke, Janet V. 'David Henry Hwang's *M. Butterfly*: The Eye on the Wing'. *Journal of Dramatic Theory and Criticism* 7, no. 1 (1992): 27–44.

Hayde, Dolly. 'On M. Butterfly by David Henry Hwang'. *North American Review* 295, no. 2 (2010): 24.

Hoeffel, Elizabeth M. Sonya Rastogi, Myoung Ouk Kim, and Hasan Shahid. 'The Asian Population: 2010'. United States Census Bureau, March 2012, http://www.census.gov/prod/cen2010/briefs/c2010br-11.pdf.

Irmscher, Christoph. '"The Absolute Power of a Man?" Staging Masculinity in Giacomo Puccini and David Henry Hwang'. *Amerikastudien/American Studies* 43, no. 4 (1998): 619–28.

Jacobson, Bill. 'Golden Child: Playwright David Henry Hwang Explores America's Attitudes Towards HIV and the Asian Community'. *A&U* (May 1998).

Jenkins, Jeffrey Eric, ed. *The Best Plays Theater Yearbook: 2007-2008*. New York: Limelight Editions, 2009.

Bibliography

Jew, Kimberly M. 'Dismantling the Realist Character in Velina Hasu Houston's *Tea* and David Henry Hwang's *FOB*'. In *Literary Gestures: The Aesthetic in Asian American Writing*, edited by Rocio G. Davis and Sue-Im Lee, 187–202. Philadelphia: Temple University Press, 2005.

Jew, Kimberly M. 'Gothic Aesthetics of Entanglement an Endangerment in David Henry Hwang's *The Sound of a Voice* and *The House of Sleeping Beauties*'. In *Asian Gothic: Essays on Literature, Film, and Anime*, edited by Andrew Hock Soon Ng, 140–55. Jefferson, NC: McFarland, 2008.

Juan, E. San, Jr. 'Symbolic Violence and the Fetishism of the Sublime: A Metacommentary on David Hwang's *M. Butterfly*'. *Journal of Intercultural Studies* 23, no. 1 (2002): 33–46.

Kawabata, Yasunari. *House of the Sleeping Beauties and Other Stories*, translated by Edward Seidensticker. Tokyo: Kodansha International, 1969.

Kerr, Douglas. 'David Henry Hwang and the Revenge of Madame Butterfly'. In *Asian Voices in English*, edited by Mimi Chan and Roy Harris, 119–30. Hong Kong: Hong Kong University Press, 1991.

Klein, Christina. *Cold War Orientalism: Asia in the Middlebrow Imagination*. Berkeley: University of California Press, 2003.

Koh, Karlyn. '(Dis)Placing Identities: Cultural Transvestism in David Henry Hwang's *M. Butterfly*'. *West Coast Line* (March 1994): 246–54.

Kondo, Dorinne. *About Face: Performing Race in Fashion and Theater*. New York: Routledge, 1997.

Kondo, Dorinne. '*M. Butterfly*: Orientalism, Gender, and a Critique of Essentialist Identity'. *Cultural Critique* 16 (1990): 5–29.

Kwan, SanSan. 'Performing a Geography of Asian American: The Chop Suey Circuit'. *TDR: The Drama Review* 55, no. 1 (2011): 120–36.

Lee, Esther Kim. *A History of Asian American Theatre*. New York: Cambridge University Press, 2006.

Lee, Jennifer. *The Fortune Cookie Chronicles: Adventures in the World of Chinese Food*. New York: Twelve, 2008.

Lee, Josephine. *Performing Asian America: Race and Ethnicity on the Contemporary Stage*. Philadelphia: Temple University Press, 1997.

Lee, Quentin. 'Between the Oriental and the Transvestite'. *Found Object* 8 (1993): 45–59.

Lee, Robert E. *Orientals: Asian American in Popular Culture*. Philadelphia: Temple University Press, 1999.

Lei, Daphne. *Alternative Chinese Opera in the Age of Globalization: Performing Zero*. New York: Palgrave Macmillan, 2011.

Lewis, David H. *Flower Drum Songs: The Story of Two Musicals*. Jefferson, NC: McFarland and Company, 2006.

Lim, Genny. '*Paper Angels*'. In *Unbroken Thread: An Anthology of Plays by Asian American Women*, edited by Roberta Uno, 11–52. Amherst: University of Massachusetts Press, 1993.

Lin, Hsiu-Chen. 'Staging Orientalia: Dangerous "Authenticity" in David Henry Hwang's *M. Butterfly*'. *Journal of American Drama and Theatre* 9, no. 1 (1997): 26–35.

Bibliography

Loo, Chalsa. '*M. Butterfly*: A Feminist Perspective'. In *Bearing Dream, Shaping Visions: Asian Pacific American Perspectives*, edited by Linda A. Revilla, Gail M. Nomura, and Shirley Hune, 177–80. Pullman: Washington State University Press, 1993.

Martin, Robert K. 'Gender, Race, and the Colonial Body: Carson Mccullers's *Filipino Boy*, and David Henry Hwang's *Chinese Woman*'. *Canadian Review of American Studies* 23, no. 1 (1992): 95–106.

McInturff, Kate. 'That Old Familiar Song: The Theatre of Culture in David Henry Hwang's *M. Butterfly*'. In *A Vision of the Orient: Texts, Intertexts, and Contexts of Madame Butterfly*, edited by Jonathan Wisenthal, Sherrill Grace, and Melinda Boyd, 72–88. Toronto: University of Toronto Press, 2006.

Moy, James S. 'David Henry Hwang's *M. Butterfly* and Philip Kan Gotanda's *Yankee Dawg You Die*: Repositioning Chinese American Marginality on the American Stage'. *Theatre Journal* 42, no. 1 (1990): 48–56.

Moy, James S. *Marginal Sights: Staging the Chinese in America*. Iowa City: University of Iowa Press, 1993.

Pao, Angela. 'The Critic and the Butterfly: Sociocultural Contexts and the Reception of David Henry Hwang's *M. Butterfly*'. *Amerasia Journal* 18, no. 3 (1992): 1–16.

Pao, Angela. 'The Eyes of the Storm: Gender, Genre and Cross-Casting in *Miss Saigon*'. *Text and Performance Quarterly* 12 (1992): 21–39.

Rabkin, Gerald. 'The Sound of a Voice: David Henry Hwang'. In *Contemporary American Theatre*, edited by Bruce King, 97–114. New York: St. Martin's, 1991.

Remen, Kathryn. 'The Theatre of Punishment: David Henry Hwang's *M. Butterfly* and Michel Foucault's *Discipline and Punish*'. *Modern Drama* 37, no. 3 (1994): 391–400.

Rich, Frank. foreword, in *Yellow Face*, edited by David Henry Hwang, vii–xi. New York: Theatre Communications Group, 2009.

Rodgers, Richard, Oscar Hammerstein II, and Joseph Fields. *Flower Drum Song*. New York: Farrar, Straus, and Cudahy, 1959.

Rogers, Amanda. 'Butterfly takes flight: The Translocal Circulation of Creative Practice'. *Social & Cultural Geography* 12, no. 7 (2011): 663–83.

Rosaldo, Renato. *Culture and Truth: The Remaking of Social Analysis*. Boston: Beacon Press, 1989.

Ross, Deborah L. 'On the Trail of the Butterfly: David Henry Hwang and Transformation'. In *Beyond Adaptation: Essays on Radical Transformations of Original Works*, edited by Phyllis Frus and Christy Williams, 111–22. Jefferson, NC: McFarland, 2010.

Rossini, Jon D. 'From *M. Butterfly* to *Bondage*: David Henry Hwang's Fantasies of Sexuality, Ethnicity, and Gender'. *Journal of American Drama and Theatre* 18, no. 3 (2006): 54–76.

Rushdie, Salman. *Midnight's Children*. New York: Knopf, 1981.

Saal, Ilka. 'Performance and Perception: Gender, Sexuality, and Culture in David Henry Hwang's *M. Butterfly*'. *Amerikastudien/American Studies* 43, no. 4 (1998): 629–44.

Selim, Yasser Fouad A. 'The Theatre of David Henry Hwang: From Hyphenation to the Mainstream'. In *Positioning the New: Chinese American Literature and the*

Bibliography

Changing Image of the American Literary Canon, edited by Tanfer Emin Tunc and Elisabetta Marino, 114–27. Newcastle upon Tyne: Cambridge Scholars.

Shimakawa, Karen. *National Abjection: The Asian American Body Onstage*. Durham: Duke University Press, 2002.

Shimakawa, Karen. '"Who's to Say?" Or, Making Space for Gender and Ethnicity in *M. Butterfly*'. *Theatre Journal* 45, no. 3 (1993): 349–61.

Shin, Andrew. 'Projected Bodies in David Henry Hwang's *M. Butterfly* and *Golden Gate*'. *MELUS* 27, no. 1 (2002): 177–96.

Skloot, Robert. 'Breaking the Butterfly: The Politics of David Henry Hwang'. *Modern Drama* 33, no. 1 (1990): 59–66.

Street, Douglas. *David Henry Hwang*. Boise: Boise State University Press, 1989.

Sturken, Marita. *Tangled Memories: The Vietnam War, the AIDS Epidemic, and the Politics of Remembering*. Berkeley: University of California Press, 1997.

Tchen, John Kuo Wei, and Dylan Yeats. *Yellow Peril!: An Archive of Anti-Asian Fear*. London: Verso, 2014.

Wada, Karen. afterword, in Hwang, *Flower Drum Song*, edited by David Henry Hwang, 99–115. New York: Theatre Communications Group, 2003.

Wang, Ban. 'Reimagining Political Community: Diaspora, Nation-State, and the Struggle for Recognition'. *Modern Drama* 48, no. 2 (2005): 249–71.

Wong, Sau-ling Cynthia, ed. *Maxine Hong Kingston's* The Woman Warrior: *A Casebook*. New York: Oxford University Press, 1999.

Wong, Yutian. *Choreographing Asian America*. Middletown, CT: Wesleyan University Press, 2010.

Woo, Miseong. 'Gender Trouble in Asian American Literature: David Henry Hwang's *The Sound of a Voice*'. *Feminist Studies in English Literature* 11, no. 3 (2003): 291–317.

Zamora, Maria C. 'Artifice in David Henry Hwang's *M. Butterfly*: Sexuality, Race, and the Seduction of Theater'. In *Nation, Race & History in Asian American Literature: Re-membering the Body*, 33–52. New York: Peter Lang, 2008.

Zia, Helen. *Asian American Dreams: The Emergence of an American People*. New York: Farrar, Straus, and Giroux, 2001.

Zinman, Toby Silverman. 'Sam Shepard and Super-Realism'. *Modern Drama* 29, no. 3 (1986): 423–30.

NOTES ON CONTRIBUTORS

Dan Bacalzo is an assistant professor of Theatre at Florida Gulf Coast University and has previously taught in the Department of Drama at New York University and the Asian American Studies Program at Hunter College. He holds a PhD in performance studies from New York University and has also worked over fifteen years as a theatre editor and critic in New York City.

Josephine Lee is a professor of English and Asian American studies at the University of Minnesota, Twin Cities. She is the author of *The Japan of Pure Invention: Gilbert and Sullivan's* The Mikado (2010) and *Performing Asian America: Race and Ethnicity on the Contemporary Stage* (1998) and co-editor of *Asian American Plays for a New Generation* (2011) and *Re/collecting Early Asian America: Essays in Cultural History* (2002).

Daphne Lei is a professor of drama at the University of California, Irvine. She is internationally known for her scholarly work on Chinese opera, Asian American theatre, as well as intercultural and transnational performance. She has published many scholarly articles and two books: *Operatic China: Staging Chinese Identity across the Pacific* (2006) and *Alternative Chinese Opera in the Age of Globalization: Performing Zero* (2011).

INDEX

Abdoh, Reza   46
Ackerman, Robert Alan   126
Aida   7, 103, 104–5, 130
American Conservatory Theatre   1, 95
American Dream   1, 11, 28, 29, 108, 112, 121, 136, 139
Asian American actors   20, 26, 36, 38, 84, 101, 127, 140–1
Asian American choreography   127
Asian American studies   87, 90, 181 n. 17
Asian American theatre   2, 5, 8, 19, 20, 36, 67, 73, 75, 107, 110, 115, 140–1, 152–5, 159–60, 165–5
Asian American Theatre Company   20
assimilation   3–4, 12–14, 17, 22, 32, 90, 92, 114, 133, 135–7, 140
As the Crow Flies   46–9
autobiography   3, 4, 12, 21, 27, 30, 32, 46, 49, 56, 75, 93–4, 96, 102, 107, 141–52

Bacalzo, Dan   4, 8, 95, 96
Baudrillard, Jean   71
Beckett, Samuel   35, 36, 37
Belasco, David   58
Berkeley Repertory Theatre   123
Boles, William C.   44, 46, 83, 84, 103
Bond, Edward   37
Bondage   5, 77–82, 89, 91, 106, 107, 111
Boston   27, 53, 82–3, 129, 165
Boursicot, Bernard   57
Boym, Svetlana   146–7, 151
Brantley, Ben   95, 105
Brecht, Bertolt   26, 94
Buchanan, Pat   66
Butler, Judith   6, 71
Butterfly (stereotype)   57–9, 62, 67–9, 71, 121, 155–9, 166

California   9–13, 18, 21, 26, 32–3, 77, 94, 95, 153
Californian Cool   10–11, 26, 32–3
Chekhov, Anton   93–4, 95

Chin, Frank   12–13, 21, 22–3, 37, 69, 127, 157
Chin, Tsai   101
Chin, Vincent   86, 180 n. 17
China   23, 25, 27–9, 31, 36, 47, 57, 60, 68, 96–8, 106, 111, 116–23, 131, 133–5, 142, 146, 148–52, 154–66
Chinatown   21, 90, 91, 130–2, 134, 138
Chinese American history   13, 17, 18–19, 21–2, 90, 140
Chinese American Trilogy   3, 9–34, 35, 38, 50
Chinese Exclusion Act   17, 18–19, 130
Chinese opera   7, 10, 18, 19–21, 23–5, 59, 91, 122, 126, 127, 133, 137–40, 177 n. 25
Chinglish   8, 115–23, 152–66
Chong, Candace Mui Ngam   159–60, 164, 166, 186 n. 47
Chong, Ophelia   46, 58
Christianity   11, 13, 27, 29–31, 35, 54, 56, 86, 93, 96–100, 120, 121,141–5, 148–51
Clinton, Bill   66, 108, 111
Cody, Gabrielle   71–2
Cold War   122, 130
Collins, Phil   7, 103
Colonial Theater (Boston)   83
comedy   6, 15, 19, 25, 52, 69, 83, 84, 86–9, 94–5, 97, 118, 122, 137, 144
Comparative Drama Conference   70, 175 n. 2
Cort Theatre   83
Cronenberg, David   72

The Dance and the Railroad   10, 20–6, 30, 91, 97, 101
dancical   124, 126
death   32, 35, 39, 40–1, 44–5, 47–9, 52–4, 62–3, 67, 113, 114, 123, 125, 133, 142, 145
deception   5, 35, 44, 56, 62, 114, 119–21

Index

Dexter, John 63, 65, 72
Disney Theatrical Group 104, 105
dragon lady (stereotype) 67
Dun, Dennis 83

East West Players 13, 19, 42, 101, 107, 140
Egi, Stan 96, 142
essentialism 70
Eugene O'Neill National Playwrights Conference 2, 19,126
Eugene O'Neill Theatre (New York City) 64, 82

face 4–5, 11, 30–1, 41, 45, 53, 68, 78, 80–1, 83, 85, 96, 100–1, 110, 113–15, 119, 144, 149
Face Value 31, 76, 82–9, 93, 94, 95, 106, 107–10, 114, 122
Falls, Robert 104, 117, 130
family 3, 4, 11, 20, 27–33, 35, 49–50, 54, 56, 76–7, 93–102, 105, 106, 114, 117, 142–52, 157
Family Devotions 6, 22, 26–33, 35, 36, 37, 38, 47, 49, 50, 51, 53, 54, 56, 77, 81, 84, 96, 101, 117
Fa Mu Lan 9, 13, 16–18
Fan, Lily 165
farce 6–7, 27, 35, 83–4, 86, 89, 106, 108
female characters 16, 38–40, 45, 54, 71, 86, 106, 133, 136–7, 139
feminism 18, 40, 67
Fields, Joseph 129
film 1, 3, 23, 36, 37, 46, 68, 72–3, 75, 76, 82, 101, 105, 109, 123, 125, 129–30, 132, 136, 140, 141
Finegold, Michael 66
Flower Drum Song (by David Henry Hwang) 7, 8, 103, 129–41
Flower Drum Song (by Rodgers and Hammerstein) 129–33, 135–8
FOB 2, 4, 7, 9, 10, 11, 12–20, 21, 24–5, 29, 30, 32, 35, 37, 38, 42, 54, 77, 80–1, 92, 115, 118, 126
Forbidden City (San Francisco) 134
form 6–7, 9, 19, 37, 46, 49, 84, 108, 124, 127, 140, 151
Fornés, María Irene 2, 9
Friel, Brian 93–4
Fu Manchu 85, 86, 87
Fundamentalism 11, 30, 96–7, 100, 143

Geffen, David 63, 72
gender 17, 38, 58, 65, 66, 70–1, 72, 80, 81–2, 93, 127, 136–7, 151
gender studies 67, 71
Genet, Jean 60
ghost 36, 37, 43, 45, 47–9, 91, 93, 99, 100, 125, 142–3, 149–50, 152
Glass, Philip 7, 76, 103, 130
Goei, G. G. 72
Goffman, Erving 6
Golden Child 4, 8, 39, 48, 93–102, 104, 106, 118 141–52
Golden Gate (film) 76
Goodman Theatre (Chicago) 116–17, 153
Gotanda, Philip Kan 7, 69
Grossberg, Michael 82
Guare, John 83
Guthrie Theater (Minneapolis) 107
Gwan Gung 9, 13, 16, 18–19, 23, 25, 92

Halcyon Theatre (Chicago) 117
Hammerstein II, Oscar 7, 103, 129, 132, 133, 137
Hearn, Lafcadio 37
Hollywood 68, 124, 125, 127, 129, 130, 134, 140
Homosexuality 66
Hong Kong 19, 116, 124–6, 134, 139–40, 154, 159–66
Hong Kong Arts Festival 123, 153
Hopkins, Anthony 72
Horibe, Cole 126, 127
The House of Sleeping Beauties 36–42, 47
Humana Festival of New American Plays 77, 82, 89
humour 15, 24–5, 52, 105, 115, 137
Hunter, James Davison 66
Hwang, Henry Yuan (father of David Henry Hwang) 1, 28, 32, 108, 111–14
Hwong, Lucia 7, 42
hyper-realism 52, 54–5
hyper-theatricality 24, 71, 87–8, 177 n. 25

identity 6, 14, 16, 30, 31, 35, 45, 48, 49, 53, 70, 76, 77, 80–1, 83, 85, 92–3, 105–6, 110, 113–16, 135, 136, 140, 146, 149, 151, 156, 162
identity politics 31, 70, 85–93, 106, 110, 115–16
Irons, Jeremy 72

204

Index

Isherwood, Charles   126–7
Ishioka, Eiko   63, 65, 72
isolationist-nationalist phase   3, 22, 36, 50, 92, 114

Jade Flowerpots and Bound Feet   105–6
Japan   36–8, 57, 108, 140, 148, 161, 163
Japanese American   7, 19, 21, 27, 36, 124
Japanese plays   3, 37–8, 46, 49, 58, 77, 91
Japanese stories   35–7
Jazz   7, 26, 42, 91–3
Jeff Awards (Joseph Jefferson Awards)   117
John, Elton   7, 103, 130
Joy Luck Club   101, 106
Jujamcyn Theater   82–3

Kawabata, Yasunari   36, 38–9, 42
Kelly, Kevin   75, 83–4, 89
Kennedy Center for the Performing Arts   95
Kim, Randall Duk   96, 101, 143
The King and I   110
Kingston, Maxine Hong   9, 12–13, 17–18, 20, 37, 106, 159
Kondo, Dorinne   70–1, 72, 151, 152
Krakowski, Jane   85–6
Kung Fu (play)   7, 21, 123–7
Kung Fu (television show)   11, 36, 125
Kurosawa, Akira   36
Kushner, Tony   67
Kwan, Nancy   129, 136

language   11, 17–19, 25–6, 37, 64, 97, 105, 120–1, 123, 125, 146–7, 153–64
Lapine, James   95, 101
Lark Play Development Center   107
Layng, Kathryn   76, 143, 182 n. 14
Lee, Bruce   123–7
Lee, C. Y.   129
Lee, Josephine   7, 8, 9–10, 19, 69, 103, 127, 145
Lee, Robert E.   133
Lee, Wen Ho   113
Lei, Daphne   8, 116
L'Heureux, John   2
Lim, Genny   153
Lim, Jennifer   116
liminality   14, 32, 46, 49, 77, 87
Lithgow, John   63, 65
Liu, Jeff   107

London   63, 72, 75, 107, 127
Lone, John   7, 19–21, 26, 37, 65, 72
Long, John Luther   58
Longacre Theatre   95, 141
Longbottom, Robert   129
Los Angeles   1, 11, 12, 13, 19, 27, 46, 50–2, 76, 101,103, 107, 124, 129, 134, 141
Los Angeles Theatre Center   46, 49
Loti, Pierre   57–8
love   3, 29, 38, 41, 43–5, 49, 51, 53, 56, 57–8, 60–1, 66, 71, 77–82, 84, 97, 98, 100, 104, 105, 119–23, 131, 133, 135, 137, 139, 142, 150, 157
Luke, Keye   129

Ma, Tzi   20, 26
Madame Butterfly   57–9, 62, 63, 64, 67, 70, 130
magic realism   10, 17, 24, 47
Mako   19
male characters   11, 16, 22–3, 38, 40, 54, 66, 67, 86, 89, 121, 122, 123, 139
Mamet, David   122
Mark Taper Forum   103, 107, 129, 139
materialism   28, 32, 49–51, 56
M. Butterfly (film)   72–3, 76
M. Butterfly (play)   1, 2, 3, 5, 6, 15, 21, 35, 38, 38, 50, 56, 57–73, 76, 77, 79, 81, 82, 84, 87, 94, 104, 107, 108, 109, 114, 116, 121, 130, 141, 147, 157, 159, 165, 166
meta-theatricality   6, 15, 26, 36, 60, 72, 79, 86–9, 104, 113, 154, 164–6
A Midsummer Night's Dream   89
Miller, Arthur   1
Miss Saigon   75, 83, 107, 108, 109, 110
Miyori, Kim   101
model minority   133, 166
Moy, James S.   61, 67–8, 127
Muller, Stephan   76
multiculturalism   76, 82, 86, 92, 108, 114, 154
music   7, 19, 20, 30, 42, 58, 62, 63, 90–2, 93, 103, 124, 125, 130
myths   2, 10, 25, 32–3

National Theatre (London)   107
National Theatre (Washington, DC)   63, 64

205

Index

Nelson, Richard   95
New Federal Theatre   20
New York City   1, 15, 20, 37, 46, 49, 63, 64, 66, 76, 82, 89, 92, 101, 103, 107, 116, 123, 142, 160, 164
New York Times   1, 15, 20, 57, 68, 112–13, 126, 150, 151
nostalgia   11, 142, 146–7, 151–2

Obie Award   107
opera   1, 57, 58, 59, 63, 76, 103, 130, 149, *see also* Chinese opera
O'Reilly, Bill   66
Orientalism   65, 67, 70, 151–2
Orton, Joe   84
Ostrow, Stuart   63, 64, 82, 83

Padua Hill Playwrights Festival   2
Pakladinez, Martin   151
Papp, Joseph   2, 20, 95, 107
Patel, Neil   151
Peer Gynt (adaptation)   76
performance studies   6, 67
Peterson, Lisa   105
Philippines   47, 94, 102, 114, 141, 143, 144, 149
Phillips, Andy   65
Pinter, Harold   35, 37
Pirandello, Luigi   4, 6, 60, 79, 86, 89
Portland Center Stage   123
post-colonial studies   67
postmodernism   71
post-structuralism   67, 70–1
power   38, 43, 49, 58, 59, 61, 69, 70–1, 77–8, 80, 81, 87, 97–100, 119, 120, 121, 142, 153, 157, 159, 165, 166
Pryce, Jonathan   75, 109
Public Theater   2, 15, 18, 19–20, 37, 64, 94, 95, 96, 107, 141–3
Pulitzer Prize for Drama   65, 107

race   50, 65, 66, 70, 76, 80–2, 83, 87, 89, 90–3, 104, 106–8, 111, 114, 115–16, 127
racial drag   114
racial politics   83–5, 87, 108, 110
Reagan, Ronald   66
realism   9–10, 17, 47, 126
resurrection   49–56
Rice, Tim   103, 130

Rich, Frank   15, 16, 20, 21, 22, 38, 40, 50, 60, 64, 65, 113, 114–15, 151
Richards, David   63–4
Rich Relations   3, 49–56, 77, 84, 122
Rodgers, Richard   7, 103, 129, 130, 132, 133, 137
Roman Vikyuk Theatre (Russia)   72
Rossini, Jon   81

Salonga, Lea   103
San Francisco   20, 21, 66, 124, 134, 138, 176 n. 10
satire   56, 106
Savran, David   26, 36
Seattle Repertory Theatre   101
Second Stage, The   49
Second World War   27, 36, 130, 161
Sejong Center (Korea)   72
sex   35, 38, 45, 59, 64, 81, 85, 86
sexuality   65, 66–7, 70, 72, 81, 127
Shaffer, Peter   6, 63, 72
Sheng, Bright   76, 130
Shepard, Sam   1, 2, 6, 9, 11, 26, 27, 33, 37
Shigeta, James   129
Shimakawa, Karen   6, 71, 72, 127
Shi Pei Pu   57
Signature Theatre (New York City)   1, 96, 101, 123, 126, 127, 142, 144, 147, 150, 151
silence   37, 43, 49, 66
Silk Road Rising (Chicago)   107, 117
Silverman, Leigh   101, 107, 116, 126, 165
The Silver River   76, 130
Singapore   93, 165
Singapore Repertory Theatre   72, 95
sitcoms   46, 52, 85, 105
Sixteen Candles (film)   68
Soelistyo, Julyana   101
Son, Diana   69, 179 n. 20
Soo, Jack   129
Sound and Beauty   37–8
The Sound of a Voice   36–8, 42–6, 49
South Coast Repertory   94, 95, 123
spiritual farce   6
The Square   105
Staiges, Tony   95, 151
Stanford University   1–2, 15, 19, 30, 107
stereotypes   12, 13, 22, 23, 61, 65, 67–9, 79, 81–2, 85–8, 90, 113, 117, 127, 130, 132, 138, 157, 166

Index

Sturken, Marita   152
suicide   39–40, 42, 58, 62, 65, 99, 145, 153
Suzuki, Pat   129
Syracuse Stage   123

Tan, Amy   106
Tarzan   7, 103, 105
Tayeh, Sonya   126
television   1, 3, 5, 11, 46, 51–4, 68, 76, 85, 88, 123, 125, 130, 132, 140
Theater J (Washington, DC)   107
1000 Airplanes on the Roof   130
Tiananmen Square   162, 164
Tony Award   1, 2, 35, 64, 65, 73, 101, 103, 108, 109, 113, 130, 141, 157
tragedy   3, 7, 24, 49, 52, 58, 72, 81, 121, 149
tragicomedy   23, 24, 52
tragi-farce   7, 27
transnationalism   49, 106, 120, 151, 154–5, 157–60, 165, 166
Trilogy of Chinese America, *see* Chinese American Trilogy
Trinity Repertory Company   76
Trying to Find Chinatown   89–93, 106, 111

Umeki, Miyoshi   129

Valdes, Ching   38
Vietnam War   62, 65, 86
Virginia Theatre (New York City)   103, 129
The Voyage   7, 76, 130

Watanabe, Greg   144
Waterston, James   116
Wen, Ming-Na   101
Wong, B. D.   63–6, 71, 75, 83
Wong, Victor   38
Wong, Yutian   127
Woolverton, Linda   104, 130

Yamauchi, Wakako   21
Yavich, Anita   151
Yellow Face   4–5, 6, 7, 15, 31, 39, 75, 89, 102, 106, 107–16, 117
yellowface makeup   5, 75, 83–5, 89, 109, 127
yellow peril   86, 108, 111, 130, 182 n. 13
Yew, Chay   105
YOMYOMF Network   107

Zaks, Jerry   83
Zinman, Toby Silverman   11

207